STYLING BLACKNESS IN CHILE

STYLING BLACKNESS IN CHILE

Music and Dance in the African Diaspora

Juan Eduardo Wolf

INDIANA UNIVERSITY PRESS

This book is a publication of

Indiana University Press
Office of Scholarly Publishing
Herman B Wells Library 350
1320 East 10th Street
Bloomington, Indiana 47405 USA

iupress.indiana.edu

© 2019 by Juan Eduardo Wolf

All rights reserved

No part of this book may be reproduced or utilized in any form or by any means, electronic or mechanical, including photocopying and recording, or by any information storage and retrieval system, without permission in writing from the publisher. The paper used in this publication meets the minimum requirements of the American National Standard for Information Sciences—Permanence of Paper for Printed Library Materials, ANSI Z39.48-1992.

Manufactured in the United States of America

Library of Congress Cataloging-in-Publication Data

Names: Wolf, Juan Eduardo, [date] author.
Title: Styling blackness in Chile : music and dance in the African diaspora / Juan Eduardo Wolf.
Description: Bloomington : Indiana University Press, [2019] | Includes bibliographical references and index.
Identifiers: LCCN 2018023309 (print) | LCCN 2018025313 (ebook) | ISBN 9780253041159 (e-book) | ISBN 9780253041135 (hardback : alk. paper) | ISBN 9780253041142 (pbk. : alk. paper)
Subjects: LCSH: Popular music—Chile—History and criticism. | Blacks—Chile—Music—History and criticism. | Music and race—Chile.
Classification: LCC ML3487.C55 (ebook) | LCC ML3487.C55 W65 2019 (print) | DDC 780.89/96083—dc23
LC record available at https://lccn.loc.gov/2018023309

1 2 3 4 5   24 23 22 21 20 19

CONTENTS

Acknowledgments vii

Accessing Audiovisual Materials ix

Introduction: Of Stereotypes and Styling 1

Part I   Styling Blackness as Afro-descendant

1. The Disappearance of Blackness and the Emergence of Afro-descendants in Chile 17

2. Tumbe Carnaval: Styling Afro-descendant 50

3. Self-Understanding as Motivation for Styling Afro-descendant 83

Part II   Other Ways of Styling Blackness

An Interlude on the Importance of Styling Blackness and the African Diaspora 105

4. Styling Blackness as Criollo: Dancing the Intimate 110

5. Styling Moreno: Taking Pride in Decent Steps 136

6. Styling Blackness as Indígena: Racial Order as Carnivalesque? 167

7. A Question of Success: Carnivalization and the Future of Styling 198

Bibliography 219

Index 231

ACKNOWLEDGMENTS

Ethnography depends upon the kindness of others, so I sincerely thank those kind individuals in Chile who allowed me to spend time with them. Special thanks to Cristian Báez, who answered my first email and whose aid was invaluable in my meeting many of the people mentioned in this book. I also acknowledge the members of the Afro-descendant organizations I spoke with, especially *Lumbanga* and its past president Azeneth Báez, as well as *Oro Negro* and its president Marta Salgado. The religious dance troupes, the *Morenos de Marconi* and *Hijos de Azapa*, deserve my appreciation for helping me to attend the preparation and celebration of both feasts of the *Virgen de las Peñas*, with special recognition to Marcos Butrón and Miguel Zegarra for hosting me there. In this space, the aid of Orlando Castillo, Emmanuel Watson, and Fr. Nelson Peña was also invaluable. For urban carnival expressions, I thank the *Caporales San Pedro de Totora* and the *Morenada Generación 90*, each of whom permitted me to document their rehearsals and performances for the 2009 *Carnaval Andino*. I owe my experiences with highland Indigenous music to Rodomiro Huanca and members of the group *Phusiri Marka*. Additional thanks to Pedro Medina Sotomayor and Marta Maldonado for making my family feel at home in the apartment they rented to us. All the interviewees listed in the bibliography deserve heartfelt thanks for their attention, as do the many others interviewed but unable to be mentioned.

My academic guides in this process were the always-supportive Drs. John McDowell, Daniel Reed, and Javier León. Providing additional guidance at different junctures were the esteemed scholars Dick Bauman and Shane Greene. For valuable Aymara and Quechua language instruction, I am indebted to Taitas Miguel Huanca and Francisco Tandioy, respectively. My scholarly haunt in Arica was the Universidad de Tarapacá, thanks to a letter of support from Dr. Marietta Ortega. Historian Dr. Alberto Díaz Araya and archivist Rodrigo Ruz Zagal made me feel welcome, sharing their knowledge and publications, while Juan Carlos Mamani Morales allowed me to visit his Andean dance classes. In Santiago, I am greatly appreciative of the hospitality and intellectual acumen of Drs. Juan Pablo González and Daniel Party.

This work could not have been completed without the financial support at different times from the Social Science Research Council (SSRC), the Institute for International Education (IIE), the Indiana University College of Arts and Sciences, the Indiana University Department of Comparative Literature, the US Department of Education Foreign Language and Area Studies Fellowships Program, the Indiana University Latino Studies Program, the Oregon Humanities Center, and the University of Oregon's Vice President for Research and Innovation.

During the writing of this book, I received additional feedback and support from various sources on parts of this project: at the University of Oregon, thanks to Carlos Aguirre, John Fenn, Lisa Gilman, Michelle McKinley, and Carol Silverman. Discussants Robin Moore and Alejandro Madrid made comments after presentations I made at the Society for Ethnomusicology that helped me clarify a few points. Special thanks to Daniel HoSang for organizing a writing and faculty support group that helped keep the process in focus. Two anonymous readers from Indiana University Press made wonderfully clarifying suggestions that editor Johanna Seasonwein helped me realize. Thanks to editors Janice Frisch and Kate Schramm at Indiana University Press, who made this book production a reality.

Throughout the entire process has been the support of family and friends. My parents, Eduardo and Teresa, raised my sisters and I with a love for Chile, exposing us to its language and culture. My extended family in Chile were always supportive, as have been my in-laws. Most importantly, I am eternally grateful to Jill for her love, patience, and understanding, and to Ceci and Quino for their hugs, which always put things in their place.

ACCESSING AUDIOVISUAL MATERIALS

AUDIOVISUAL MATERIALS ARE AVAILABLE FOR THIS VOLUME AND can be viewed online at https://purl.dlib.indiana.edu/iudl/media/g45148gm6z. Information and links for each individual entry follow.

Video 2.1. Oro Negro performing tumbe carnaval for the pasacalle during the Pascua de los Negros celebration, January 6, 2009. Arica, Chile. Percussionists of the comparsa playing one version of the tumbe carnaval rhythm, accelerating the rhythm after a unison break. The "Eeee . . . tumbe!" chant begins halfway through the excerpt.
  https://purl.dlib.indiana.edu/iudl/media/366613p19n

Video 2.2. Oro Negro performing tumbe carnaval for the pasacalle during the Pascua de los Negros celebration, January 6, 2009. Arica, Chile. Dancers performing several sequences of steps, including motions that invoke the cutting down of sugarcane.
  https://purl.dlib.indiana.edu/iudl/media/089227nr7c

Video 2.3. Oro Negro performing tumbe carnaval for the pasacalle during the Pascua de los Negros celebration, January 6, 2009. Arica, Chile. Features percussion break and the hip motion designed to mimic the "tumbe" itself, that is, the act of knocking down one's dance partner.
  https://purl.dlib.indiana.edu/iudl/media/k22534gx9k

Video 4.1. Couples dancing valses sung by Diego Baez, accompanied by Segundo Quintana on keyboard and Richard Tajadillo on cajón at Lumbanga's 2009 anniversary celebration. Marcos Butrón and Francisca "Rosa" Rios dance together, as well as Carmen Baluarte with her father, Carmelo.
  https://purl.dlib.indiana.edu/iudl/media/999n108429

Video 4.2. Baile de Tierra performed by ONG Oro Negro during the Afrodescendant salute to the authorities, September 18, 2009. Chilean Independence Day parade, Arica, Chile.
  https://purl.dlib.indiana.edu/iudl/media/x02138kr4v

Video 5.1. Hijos de Azapa dancing in the plaza at the sanctuary of the Virgen de las Peñas during the Fiesta Chica, December 12, 2008. During their sixtieth anniversary, these morenos de paso combined their veteran retired dancers with that year's current troupe. This excerpt features the veteran caporal's solo pass flanked by the veteran troupe playing their matracas.

https://purl.dlib.indiana.edu/iudl/media/v83801qs4p

Video 5.2. Hijos de Azapa dancing in the plaza at the sanctuary of the Virgen de las Peñas during the Fiesta Chica, December 12, 2008. During their sixtieth anniversary, these morenos de paso combined their veteran retired dancers with that year's current troupe. This excerpt features that year's caporal's solo pass flanked by that year's current troupe playing their matracas.

https://purl.dlib.indiana.edu/iudl/media/227m70nv03

Video 6.1. Morenada Achachis Generación 90 on the first day of the Carnaval Andino, February 6, 2009. This opening sequence features the announcer's comments that are included at the opening of chapter 6 as well as the bloc of cholas called *Podersosas de Corazón* (Strong of Heart) dancing with matracas in the shape of a heart. Accompanied by the Bolivian Banda Poopo.

https://purl.dlib.indiana.edu/iudl/media/v93504sv3p

Video 6.2. Morenada Achachis Generación 90 on the first day of the Carnaval Andino, February 6, 2009. This clip features dancers in moreno masks.

https://purl.dlib.indiana.edu/iudl/media/d56z90448b

Video 6.3. Caporales San Pedro de Totora on the second night of the Carnaval Andino, February 7, 2009. Example of female basic step and a choreographic sequence.

https://purl.dlib.indiana.edu/iudl/media/524j62tb9q

Video 6.4. Caporales San Pedro de Totora on the second night of the Carnaval Andino, February 7, 2009. Example of male choreographic sequence. Daniel Barria is the leader on the troupe's right side, closest to the camera.
   https://purl.dlib.indiana.edu/iudl/media/co8h441x7n

Video 6.5. Saya Interlude of the presentation in front of the judges. Caporales San Pedro de Totora on the second night of the Carnaval Andino, February 7, 2009.
   https://purl.dlib.indiana.edu/iudl/media/494v53m23x

STYLING BLACKNESS IN CHILE

Figure I.1. Oro Negro performing tumbe carnaval at a pre-carnival celebration in November 2008, Arica, Chile.

INTRODUCTION

Of Stereotypes and Styling

Carnival in the Andes can overload the senses, and the annual large urban carnival in Arica, Chile, is no exception. Thousands of dancers, dressed in colorful costumes and belonging to dozens of troupes, are accompanied by hundreds of musicians on brass, wind, and percussion instruments. For three days, the festivities begin under the hot summer sun in the early afternoon and do not finish until the cool hours of the following dawn. Many of the genres performed are the same as those found in other parts of the Andes and associated with highland festivals: *caporales, morenada, tinkus,* and *tarkeadas*. By 2004, however, one type of performance had emerged with a unique connection to city life: the *tumba* or *tumbe carnaval*.[1] Tumbe carnaval musicians play multiple rhythms simultaneously with their hands and sticks on barrel-shaped drums, accompanying columns of mostly female dancers wearing head wraps and swishing the ankle-length skirts they hold in their hands (see fig. I.1). Their songs and choreographies reference part of the history and experiences of the local coastal people of African descent, who harvested olives, cut sugarcane, and worked as laundresses, first as slaves and later as free people in a territory controlled by various national governments.

As music-dance, the tumbe carnaval shares many characteristics with other expressions connected to the African diaspora throughout the Americas.[2] What sets it apart is its emergence in Chile, a country that, until recently, was often characterized as not having a Black population at all.[3] During a visit to Chile as a young man in the 1990s, I was sitting in a plaza in the capital city of Santiago when an odd feeling came over me. I realized that I had just seen the first person that I would identify as Black by phenotype in Chile. The moment produced a feeling of incongruity within me, for while I was born in Chile, I had formed most of my ideas about race in the United States, where I was raised by my Chilean parents. As a way to learn about my heritage, I had learned to play several Latin American musical genres on the guitar. While I had heard about the African influences on Cuban *son* or Brazilian *bossa nova*, I never encountered a similar narrative about Chilean genres like the *cueca* and the *tonada*. I mentioned my experience in the plaza to immediate and extended family members later that day, as we gathered around the table for afternoon tea. One response was that "he must have been a Brazilian." Another offered, "Or Cuban—a lot of Cubans came to Chile with Allende's election." Whatever the case, the idea was clear: if he was *negro* (Black), he must not have been Chilean. The experience stuck with me; it was the first time I seriously thought about Chile in relation to a Black population.

After that day, I noticed similar points consistently reiterated in the media and in texts on Chilean folklore: there are no Black people in Chile; any Black people in Chile are foreigners; Chile may have had African slaves, but they are long gone and had no significant impact on the national culture. This litany reaches at least as far back as the nineteenth-century writings of Chilean historians like Diego Barros Arana. Race is a social construction with historical consequences (Wade 2010,12–14), so Chilean intellectuals like Barros Arana contributed to the social work of constructing an image of Chile whose people were free of Blackness, attempting to demonstrate the country's superiority to similarly minded domestic and international audiences. Indeed, several ideas of what constitutes Blackness in Chile today, whether referencing certain phenotypical features or characteristics such as music-dance prowess, resonate with cosmopolitan conceptions of Blackness, reflecting long-time interactions with Europe, the United States, and other parts of Latin America.[4] Yet even with this influence—or arguably reinforced by it—comes the understanding that most Chileans see their country as a place where Blackness is particularly Other and not part of the Chilean experience.

The tumbe carnaval has begun eroding this impression, illustrating music-dance's potential as an especially influential resource for the construction of social ideas. Even though the presence of Afro-Chileans first came to international attention in 2000 during preparations for a United Nations conference, performances of the tumbe carnaval since 2003 have consistently captured the imagination of local and national media and have become the contemporary representation of a Chilean Black culture. Growing acceptance of tumbe carnaval performance also encouraged some families in Arica to participate in and identify with one of the city's increasing number of Afro-descendant activist groups.[5] In fact, a televised appearance of the tumbe was what enticed me to visit and eventually do fieldwork with members of Arica's Afro-descendant population. Yet this expression has not changed everyone's opinion; many Chileans see the recently visible Black population as an anomaly unique to Arica or as a result of immigration. As of January 2019, the Chilean government still does not give individuals the possibility of identifying as Afro-descendant/Black on its national census—the only country remaining in South America to not offer such self-identification.[6]

Inspired by the growing awareness of Afro-Chileans that tumbe performance created, I focus on how music-dance has been used to understand and shape different manifestations of Blackness in and around Arica, a coastal city along Chile's northern border. This is a music-dance ethnography based on travels I have made to this region since 2006, with an extended stay in Arica between 2008 and 2009. While ideas about Blackness in Chile are certainly not limited to this territory, the Arica-Parinacota region is where Afro-descendant activists first began to call for the Chilean state to officially recognize them as a unique and separate ethnoracial group within Chile. This region is where the tumbe carnaval emerged as a way of embodying the African heritage of a population historically associated with Blackness. Because of the connections between tumbe performances and the lobbying efforts of Afro-descendant activist organizations, the regional and municipal governments of the Arica-Parinacota region established a special line of funding for Afro-descendant cultural projects, as well as an Office for Afro-descendant Development—both unique in Chile.

The developments in Arica have implications for all of Chile, however. The political successes that the tumbe carnaval has helped achieve can be attributed to what sociologist Tianna Paschel (2016) calls the "multicultural alignment" in Latin American politics. Beginning in the late 1980s, many Latin American governments adopted this orientation, which ascribes specific protections and rights to communities based on cultural attributes that are significantly different from a state's mainstream urban society. For many Indigenous groups, this cultural difference has been established through a specific language ascribed to that group. Chile demonstrated its adoption of this position with the passing of its 1993 so-called "Indigenous Law." This law recognized several different Indigenous communities and set specific guidelines for how a specific government agency officially could recognize individuals as Indigenous, making them eligible for various government programs.[7] Black communities generally do not have a separate language, so if they wish to follow this multicultural logic, they must seek other markers of difference, often in the form of music and dance. In Chile, the tumbe has come to serve as the most visible marker of cultural difference for Afro-descendant activist organizations in Arica. A better understanding of the tumbe carnaval will help clarify the dynamics of performing cultural difference and their relationship to multicultural politics throughout Chile.

As I spent time in Arica, however, it became clear to me that the tumbe was not the only music-dance genre connected to Blackness in Arica. Individuals that I initially met as performers in Afro-descendant organizations also played important roles in other aspects of the city's musical life. Some Black families were important members of religious dance troupes. Many individuals sang along to popular songs in private festivities, and others participated in dances during large public carnival celebrations. Unlike the tumbe, such activities did not seem to emphasize their relationship to their African heritage. Instead, these music-dance genres were connected to other types of heritage—oriented toward national, religious, or other ethnoracial ways of identifying. The multiplicity in Black individuals' music-dance behavior illustrated that Blackness can be performed in a number of ways and emphasized the different relationships that Black performers have had with other groups of people over time. I characterize the building of these relationships between performers as *styling*.

Styling Explained

In everyday parlance, style is a term often used loosely to refer to multiple aspects of music-dance performance. This laxity is understandable, given the challenge of consistently separating out style from other analytical concepts, but if scholars are not attentive to such distinctions, I believe they overlook important analytical tools. As Harris Berger has argued, style terms function to "draw our attention to the distinctive affective and valual quality" of performances, but their use remains undertheorized (2009, 23).[8]

Historically, intellectuals have defined style along at least two lines, both of which can be problematic but prove useful as starting points.[9] First, style can distinguish *how* things are done versus *what* is being done. This type of understanding is often rooted in literary or aesthetic approaches to analysis. The assumption here is that stylistic differences become clear in the ways in which different authors produce the same type of text or form (e.g., a novel or a sonnet). A second common understanding of style comes out of ethnographic disciplines; it emphasizes style as the underlying principles that serve as rules of practice for a specific group. In all cases, scholars have used style as a tool to identify an individual artist, a group of artists, or a culture. As Anya Royce put it, style is understood as what "people rely on to mark their identity" (2002, 18).[10]

Over time, scholars have, of course, recognized the shortcomings of these two orientations toward style, particularly in the way that they essentialize forms or human behaviors. Intellectuals have developed a more nuanced sense of how people and artistic forms change over time, and how contexts influence performances. The scholarly response has been a shift to thinking about such categories in terms of "discourse."[11] Using this language-based metaphor emphasizes style's emergent quality—the idea that styles do not interact with one another in fixed ways but are constantly in flux because of this "dialog." While discourse as a concept is a language-based metaphor, it does not necessarily work only on the basis of language. Discourse can take place through other types of actions, with or without words.

My concept of style developed under the influence of a vein of performance studies rooted in folkloristics and the ethnography of speaking. More specifically, it is influenced by Richard Bauman's work on the concept of genre. Bauman has defined genre as "a speech style oriented to the production and reception of a particular kind of text" (2004, 3–4). In keeping with the discursive turn, Bauman argues that the emergent nature of genre means that every performance shapes how a specific genre is understood over time, and that genre is produced via the comparison of texts in relationship to one another, that is, via intertextuality.[12] Differences between texts are what Bauman (7) and Briggs have called the "intertextual gap," and performers must constantly negotiate these intertextual gaps in performance.

Synthesizing these ideas, I advocate for the understanding of style as an emergent category for the production and reception of the relationship between performers, analogous to the way genre functions for texts. From this perspective, analyzing style becomes a matter of understanding how performers do music-dance and inviting comparison or contrast with other performers; it addresses the perceived "gap" between these performers.[13] John Chernoff asserted that "style is another word for the perception of relationships" (1979, 125), but his emphasis was on the relationships within the constantly reinforced social order of a given culture. Instead, I envision a more dynamic perspective in which such perceptions are constantly in flux. Style not only applies to a social order within a constrained culture, but, I argue, between multiple sets of performers, both within and across cultures.

Placing the emphasis on the relationship between performers brings the issue of agency to the fore. Here I want to invoke sociolinguist Nikolas Coupland's use of the term styling, which he defines as "the activation of stylistic meaning" (2007, 2). From my perspective, styling emphasizes the performers' intentions to shape and highlight their relationships to other performers through the resources of performance. Of course, like all aspects of performance, the success of a specific styling depends on whether the intended audience accepts the proposed relationship based on its members' experiences. Note that the intended audience often includes the performers themselves.[14] The resources that performers use when styling are not necessarily exclusive nor independent of other analytical tools, such as genre. In many disciplines, style has been understood as a category that encompasses genre, but I understand these as different and complementary frames through which performance can be analyzed. The reason I emphasize styling here is my interest in how relationships between performers are framed in ethnoracial terms, particularly Blackness. Humans are complex, and rather than having a single way of understanding themselves, they often take various context-dependent approaches to engaging with who they are in relationship to others. Styling accounts for individuals who participate in multiple forms of music-dance performance, each of which frames Blackness in relationship to different sets of performers.

Styling Blackness

Given that Chile's mainstream society has generally denied any association with Blackness, tumbe performers have sought to present the genre in a way that will resonate with broader contemporary cosmopolitan understandings of what it has meant to be Black. For many, including global organizations like the United Nations, Blackness has become framed as an African diaspora that, in the Americas, was epitomized by certain groups of performers from countries like Brazil and Cuba and, more recently, Peru and Uruguay. These groups of performers tend to stress their connection to Africa and similarities with African performers of music-dance. Performing tumbe carnaval gives local individuals the opportunity to engage with ideas about African heritage through lived experiences of music-dance. Simultaneously, these individuals offered those performances to an audience as experiences open to interpretation. I argue that tumbe performers successfully use embodied signs—whether sonically through rhythms, visually through costuming, or kinesthetically through dance—to call attention to their similarities with performers who are already prominently established as part of the African diaspora. The performers' affinity for these signs helps them shape their heritage in Afro-descendant terms. This affinity does come not out of a deep understanding of history but rather from the experience of performing itself relative to the way that they identify. Performances that resonate with what feels right—what Floyd (1995) and Ramsey (2003) have referred to as "cultural memory"—are full of what Turino (2008, 2014) refers to in Peircean terms as dicent indexes, signs that are understood to be a direct consequence of the object they signify.[15] In the case of the tumbe carnaval, for example, characteristics of styling Blackness as Afro-descendant are often interpreted as a direct result of the historical presence of Africans in the region. The challenge with these interpretations is that rarely are such signs straightforward. As I explored tumbe carnaval performance, I became more conscious of the way in which it resulted from an awareness of cosmopolitan Afro-diasporic expressions that interacted, complemented, and competed with local Afro-descendant experiences. In the understanding of Afro-descendant activists, performing the tumbe facilitates their acceptance as one of the "communities of style" that ethnomusicologist Veit Erlmann (2000) has argued make up the African diaspora—which include shared experiences of music-dance practice. Based on these ideas (and to draw attention to the active nature of this process), I describe the tumbe carnaval as an example of *styling* Blackness as Afro-descendant that tends to emphasize performers' relationship to African performers, often through proxies in other parts of the diaspora. Heidi Feldman (2006) described a similar dynamic in Peru with her idea of the Black Pacific (which here I expand on as the Black Periphery) as one model of styling Blackness in the African diaspora.

A complete understanding of the African diaspora, however, must account for the gamut of experiences and strategies in which those of African descent have been and continue to be engaged—that is, how Blackness has been shaped locally in relationship to many different groups of performers, not just Africans. When I encountered individuals performing multiple music-dance genres in my ethnographic work, I realized that certain performances in Arica had previously styled Blackness in ways that reinforced its absence in Chilean culture because these stylings emphasized the performers' relationship with non-Black performers. To understand these approaches to styling Blackness, I use local, historically significant ethnoracial categories as metaphors for the relationships between the Black performers of these other music-dance practices and non-Black performers of the same or related genres. For example, over time, the term *criollo* in Latin America came to represent what was locally created that demonstrated both difference from and significant similarity with certain European aesthetics. These criollo expressions were often the first shared ways of identifying nationally. Styling Blackness as criollo, then, references Blackness in relationship to performers of these national music-dance practices. The implication that emerges here is that, as in other Latin American countries, the larger society co-opted characteristics associated with Blackness to create difference between Chile and the Europeans that had colonized the Americas. Of course, Chile's peers—and even the former colonial powers—still needed to appreciate these practices, so the aspects of Blackness that were viewed negatively needed to be erased or glossed over. While some Chilean intellectuals followed the regionally popular idea that the appearance of these music-dance characteristics were part of a racial mixture, or *mestizaje*, this idea did not gain as much traction in Chile as in other parts of Latin America. The result was that Blackness was erased from these expressions and envisioned in the national imagination as *criollismo*, a process of cultural "Whitening." As in the case of styling Afro-descendant, my interest here is not concerned with following historical transformations but rather with understanding how certain music-dance practices function within contemporary Arica for individuals that may also style Blackness in other contexts.

I follow the same type of analysis for styling Blackness as *moreno* and styling Blackness as *indígena*. In Chile, moreno has become a term that people can use to avoid describing an individual as Black, which has negative connotations in Chilean society. This use implies that this person may be Black but is nevertheless decent. Styling Blackness as moreno, I argue, references how Black performers create a relationship with other respected performers, particularly in the realm of religious practice. As with styling criollo, this behavior tends to erase Blackness. Finally, my analysis of styling Blackness as indígena returns to a political framing that invokes the multicultural alignment. Here, groups of Indigenous performers co-opted characteristics of Blackness, often in a potentially negative way, to mark differences from mainstream Chilean culture. Since these practices ultimately associate this difference with Indigenous people, Blackness can still be erased. Some individuals, however, identify both as Indigenous and

Afro-descendant, meaning that performers can find themselves styling Blackness in paradoxical ways. The success that Indigenous groups have had in obtaining some rights, based on multicultural alignment policies, means styling Blackness as Indigenous has had an important influence in the ways that certain music-dance expressions are interpreted, and also how Afro-descendant groups have developed strategies to attain their own rights.

This book, then, is more specifically about the multiple stylings of Blackness in music-dance found in Arica, with an eye toward the implications of these experiences and strategies for styling Blackness through music-dance in the rest of Chile and the African diaspora. I examine how Black performers style themselves in relation to a range of performers from Africans to Indigenous and how each of these relationships reflects a different heritage narrative. Each of these narratives not only brings us to a deeper understanding of the dynamics of diaspora as a whole but also helps us rethink the personal aims and political consequences for peoples of African descent who perform these music-dance genres.

The Politics of Styling Blackness through Music-Dance

Earlier I mentioned the tumbe carnaval's success at raising awareness of the presence of people of African descent in Chile. Given Chile's history of distancing itself from Blackness, however, some people dismiss tumbe carnaval as inauthentic or foreign, either in terms of being contrived or in terms of not being Chilean enough, given Arica's historical relationship with Peru (discussed in chap. 1). This study of styling Blackness helps bring to the fore several issues that mitigate these criticisms. First, many individuals who identify as Afro-descendant participate in this cultural expression. While some critics might call the tumbe a case of strategic essentialism, many Afro-descendants feel represented by this form of music-dance, sensing that it resonates with their personal experiences of Blackness, that is, their own cultural memory.[16] Perhaps just as important socially, many individuals point to the community-building aspects of performing tumbe in a *comparsa* (a music-dance troupe) as a key benefit of participating, particularly when it reunites Afro-descendant extended family members in a space where their Blackness is valued. In my fieldwork, several individuals in Afro-descendant organizations related the negative comments about

Blackness that they encountered in their daily lives (see chap. 3). These comments underscore the desire for spaces to exist that see Blackness in positive terms. While not every Afro-descendant I interviewed claimed being discriminated against, many did experience some form of discrimination. A growing intolerance against immigrants in Chile (Tijoux 2016) suggests an even greater sense of ethnoracial exclusion present in the entire country than the discrimination I encountered in Arica, where the more visible presence and interaction with Afro-descendants has made a difference. Note that thinking about granting protections and rights based on racial discrimination differs from the multicultural alignment, offering instead what Paschel (2016) has called the "racial equality" alignment that has only more recently become prominent in Latin American politics. It does not rely on the establishment of the cultural difference of a community but rather on quantitative proof of discrimination. These types of statistics are difficult to gather without the kind of information usually collected by a census. Until enough information has been gathered, the multicultural alignment remains the primary orientation for seeking justice for Afro-descendants in Chile, and performance of difference through the tumbe carnaval and the recognition of other ways of styling Blackness in music-dance remains an important tool for Afro-descendant activists.

With this analysis of multiple ways of styling Blackness, I have ultimately written this book as an intervention against the perceived absence of Blackness in Chilean culture. Given my position as an academic researcher from a US institution, such an act might be considered problematic—an imperialistic projection of US ethnoracial attitudes onto a Latin American country with a different set of histories and attitudes. In writing this ethnography, however, I have sought out what is valued in music-dance performances based on content and context, drawing from local performers' and audiences' experiences. I have tried to privilege their voices while using my own judgment to make historical and cosmopolitan connections that may not always be obvious. The multiple ways of styling Blackness appear in relation to different performance experiences, both in the discourse surrounding the performances and in how their performers identify them. That the same individuals could espouse multiple perspectives in different contexts reflects the complexity of human interactions. Of course, my own position as a US researcher is also complicated by a familiarity with Chilean culture as a child of Chilean parents—my own form of cultural memory. I cannot escape my personal desire for understanding the way that I might construct my own heritage. To be more transparent, I try to address these motives throughout the text via my experiences as a participant-observer. This awareness of my own position means that I must consider my own interest in Blackness, given that I do not identify as Black/Afro-descendant. I offer some possibilities toward the end of the book as I tackle the thorny issues of non-Black participation in contemporary stylings of Blackness. While I do not pretend to have completely addressed these issues in this ethnography, I believe that my research illustrates how Blackness is integrated into music-dance performances in Chile and contributes to an understanding of how cultures of Blackness participate in Chilean culture more broadly. Furthermore, my theoretical framing of styling to describe these contemporary processes is particularly fruitful to illustrate the mechanisms for how expressive culture may have treated Blackness in the past and how it may be treated in the future.

One final point based on experience: as mentioned, during my time in Arica, I witnessed and listened to reports of discrimination toward Black individuals in Arica. Such reports are often discounted as anomalies, unique situations that only foreigners might occasionally face. Many Chileans want to think of themselves as welcoming of visitors and free of racialized behavior—but with the understanding that people who are racially different are foreign. One can conclude from this reporting that as long as Chileans continue to see Blackness as Other, then discrimination against individuals seen as Black will continue to be taken lightly. As Blackness in the population of Chile is only bound to increase through self-identification and immigration, the number of reported cases of discrimination will likely increase. I aim to contribute to a better understanding of Blackness in the Chilean experience so that Chileans will be more attentive to the ethnoracial dynamics within their society. Such an awareness should bring a greater acceptance of Black individuals as full Chilean citizens and help to complement the myriad of experiences that constitute Blackness.

The Organization of This Book

Following the logic described above, I have organized this book into two main parts. In part one (chapters 1–3), I describe how Latin American framings of the African diaspora that developed during the 1990s brought the existence of Afro-Chileans living in Arica to the attention of the international community. As a reference for these understandings, in chapter 1,

I offer a brief history of how Blackness was initially constructed in colonial Chile. After independence, intellectuals helped erase presence of Blackness through their ideas of nationalism, which were reflected in Chile's music-dance. This framing helps to illustrate the importance of music-dance to the perception of Blackness and introduces the categories that will be useful in explaining the styling of Blackness in later chapters. It also sets the stage for the emergence of the most important expression in terms of styling Afro-descendant: the tumbe carnaval.

In chapter 2, I describe how the tumbe carnaval was first interpreted and offer a close analysis of its performance as it had developed up to 2010. Blending ideas found in performance studies and Peircian semiotics, my goal here is to illustrate details of how individuals used visual, aural, and kinesthetic signs available in music-dance performance to emphasize the relationship between the Blackness of a population in Arica with other regions of the African diaspora. I understand this relationship as the essence of style. Through semiotics, I illustrate how the tumbe carnaval works both with and against cultural memory to style Blackness as Afro-descendant heritage in the wake of emerging cosmopolitan understandings of the diaspora. I also explain how this understanding of styling resonates and contributes to scholarly understanding of the African diaspora.

In chapter 3, I explore the impact of tumbe carnaval styling at both the group and individual level. The concept of styling stresses the agency of performers in attempting to shape how relationships are perceived. Its semiotics are not simply semantic data; they also function as tools for thinking about these relationships in an embodied way, both on the individual and social level. Since I argue that tumbe carnaval styled the Blackness of a population living in Arica as Afro-descendant, here I show how participation in the tumbe—and the Afro-descendant organizations more generally—changed the way individuals and groups understood their relationships with the diaspora and each other. Tumbe clearly brought people together under a new category, yet this feeling of relatedness is complicated by the persistence of certain stereotypes as well as differences in the politics of what this way of identifying means. This complex situation reinforces the idea that the tumbe was not a performance independent of its larger social context. Rather, it was a type of performance that helped shape and was shaped by its environment. When ways of styling are called into question, older ideas underlying heritage and race, such as family lineage, come forward.

In part two (chapters 4–6), I examine how self-identified Black families in Arica participate in music-dance expressions that style their Blackness in other ways: as criollo (chap. 4), as moreno (chap. 5), or as indígena (chap. 6). Historically, these expressions preceded styling Blackness as Afro-descendant in the tumbe, yet I encountered these stylings as contemporary during my fieldwork. Each offers a different perspective on the heritage of Blackness within Arica, and I connect each perspective with a general theoretical principle that helps describe these stylings: cultural intimacy, decency, and the carnivalesque, respectively. With these multiple perspectives in mind, chapter 7 concludes the book with some detail on more recent developments in the status of Afro-descendant organizations in Arica. I examine the tenuous relationship between the Chilean government's cultural policy with respect to Afro-descendant music-dance heritage, its political stance toward its citizens who identify as Black/Afro-descendant, and what it means for people who identify as non-Black to participate in the tumbe carnaval. By discussing these issues in the wake of the previous chapters, I offer food for thought on the continuing styling of Blackness in music-dance in Chile and beyond.

Notes

1. Whether this expression should be called *tumba* or *tumbe carnaval* was a source of debate during the bulk of my fieldwork. This discrepancy has been present since 2002 because of the ambiguity in the naming of the expression among the initial informants. In 2010, amid another division in the performing troupe of Oro Negro, a claim was made that "tumba carnaval" referred to the historical performance of the expression while "tumbe carnaval" referred to the contemporary practice described here. Beyond this attempt to protect the initial group of performers from critics, I have not seen this distinction to be significant among performers or the media. In citations, I respect the speaker's preference, but by 2016, conversational usage in Arica seems to have settled on tumbe carnaval or simply tumbe. For ease of use, then, I shall use tumbe carnaval to simplify orthography and match popular usage.

2. In English, unlike other languages, no single word reflects the interdependence of these two expressive forms. I use the hyphenated term "music-dance" to reflect this quality in the genres discussed in this book.

3. Following several other authors (e.g., Feldman 2006, Fox 2006), I use the capitalized forms of Black and Blackness. This gesture is intended to convey a category of human beings, who, beyond association with skin color, face challenges and identify politically with the term. It also calls into questions any strict division between race and ethnicity. I capitalize Indigenous for similar reasons.

4. My use of the word "cosmopolitan" is modeled after Turino (2004, 235): "a type of transstate cultural formation dispersed among a number of countries and often including only certain segments of the population."

5. Afro-descendant is the direct translation of the currently preferred Spanish term *afrodescendiente*.

6. In April 2016, Chile's House of Representatives unanimously approved a resolution asking the government's Institute of Statistics (INE) to incorporate a question on the next census. However, the resolution did not have the force of law, and the institute's director stated that it was too late to include this question for the upcoming census. (https://www.camara.cl/prensa/noticias_detalle.aspx?prmid=129064)

7. Currently the recognized communities include: Aymara, Atacameños, Diaguitas, Kolla, Mapuche, Rapa Nui, Quechua, Kawesqar, and Yagán.

8. I agree with Berger's general critiques about the way style has been used in the past and the importance he gives to the concept of stance in terms of its relationship to experience. I worry, however, that Berger's concept of stance tries to encompass so many aspects of performance that the term's contribution becomes clouded. Berger still admits the importance of style, and my presentation of styling should address some of his concerns.

9. For reviews on the literature related to style in ethnomusicology, see Blum in Myers (1992) and Feld (1988). For a more recent book-length work that engages style, see Rommen (2007).

10. Rogers Brubaker (2004) argues that the generally "weak" construction of the "identity" concept is not necessarily helpful. I will discuss Brubaker's solutions to this challenge later; here, what is important is understanding identity as process.

11. Timothy Rommen has summed this up nicely by stating that, "style itself functions as discourse" (2007, 36).

12. Note that Julia Kristeva is credited with coining the term in relation to Bakhtin's work. See the entry "Intertextuality," in Joan Swann, Ana Deumert, Theresa Lillis, and Rajend Mesthrie (2004, 153–54).

13. This idea suggests the term "inter-performer-ativity" in parallel to intertextuality, but it is just too cumbersome. I do not espouse an "intertextuality between performers" as I would argue that obscures the agency of the performers.

14. Again, I am drawing on Bauman's ideas of performance, particularly in the sense that a performance is held accountable to an audience—what Coupland refers to as high performance. Note that Coupland himself considers another term, identity stylization (2007, 149–54), which parallels some of the characteristics of styling as I envision them. One key difference, however, is that stylization seems to imply a type of false artifice on the part of the performer, which I am trying to avoid here.

15. "Cultural memory" is a term that Samuel A. Floyd Jr. (1995, 8) refers to as "a repository of meanings that comprise the subjective knowledge of a people." Floyd explains that people who belong to a cultural group may feel that some principle or practice is "true" or "right" without "direct knowledge or direct training."

16. The concept of strategic essentialism is commonly associated with the work of postcolonial scholar Gayatri Chakravorty Spivak. Spivak has called the idea that stereotypes can be used to project the stereotyped group in good light as "a strategic use of positivist essentialism" (1996, 214).

PART I
STYLING BLACKNESS AS AFRO-DESCENDANT

1

THE DISAPPEARANCE OF BLACKNESS AND THE EMERGENCE OF AFRO-DESCENDANTS IN CHILE

> Music has been very important symbolically. I would say that it is a part of our culture, of cultural expressions, that has empowered us. Because, in the North, people like music very much, and we have noticed that they, when we go out in our *comparsas*, when we present our festivities, they follow us—with a lot of joy, with a lot of respect, which is something very honorable in the community, and we have noticed that foreigners knock themselves out taking pictures, but thinking that we are a group on tour in the city. When we tell them that we are Chilean Afro-descendants, they exclaim—Oh, I did not know! And they begin a series of interviews and, in truth, music has been our great achievement and helped plant us in the minds and awareness of people.
>
> (**Marta Salgado**, president of Oro Negro, interview with author, September 5, 2009)

AT THE TIME I INTERVIEWED MARTA SALGADO, THE *tumbe carnaval* had been in the public spotlight for six years, and her praise of this music (and dance, for she has often danced as the standard bearer of the group) was based on her own experiences of its growing positive reception. To fully appreciate the effect tumbe performances have achieved and to understand the rationales behind styling Blackness as Afro-descendant, one needs to have an idea of the historical trajectory of Blackness within Chile. In this chapter, I weave some of the history of Africans and their descendants in Chile with the evolution of concepts of Blackness in the country to frame the emergence of the tumbe carnaval. This information will also be useful later as I describe music-dance genres associated with Blackness other than tumbe.

The trajectory of Blackness as a concept in Chile began as Africans arrived with the colonizing Spaniards to the Americas and were given a designation within the developing system of *castas*—categories that combined ideas of class, ethnicity, and race—which included the category Black. When Chile became a republic and slavery was abolished, the government generally stopped recording this information in the name of fairness, but intellectuals writing during the nineteenth century continued to stigmatize Blackness and downplay its role in Chilean society. During the twentieth century, popular culture played a particularly important role in shaping the country's racial attitudes, so developments in music-dance contributed to the "erasure" of Blackness in Chile throughout this period. These attitudes became more flexible with the end of the Pinochet dictatorship, a time frame that coincided with the adoption of the Multicultural Alignment and new lines of thought regarding Blackness throughout Latin America. This meeting of moments set the stage for what seemed like the sudden appearance of Chilean Afro-descendant groups and the tumbe carnaval, the music-dance that is most identified with the movement.

Castas and a Brief History of Afro-descendant Slavery in Chile and Arica

The history of ideas about race in Chile follows many of the trends that were present in the rest of Latin America. In general, an individual's status in Latin American colonial society was legally established through association with their casta, a category that depended on a number of factors. Not solely racial, castas combined ideas of lineage and phenotype with geography and culture. The three main, or "pure," categories in colonial Spanish America were *español*, *indio*, and *negro* (Spanish, Indian, and Black), with español at the top of the hierarchy. From the Spanish perspective, the geographically named casta of español was presumed Catholic, while indio (from Indies, also geographically named) was conceived as a pagan in need of conversion and spiritual guidance. In return for their salvation, they would give their labor. The phenotypically named negro, however, was assumed infidel and generally appropriate for enslavement.[1]

From these primary categories, more castas emerged based on the concept of "mixture." The secondary categories were *mestizo* (the mix between Spanish and Indian), *mulato* (the mix between Spanish and Black), and *zambo* (the mix between Black and Indian). Additional tertiary categories varied locally depending on further combinations of these six categories

(Mörner 1967, 58–59). The casta of indio tended to be afforded more legal protections than the casta of negro, but other factors also came into play by considering an individual's social status. For example, Black slaves with a trade could sometimes earn additional money and eventually purchase their freedom. Together with slaves who were voluntarily given their freedom by their owners as well as Black children whose parents were already free, these individuals made up a class of free Black people who were present in Latin American societies from quite early on. These free Black people could be referred to as *moreno* or *pardo* to distinguish them from *negro* (Forbes 1993, 121). Beyond one's status as slave or free, one's place of birth also had an influence on one's casta. Environment was supposed to have an impact on one's character, so that European-born Spaniards, referred to as *peninsulares*, were given higher status than those of Spanish descent born in the Americas, most often named *criollos*. Interestingly, the term *criollo* appears to have originated to contrast a Black person who had been born within Spanish society (also called *ladinos*) with the *bozal*, who was born on the African continent (Lockhart 1994, 198). These terms were often combined to refine the broader casta categories, for example, *negro bozal*.

The abundance of casta categories—due to local variations and socially mitigating factors—has led some to debate how important the concept of race was in colonial Latin America (Wade 2010, 29; Burns 2011). However, some colonial-period writings directly connect the castas with physical appearance and temperament, a sign of racialized thinking. In 1789, Jesuit priest and historian Felipe Gómez de Vidaurre listed the castas he recognized in Chile, together with descriptions of their behavior. For example, he characterized mulatos as being "of regular stature, of weak constitution and beautiful qualities of spirit, if you overlook the arrogance that is their inclination." Similarly, for zambos, he stated, "The color of these is copper, their frame large, robust, brawny, their hair not long but not so curly. The qualities of spirit are ordinarily bad, disloyal, extremely cantankerous, cruel, traitorous, and so, people whose company you ought to avoid."[2] Gómez's descriptions suggest that phenotypical characteristics played a role in the system. They were particularly limiting for those individuals who were phenotypically and temperamentally associated with the castas of indio and negro (Wade 1993, 9). Gómez discussed criollos separately from the castas, noting their similarity in appearance to Spaniards and, given the right upbringing, their tendency to be logical, honest, and concerned about their reputation. Such descriptions of Chilean society provide the basis for the metaphors I use to describe the styling of Blackness in part 2 of this book.

With this understanding of casta terminology, one can more deeply engage with the limited historiography about Africans and the nature of slavery in Chile. This literature began to expand, albeit mostly focused on Chile's capital, Santiago, after the recent appearance of Afro-descendant activist groups.[3] From this new scholarship, it is worth elucidating a few points. First, while the overall number of slaves in Chile was relatively low, the same could be said of the overall population of Europeans and their descendants. Thus, the relative percentage of Afro-descendants, recognized within the categories of negro and mulato, could be locally significant. For example, using baptismal records in Santiago, Jean-Paul Zuñiga (2009) has calculated that during the period of 1633–44, there were approximately 430 slave owners for the approximately 1,685 slaves in a city with roughly 300 families. Since most of the owners had four or fewer slaves, Zuñiga asserts that slavery was a reality in most households. Both he and Frederick Bowser (1974) argue that slavery in the viceroyalty of Peru was understood as a socioeconomic asset to the household, so that even people with meager resources were willing to invest in the purchase of a slave.[4] Furthermore, the work of both Zuñiga and Celia Cussen (2009) shows that slaves in colonial Santiago were involved in a variety of tasks and professions, from shoemaker to carpenter. During its early period, Santiago was a mixture of urbanity and rurality, so the tasks of a "domestic" slave could also involve tending fields or working small mining extractions. Those slaves with the most lucrative professions—who often became well-connected with the more influential people in colonial society—were more likely to be able to purchase their freedom, although few slaves could achieve this status. Even after a slave was freed, Cussen argues, slavery continued to cast a long shadow. Former slaves thought about how to free enslaved companions and family members, and they still faced the stigma of race, since they were persistently marked in documents with phrases such as *pardo libre* (free Black) (Cussen 2009, 134).

The stigma associated with Blackness might explain why it is so difficult to trace the history of African descendants after their manumission. To begin with, Zuñiga believes that Africans in Chile had a difficult time identifying with one another precisely because they were spread out in the assimilating environments of individual households rather than held in large groups. In other countries, the membership of certain institutions, such as specific religious brotherhoods, was predominantly African. In Chile, the membership of brotherhoods was much more diverse. William F. Sater

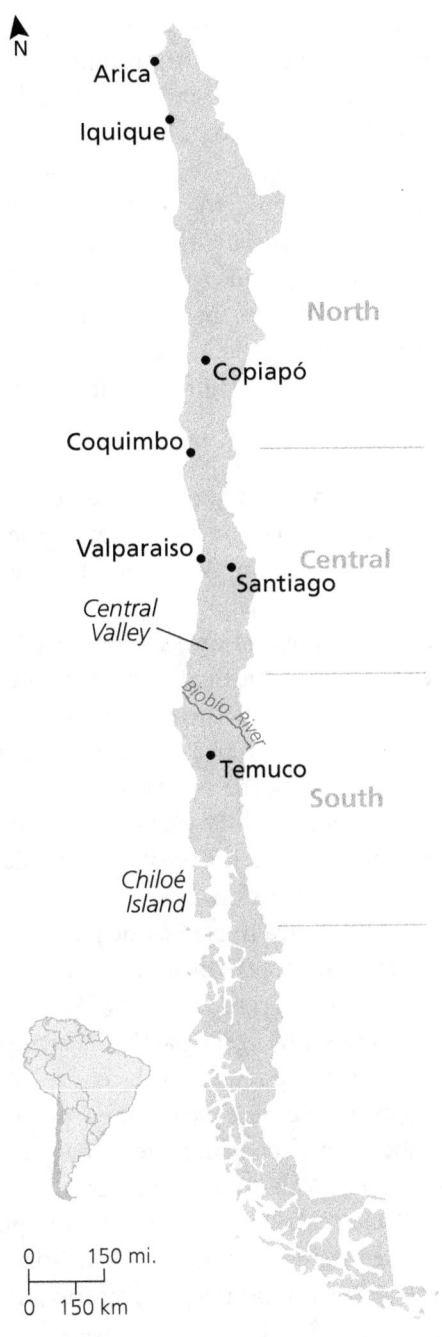

Map 1.1. Major cities within the three general cultural regions of mainland Chile. Cartography by University of Oregon InfoGraphics Lab, Department of Geography.

argues that, in Chile, "miscegenation . . . annihilated the black" (1974, 37), an argument that he supports by citing several case studies in which documents showed a decline in the Black population, while the mixed population designated as mulatos and zambos increased. Like Sater, many people have focused on the concept of racial mixture to explain the so-called absence of Blackness in Chile, thereby downplaying the role racism played in the process. Chilean society, however, consistently valued Spanish over Black heritage, giving little motivation for people to recognize their Blackness. George Reid Andrews (1980) discovered that, for Argentina, these arguments based on miscegenation can be called into question on closer scrutiny, and I believe that a similar situation is possible for Chile, if the appropriate records can be located.

Of course, this description of the history of people of African descent in Chile principally refers to colonial Chile, a region focused on Santiago that geographically ranged from north of the Bio-Bio River to the city of Copiapó. Populations varied within this region. According to a census in 1777–78, Santiago's population was approximately 18 percent negro and mulato. Coquimbo's negro and mulato population was higher (at greater than 20 percent), and the southern valley, including Colchagua and Maule, was approximately 8 percent (Cussen 2006, 53). The region in and around Arica, however, has a slightly different history: Arica only came under Chilean control in 1880, after Chilean troops took the city as part of the War of the Pacific (1879–83). After a dispute of almost fifty years, Arica was finally ceded fully to Chile via treaty in 1929. Thus, Arica's history with slavery is intimately tied with that of Peru, and by extension, Bolivia.

The Spanish founding of the port of Arica in 1546 came just a year after the Spaniards discovered silver in the mines of Potosí, in the highlands of what would later become Bolivia (Vásquez Trigo 2002, 20). Arica initially served as the principal port for the mines, giving it a particularly important status within Spanish colonial America in the seventeenth century. According to a 1614 census, some 1,300 Black people were part of the 1,784 residents in Spanish colonial society, a number that already included African descendants of the fourth generation (Briones Valentín 2004).[5] Arica's status as a port, combined with the high Black percentage of the urban population during this early period, led to some interesting situations. Militias of free Blacks were enlisted to protect the port from pirates, and legend has it that Arica even elected two free Black mayors, who were removed from their posts due to racism (Salgado Henríquez 2014, 69–70). The Black population continued to be significant until the second half of the nineteenth century. The urban slave situation along colonial Peru's coast was like that of colonial Santiago in that many slaves were artisans and the "domestic" slave often performed tasks in the garden. As with Santiago, the Indigenous presence in Arica's surrounding regions was still important and performed much of the agricultural labor.

Beyond Castas: Chile's Independence and Republican Ideas of Racial Mixture

During the colonial period, the concept of racial mixture could be threatening to those groups at the top of the social hierarchy, as it provided the possibility—albeit very limited—for individuals to contest and reposition themselves within that structure. With the arrival of independence in the nineteenth century, however, some members of the new governments wanted to show they had thrown off ideas about the division between races. Racial attitudes toward Blackness, however, continued to surface in the writings of intellectuals and historians, and also appeared in political cartoons addressing the question of Arica's sovereignty in the wake of the War of the Pacific. In this section, I explore the racial attitudes of the period through the writings of Diego Barros Arana and Nicolas Palacios as well as the propaganda images that appeared in Chilean magazines as the fate of Arica was being negotiated.

In 1818, Chile's first supreme director Bernardo O'Higgins stated that castas should not be an issue in the new republic, and the state did not ask a racial identification question after its 1813 census (Loveman 2014, 79, 112). Such actions reflected an attitude that the state should stand for liberal values that would allow every man to participate in society independent of race (so long as he could obtain property and literacy). Later in the nineteenth century, certain intellectuals, like historian Diego Barros Arana, saw leaders like O'Higgins as iconic of the Chilean state, and their values (such as the rejection of race labels) as Chilean values. Ironically, Barros Arana's historiography still revealed racialized thinking. He asserted that "Chile was undoubtedly the colony of the King of Spain that had the highest relative population of pure White race" (1886, vol. 7, 447n19). In this worldview, the "Araucanian Indian" could still function as the incarnation of the values of bravery and resistance, a historical "noble savage," as portrayed in colonial-era literary works.[6] Barros Arana noted, however, that while not always physically obvious, racial mixture, or *mestizaje,* included both races' worst qualities (Barr-Melej 2001, 60). Coupled with the lack of education and work in Chile, the country's mestizos were, according to Barros Arana, uncivilized, superstitious, improvident, and liable to gamble, drink, rob, and fight (1886, vol. 7, 441).

Unrest began to foment among the Latin American working class as it became clear that, despite this discourse of liberal values, the state had concentrated power and capital in the hands of oligarchs and foreign investors (Turino 2003, 180). In response, many elites and intellectuals at the beginning of the twentieth century appealed to the language of nationalism, praising a country's racial mixture as positive to appear more inclusive. The result was that, by the mid-twentieth century, the elite in many countries saw their states as racial democracies—claiming themselves to be free of discrimination because, they argued, all their citizens were racially mixed to some degree and, as such, were equal. While this discourse could serve as a unifying argument at the state level, it also effectively denied the ethnoracial inequities still present in everyday practice.

The most famous proponent of mestizaje in Chile was Palacios, a doctor and writer. In his 1904 work *Raza Chilena* (The Chilean Race), he asserted that this mixture of European descent with the Araucanian Indian applied generally to Chileans. Palacios uniquely claimed that the European component of Chilean mestizaje had noble Teutonic roots, which, in his eyes, elevated the status of the lower-class Chilean mestizo, or *roto* (see fig. 1.1) above other forms of Latin American mestizaje. Palacios insisted that the Spanish conquistadors saw admirable values—reflections of themselves—in their Native adversaries.[7] Sociologist Patricia Richards makes the case that, while Chilean elites incorporated imagery of past noble Araucanians into the national imaginings of mestizaje, the contemporary Mapuche have always been excluded (2013, 43). Thus, for most of the twentieth century, Chilean ideas of mestizaje implied mixture with Indigenous peoples without confronting the implications of that mixture.

Black slaves and African lineage play an insignificant role in both Barros Arana's and Palacios's conceptions of mestizaje. Palacios recognized the arrival of slaves to Chile, stating that they were primarily an urban phenomenon. While the Jesuits brought African slaves to work in rural environments, Palacios argued that the slaves were all sold off to foreign buyers when the Jesuits were expelled from the country. Furthermore, Palacios claimed that colonial leaders severely limited the ability for slaves to

Figure 1.1. Copy of the "Roto Chileno," originally known as "Hero of the Pacific," modeled after the late nineteenth-century sculpture by Virginio Arias. The plaque reads "Genuine Expression of the Chilean Race" with the date of the Battle of Yungay. Arica, Chile.

reproduce. What is most revealing, however, are the negative "cerebral" (Palacios's term) qualities that he associated with Blackness: a lack of mental control, predominance of imagination, and baseness of ideals. Given Palacios's intention of elevating the roto based on their positive qualities, he was reluctant to claim the presence of African blood in his vision of Chilean mestizaje.[8]

Earlier, Barros Arana had taken a more charitable view toward Blackness, admitting that slaves could be "intelligent" and "faithful" (1886, vol. 7, 447) and assuming a moral position against slavery. He believed that slavery in Chile was milder than in other parts of Latin America, yet he admitted that slaves could be subjected to harsh punishments there. In his 1884 *Historia general de chile*, he stated that the majority of Black individuals present in Chile at the beginning of the nineteenth century were mixed (mostly with Whites) and free, often pursuing a trade that did not require them to read and write. Yet, for Barros Arana, that is where the role of Black people in Chile's history ends. Thus, his primary contribution to the discussion of Blackness was the explanation he offered as to why there were few African slaves there. He asserted that the cost of procuring slaves from Lima, Peru, was high, which meant that the total number of slaves to reach the colony was small compared to other regions of Spanish colonial America. Barros Arana also stated that, as other routes for procuring slaves became available, it was more profitable to sell slaves to Peru than to keep them in Chile.[9] Such arguments established an initial historical narrative that slaves were few and often not in Chile to stay.

Examining the works of Barros Arana and Palacios, therefore, offers complementary yet slightly different perspectives on race in Chile. Both authors acknowledge the existence of mestizaje, and both dismiss the importance of Blackness to that mixture. Barros Arana downplayed the existence of mestizaje to highlight the values of the criollo founding fathers, while Palacios thought that the mixture was widespread and something to be valued in the national imagination. At their core, however, both views foregrounded European contributions to Chile's ideas of racial mixture, and the degree to which Blackness was seen as not Chilean was clearly demonstrated when Chile compared itself to neighboring states in imagery.

While the general discourse on Blackness in Peru was similar to that of Chile, Peru did not fully abolish slavery until 1855, a generation later than Chile, with the result that people tended to be identified as Black in Peruvian-controlled Arica throughout the nineteenth century. Peruvian census data available for Arica in the years 1817, 1843, and 1871 has allowed researchers to observe that the Black population remained significant, although less so as the century passed. One particularly interesting observation made by Díaz Araya, Muñoz, and Lanas (2013) is that some 71 percent of the women in Arica in 1813 were Black. Sater (1974, 37) suggested that one reason more individuals could hide their Blackness in Chile was that "twice as many Black men as women were imported into Chile," forcing more interracial relationships in the central region. By contrast, in Arica, the probability of relationships between Black men and Black women appears to have been greater. The implication is that identifiably Black phenotypes continued to persist in the local racial imagination. More historical work needs to be done to see which other social structures during this time frame also reinforced Black ways of identifying, but historian Vivian Briones Valentín (2004) has pinpointed at least one more: location. She noted that the Lumbanga neighborhood in Arica was locally recognized as a place where many Black families resided, such that cultural practices shared by Black residents were likely to have been passed along there. In fact, contrary to the belief of many locals, Díaz Araya, Muñoz, and Lanas (2013, 333) discovered that, during the nineteenth century, 68 percent of the Black population lived in the city limits of Arica rather than in its surrounding valleys.

A key factor in changing Black demographics in Arica was the War of the Pacific (1879–1883). Chile's military victory over Bolivia and Peru resulted in Bolivia ceding to Chile the territory that gave it access to the Pacific Ocean. Peru also had to give up the Tarapacá region to Chile under the Treaty of Ancón, although the agreement stated that after ten years of Chilean administration, residents of the region would be able to vote on whether they would remain under Chilean sovereignty. However, this plebiscite never happened. In 1929, negotiations resulted in the city of Tacna being given to Peru, while Arica went to Chile. During the intervening fifty-year period, however, both sides tried to stack the odds in their favor, whether by persuasion or by violence. Given that the erasure of Blackness from the Chilean national imagination was already firmly rooted by the end of the nineteenth century, Chilean sympathizers believed that if someone was Black, they were Peruvian and therefore inclined to vote for Peru in the event of a plebiscite. Political cartoons in the Chilean press often depicted Peru as Black (see fig. 1.2), stereotypically in love with pomp and costume but also cowardly. Even more ominous is how such stereotypes guided actions. In some cases, the state employed the Chilean police force

28 | *Styling Blackness in Chile*

Figure 1.2. A *Sucesos* magazine cover from 1920 depicting a White Chilean soldier chasing a Black Peruvian soldier. Part of the Alfredo Wormald Cruz Heritage Collection, Main Library, Universidad de Tarapacá. Digitalization courtesy FONDEYCT project 1151514, Luis Galdames, director, assisted by Rodrigo Ruz and Alberto Díaz.

to engage in violence aimed at voters who they believed were inclined to favor Peruvian sovereignty. In other cases, private organizations called *ligas patrioticas* committed such atrocities.[10] Many families now identifying as Afro-descendant in the Arica region have stories of family members who fled to Peru or hid in the valleys to avoid persecution (Canto Larios 2003, 55–57). Given the absence of additional census data, the presumed result was the steep decline in Arica's urban Afro-descendant population, while the remaining individuals congregated in isolated pockets in the adjoining valleys of Azapa and Lluta. Concordant with this dispersal of Afro-descendants from urban Arica was the imposition of the Chilean educational system and government ideologies that equated Chileanness with Whiteness. As a result, those residents who stayed and were perceived as Black became understood as anomalies, structurally and institutionally. One of these structures was the production of popular music-dance.

The Singing *Huaso*: Interpreting Racial Mixture in Chile's Music-Dance

The writings of Barros Arana and Palacios and the cartoons in Chilean magazines are two arenas that reflected Chilean conceptions of national character and race. For an idea such as the absence of Blackness in Chile to be so widespread throughout the society, it had to be reinforced through repetition and in multiple modes of experience, what ethnomusicologist Thomas Turino refers to as redundancy (2008, 197). Music-dance provides one way that humans can reinforce, refine, and generate ideas about race, thus contributing to the redundancy of accepted social norms to make them seem natural and ever-present. In addition to live performances, the new circulation of recorded music-dance in the early twentieth century also helped the spread of these ideas. Here I offer a brief historic overview of the types of music-dance performance that supported and complemented Barros Arana's and Palacios's racialized vision of the state and the nation. Contemporary ethnographic reactions to these performance types will be the focus of most of the book.

The first prominent music-dance performances representing the Chilean state were military marches and hymns. Listeners were familiar with military bands as signs of imperial power, and the newly independent Latin American countries aspired to international respect like that accorded to imperial powers. Local composers modeled these pieces after European examples, such as France's *La Marseillaise* (Turino 2003), while lyricists made references to local geographic names and features to help listeners identify the state specifically. When it came to referencing the people of Chile, the model was like the one that Barros Arana espoused—the citing of values to be associated with the criollo founding fathers and the battles that they fought—yet the noble Araucanians of the past were not forgotten. The first set of lyrics to the Chilean national anthem in 1819 included references to three brave Native leaders during the Arauco War: Lautaro, Colocolo, and Rengo. Their valor was invoked as something to be imitated, implying it was not in the Chilean blood. In the 1847 revision of the anthem, however, lyricist Eusebio Lillos added the line, "With the blood of the Araucanian, we inherited bravery" (Pedemonte 2008, 156). These types of patriotic songs were composed throughout the nineteenth century, and, from the perspective of ideas about Chile's racial formation, the songs resonated with Barros Arana's vision of the state: music that sounded European with lyrics about liberal ideals.

Paralleling attempts to include the mixed characteristics of the general population into the nation's imagination, intellectuals in the early twentieth century began to focus on the practices of an imagined Chilean "folk." A redundant complex of signs emerged from various sources: researchers who focused on Chilean folklore through the collection of texts, fiction writers known as *criollistas* who tried to depict "typical" Chilean scenarios with a progressive eye, essayists who tried to describe Chile's character, and musicians who began to perform and record specific genres associated with Chile.

The academic folklorists thought of their work as scientific, but the sciences were under the influence of racial ideas and perpetuated the concept of an absence of Blackness in Chile. In 1909, Rodolfo Lenz advocated to his fellow researchers that their job was to determine what elements of Chile's folklore were from the Spanish "fatherland" and "what indigenous elements were accepted in the great mix of races" that had such a "happy result" in Chile (1909, 10). While these folklorists collected materials from different regions in Chile, an important body of work focused on a region that included Santiago, its surrounding countryside, and parts south to Temuco and surrounding areas. In addition to both urban and rural examples of language, trades, stories, and legends for this "central" region, folklorists identified and collected several gender-marked music genres and one music-dance genre danced by a couple. Men known as the popular poets generally chanted Spanish verses, whether memorized or improvised, in four- or ten-line stanzas, while women played the guitar and sang in high-pitched voices. These *cantoras* (female singers) played a diverse repertoire that included a genre meant for listening, the *tonada*, as well as a popular dance genre dating back to the era of independence called the *cueca*. The presence of these forms within folklore collections would both provide the raw material for and vindicate the use of certain genres that artists interpreted on commercial recordings marketed as Chilean.

Like the academic folklorists, fiction writers included several different characters to represent Chilean society. One of these characters was the *huaso*, a rural Chilean horseman of the central region who was ambiguously situated in Chile's socioeconomic structure. The huaso was not an elite landowner nor a peasant laborer. Instead, the huaso represented the tenant farmer, who was seen as loyal to his patron and thankful for not having to roam in search of labor. His prize possession was his horse. During the nineteenth century, the huaso was understood as a country bumpkin, and today Chileans still use the word to describe someone too dense or unaccustomed to urban modernity. At the same time, the huaso began to appear in literature that attempted to show typical Chilean scenes. The final scene of an 1885 stage adaptation of one such story, Martínez Quevedo's *Lucas Gómez*, features two cantoras playing cueca on harp and guitar while a huaso dances with a *campesina* (country girl). Such depictions began to set up a cluster of signs (huaso-guitar-cueca) that would find success in future performances.[11]

In addition to his socioeconomic ambiguity, the huaso was initially racially ambiguous. In his 1872 *Chile Ilustrado*, journalist Recaredo Tornero described the huaso as having barely ten percent of European blood. Tornero did not even mention the possibility of African blood, saying specifically that there are only two races in Chile: Spanish and Indian (446). He ascribed strength to the huaso but also a laziness derived from being content with a difficult but steady life. Such comments are consistent with the way that the nineteenth-century writers known as the *costumbristas*, those dedicated to depicting these typical scenes, would have portrayed them. The next two generations of writers, however, associated the huaso with another set of qualities. He was to epitomize common sense, reject putting on airs, and value the simple, rural life and the Chilean countryside. Known as the criollistas (criollo writers), these writers used European narrative models within Chilean rural settings to write stories that featured the huaso as a central character. Like the folklorists, the criollistas did not focus only on the huaso character, but he emerged to become the most prominent. By this time, the term "criollo" was largely understood as "home-grown" and had become synonymous with Chilean in local usage. While the huaso might not have been racially distinguished from the roto at the beginning of the twentieth century, physical descriptions of the kind that Tornero offered played less of a role as the years went by. The huaso became racially unmarked, and, as scholars of race have emphasized, the unmarked in society becomes associated with the dominant cultural mainstream, accompanied by assumptions of Whiteness.[12]

The appearance of the huaso on stage in music-dance performance played a key role here. In 1921, Jorge Martinez and Julio Cartagena took to the stage dressed in boots, spurs, and the embroidered mantle called a *chamanto*. Calling themselves the Huasos de Chincolco, they played guitar and sang *tonadas*, music that was formerly considered the repertoire of cantoras. They achieved moderate success, but praise focused on the way they could evoke the countryside with their costume and songs. While several other performers experimented with this format, it was Los Cuatro Huasos, founded in 1927, that established the model for all such groups to follow. This quartet of respectable, urban young men included three college students and a bank employee. At the urging of one of their mothers, they borrowed outfits and guitars to perform as huasos for a benefit (Rengifo 2008), which highlights the novelty of the format. The debut of the group proved so successful that they were hired for a regular engagement at a theater, eventually appearing on the radio, recording, touring, and acting as representatives of a repertoire that would collectively become known as *Música Típica Chilena* (Typical Chilean Music). This repertoire consisted initially of songs learned from their female family members, to which they applied the aesthetic standards of popular music. They traveled internationally to Peru and Argentina, and even had an extended engagement at the Waldorf Astoria in New York City in 1939. The national and international success of the group led to the acceptance of the huaso as an important symbol for Chile, and similar groups like the Huasos Quincheros also thrived. Even today, one finds such ensembles throughout Chile (see fig. 1.3). Composers such as Nicanor Molinare and Clara Solovera were inspired to write new compositions for these groups, songs that emphasized quaint rurality and patriotism.

Musicologist Juan Pablo González Rodríguez and historian Claudio Rolle (2005, 375–377) have suggested several reasons for the success of the Cuatro Huasos. Principally, they argue that the Cuatro Huasos appeared at a time when Chile's cities were growing quickly and the organization of labor unions was beginning to threaten the established social order. The Cuatro Huasos seemed to appeal to both sides of that order. Workers recently arrived in the city, recognizing musical elements that they had heard in the countryside, found solace in the singing huasos' idealized nostalgia for a rural life they had left behind. The elite, for their part, found a

Figure 1.3. Folklore group *Cantares de mi Tierra* dressed as male huasos and female *chinas* (rural companion of the huaso) performing a cueca at the May 21, 2009, celebration held on the steps of the *Casa de la Cultura*, Arica, Chile.

reification of the established order, a national musical symbol of how good things had been in the past.

Rural and temporal associations aside, the commercially successful huaso performers came from middle- or upper-class families and were phenotypically unmarked. Instead public intellectuals defined the singing huaso's physical features by contrasting him with other performers.[13] In 1939, well-known Chilean composer Pedro Humberto Allende praised the huaso groups for promoting Chile's national music because otherwise, he stated, "we see that the tangos, the rumbas, and the out-of-tune music of the North American blacks displaces our noble Chilean tonadas and cuecas."[14] Allende specifically and negatively singled out the Blackness of the North American musicians as opposed to the tango or the rumba, which seem to be simply dismissed due to their foreignness. Allende framed this criticism in this way even though, as González and Rolle (2005, 506–14) point out, Blackness in Chilean popular music was largely framed by foreign acts like Josephine Baker, and her visits to Iquique in 1928, and Afro-Cuban bandleader Isidro Benitez, and his presence in Santiago beginning in 1926. Conservative critics described these artists as primitive, out-of-control, and socially corruptive, while aficionados saw these artists as modern, cosmopolitan, and sensual. The association of either set of behaviors with Blackness was consistent with the division among cosmopolitan racial attitudes.

Furthermore, intellectuals described the criollo huaso and his music in Spanish terms that continued to exclude Blackness in Chile. In his award-winning collection of essays, Luis Durand asserted, "Ultimately, criollo music made black melodies autochthonous to the Americas, although in Chile, this phenomenon did not happen, because the black race did not prosper here due to the climate that was averse to it" (1942, 186). He went on to state that the tonada was from Spain, brought by the conquistadors, but transformed locally to absorb aspects of Chilean life. Oddly, Durand argued for Basque influence as well, even though he denied any shared musical traits with the Basque. By 1962, folklorist Oreste Plath stated that the huaso was well-defined: "He is assuredly a man of Basque-Arab Spanish wisdom that professes a great love for earth and horse. . . . His speech is proverbial. His tongue seasoned with the cumins and peppers of Andalusian mockery and criollo sarcasm" (151). By contrasting the huaso with Blackness and associating him with Spanishness, essayists like Allende and Durand complemented the signs grouped around the huaso-guitar-tonada-cueca cluster, and, like Barros Arana and Palacios, minimized any sense of racial mixture in these performances.

Bringing the Ethnoracial Other into Chilean Music-Dance

While huaso groups continued to be popular within typical Chilean music in the 1940s, educators began to promote a specific model of performing Chileanness. With the founding of the Institute of Folkloric Music Research in 1941 (González Rodríguez 1997, 63), the broader work of academic folklorists, which had always spanned more than just the tonada and cueca, became material for educational purposes. Particularly at the university level, students were instructed in the techniques of the documentation and collection of folkloric material and how to use this material as a basis for *proyección folclórica* (staged folklore).[15] This concept of putting folklore "on display" was meant to expose (primarily urban) Chileans to folkloric expressions that they otherwise might not encounter. Educators organized summer programs in which participants learned to dance or play several folk genres from the different regions of the country. The culmination of these camps was a performance of these dances in costumes associated with a region, people, or community, sometimes in front of a backdrop invoking the setting. Over time, these workshops were converted into academic courses and were implemented at all levels of the Chilean educational system. Even today, most school children perform a folkloric dance in its corresponding attire during Chile's annual Independence Day celebrations.

The institutionalization of folklore collection and performance had two fundamental consequences. First, it created a sense—which many Chileans still have today—about the proper way of collecting folklore and representing it "authentically."[16] Particularly prized was the concept of fieldwork: interviewing folk artists within a community and witnessing an expression within its associated context. Staged versions of folklore were then assumed to mimic these documented performances. Second, a canon for such performances was created that generally referenced three geographic regions of Chile and two ethnoracial groups therein: the North, Central, and South (or more specifically Chiloé) regions, plus the Mapuche and Rapa Nui (Easter Islanders).[17] In the minds of many Chileans, this canon expanded the range of possible expressions that could represent Chile. Since the majority of Chile's population resided in the Central region, many Chileans understood music-dance outside this huaso-imagined region as extremely different from their own experience. These concepts played a role in the way that Afro-descendant music would later emerge in Arica.

The institutionalization of folklore set the stage for what Juan Pablo González and others have dubbed the "neofolklore" era, a period from the early to late 1960s. Like the huaso groups, the neofolklorists modified folklore materials to perform and compose their repertoire. These artists, however, incorporated genres from outside Chile's Central region while more overtly including some techniques and timbres of international popular music. For example, a large number of Latin American folk genres, particularly from Argentina, were incorporated into this movement. The neofolklorists were mostly young and urban, interested in captivating listeners like themselves. They tended to dress as cosmopolitan artists in suits and appeared on the covers of magazines aimed at teenage audiences. As González points out (1998, 18), the major contribution of this phase was to expose the public to a wider variety of folklore genres from different regions of the country and to revive some older, neglected genres using cosmopolitan and commercial aesthetic practices. Critics, of course, complained about a lack of authenticity and perhaps knowledge of the genres being performed, although they were grateful for the renewed interest in folklore and the additional creative license that these artists had carved out for performers.

Such tensions with critics partially fueled artists who wanted to utilize other folk resources to represent groups of people outside the realm of the urban cosmopolitan sphere. Some of these artists performed and composed in Chilean folkloric genres, attempting to invoke rurality, but many took to performing international folk musics, particularly highland Andean genres (from Argentina, Bolivia, and Peru). The Andean focus started to nuance Chile's Northern region as a place with a presence of Aymara and Quechua indigenous peoples, whom the state had overlooked. This focus on the plight of the Other that was the source of these forms of music meant that the lyrics gradually became more political. This group of artists formed a key part of what eventually became known as the *nueva canción* (New Song), named after the music festival that brought many of these artists to national attention. The New Song Movement, with its heavily Andean influence, became the soundtrack for the Popular Unity party and eventually the election of Marxist president Salvador Allende.

These three movements (proyección folclórica, neofolklore, and the nueva canción) more strongly introduced the concept of local difference into Chile's musical imagination. They presented genres from outside Chile's Central region and offered images of characters beyond the huaso. Such representations were complicated, because the performers often were university students in Santiago that had limited exposure to the groups of people they were supposed to be representing. They created a space that allowed for an alternative to the criollo huaso as a way of imagining the nation. These Others within Chile's imagination initially tended to be described in geographic and cultural terms: the Chilote boatman, the rural rover (whether shepherd, cattle driver, or cattle rustler), and a historical approach to Chile's north that featured the Chilean soldier in the War of the Pacific or miners and other early actors within Chile's Labor Movement (González Rodríguez 1997). With the New Song Movement, new ethnoracial categories of Aymara and Quechua joined the ever-present but distant Mapuche, and music-dance genres associated with Indigeneity more notably became a part of Chile's musical soundscape.

An Opening for Blackness: Neoliberalism and the Multicultural Turn

While the presence of Indigeneity became more significant in the forms of music described above, with few exceptions, Blackness remained something forgotten or foreign.[18] During this same period, however, several additional historical studies on slavery began to subtly change perspectives on the role that institution played in Chile's history. In 1942, Guillermo Feliú Cruz published a book that asserted the absence of Blackness in Chile's culture, claiming that the slaves "did not leave footprints behind" nor "distinguish themselves in an industry or craft" "as they passed through Chilean society" (1942, 117). In fact, Feliú Cruz painted an idyllic picture of enslavement in the period just prior to abolition, in which the slaves had lost their greatest vices of sex and violence, and slave owners no longer had to resort to cruel punishments to create a system of mutual respect. To illustrate the benefits of this system, Feliú Cruz offered the story of José Romero, a mulato whose military prowess during the fight for Chilean independence was commemorated by the erection of a monument in Santiago in 1862. This position had the effect of both recognizing and erasing Blackness in Chile's national narrative, merging it with the values of the criollo founding fathers. Similarly, Gonzalo Vial Correa noted the presence of Juan Valiente, a Black conquistador who received an *encomienda* during Chile's colonial period, although he agreed that Blackness had little effect on Chilean society.[19] This paradoxical approach slowly opened the door to Vial's minor acknowledgment that "our race has, well, something of the Black" (1957, 126), while still asserting that it had been absorbed in the mestizaje process. This process resonates with the idea of "styling criollo" that I describe in chapter 4.

In 1959, a major advance was made in historical scholarship about slavery. Historian Rolando Mellafe set the new bar for the scholarly study of slavery in Chile with his book *La introducción de la esclavitud negra en chile: Trafico y rutas*. Looking beyond censuses, Mellafe carefully examined documents like bills of sale in the colonial period to give a more complete picture of the demographics of slavery in Santiago. Mellafe took slavery in colonial Chile seriously, dismissing theories about how Chile's climate had made Black labor untenable, and he demonstrated that slavery played an important economic role (Cussen 2006, 52). Unfortunately, until recently, few scholars followed Mellafe's call to continue his work, and social attitudes did not generally change.

The 1973 military coup that eventually led to General Augusto Pinochet's rise to power did not encourage the situation. The political upheaval cut short the development of the Nueva Canción, and Andean music inside Chile, which had been so closely associated with the Popular Unity government, disappeared from public view for a time. The Pinochet regime resorted once again to música típica as its main form of representation, appointing the leader of Los Huasos Quincheros, Benjamin MacKenna, as the secretary for cultural relations (Jara Hinojosa 2016). This espousal of criollo music resonated with the government's position on race. A government agriculture minister famously stated in 1978, "There are no Indians in Chile, there are only Chileans."[20] Despite the repressive nature of the Pinochet period, Andean instruments began to reappear, fueling a relative of the Nueva Canción called Canto Nuevo (New Singing).[21] The lyrics of Canto Nuevo were politically more subdued than before the regime and dealt with environmental issues and the daily challenges of urban life. The persistent use of Andean music meant that many Chileans, particularly those who opposed the regime, started to envision the country as Andean rather than criollo.[22]

Yet within this space of Canto Nuevo, the first musical acknowledgments toward the history of the Black population in Arica appeared. In 1979, Osvaldo Torres recorded a song entitled "Lumbanga de Arica (Viejo Bantu)," which narrated the story of an old Bantu slave from the Congo that was brought to Arica. Torres wrote the song based on his travels through Chile's North region, and although his album was well received, the song did not gain special attention until Afro-descendant groups began to claim it as their own in the 2000s. The group Arak Pacha, which formed in Arica, has recorded several tunes that reference Blackness, albeit within identifiably Andean genres. Most directly related to Arica was the 1987 *wayno* titled "Totoral—A Rosa Güisa," dedicated to the reed-weaving artisan and beloved personality in Arica who became an icon for the Afro-descendant movement, despite also having Indigenous roots.[23] At the time, however, the songs' Andean contexts overpowered these songs, a process I discuss in chapter 6 as styling indígena.

Despite these musical forays into Arica's Blackness and the growth of Chilean Andean music, the dictatorship did not consider social issues in ethnoracial terms. Instead, it focused on silencing political opposition and addressing economic issues in the usual terms of class. Pinochet's government followed the free market policies suggested by the infamous "Chicago boys," a group of Chilean economists.[24] These policies would anticipate a later, larger "neoliberal" turn—an orientation adopted by many Latin American countries in the late 1980s through the 1990s that favored free markets with little regulation as a means of development. By the 1990s, after multiple recessions and setbacks, international observers hailed Chile's economy as successful, but over the last decade or so, this success has come under critique by those who recognize that such policies often shifted social commitments like health care and education from the state to community or nongovernmental organizations. This shift meant that the "benefits" of neoliberal economic policies were often unevenly distributed. These criticisms also make note of the significant human rights abuses that took place during the Pinochet era.

While these issues affected all of Chilean society, "neoliberalism represents a continuation of coloniality and systemic racism" (Richards 2013, 74), and as such, Indigenous communities were notoriously victimized. As the 1989 plebiscite approached, Pinochet's opposition courted these communities with promises of governmental changes. In 1993, after Patricio Alywin's successful election to the presidency, the Chilean government passed the so-called "Indigenous Law," which created the National Council for Indigenous Development (CONADI), a government agency within the Ministry of Planning. While ostensibly designed to put power in the hands of indigenous leaders, some Indigenous individuals that I spoke with told me that the CONADI effectively eliminated Indigenous activism by offering activist leaders government positions. With these leaders now working for the government, fewer community members could hold the CONADI accountable to the community. In general, the newly elected 1993 Concertación government did not change the neoliberal economic policies of the Pinochet regime, so the CONADI's programs were tailored in ways to both acknowledge Indigenous ways of identifying while simultaneously encouraging free market initiatives. This alignment of economic policy with an interest in promoting cultural difference resonated with the way that other Latin American governments interacted with their ethnoracial minorities, a phenomenon that several scholars have referred to as "neoliberal multiculturalism" (Richards 2013, 11).[25] Latin America's renewed interest in recognizing and promoting these communities during this period has also been referred to generally as the "multicultural turn."[26]

In terms of music-dance, this neoliberal multiculturalism plays out in several ways. On the one hand, the CONADI offers resources for cultural projects, often framed as the "rescue" of fading traditions. These projects culminate in audio or video recordings, concerts, and/or books. Given their limited distribution, the importance of such projects is difficult to interpret. Over time, however, they arguably contribute to an increased acceptance and appreciation of Indigenous cultures and act as resources for the elaboration of Indigenous expressions. On the other hand, in line with the government's neoliberal policies, the state is particularly supportive of cultural expressions that may serve as a source of economic ingress via tourism or other means. In Arica, for example, much municipal and regional support is given to the carnival Con La Fuerza del Sol. The growth in the number and size of dance troupes representative of Indigenous culture as part of this carnival can be understood both in terms of an increased interest in the culture itself as well as a possible increase in tourism for the city.

The Afro-descendant movement for ethnic and cultural recognition in Chile appeared within this "neoliberal multicultural" context. While such policies were oriented primarily toward Indigenous groups in Chile, Afro-descendant groups have been included as part of the multicultural turn in other parts of Latin America. This inclusion coincided with a reframing in the way in which people had understood Blackness in the region, which inevitably influenced how the Chilean Afro-descendant movement emerged. I now consider this change in orientation before discussing its impact in Chile.

Blackness Reimagined: From Black to Afro-descendant

In 2000, Chile hosted a Latin American regional conference for the United Nations that anticipated the now-famous 2001 Durban International Conference on Racism, Xenophobia and Discrimination. It was not the original choice of location, and critics of the change worried that the lack of Blackness in Chile would result in little attention paid to the concerns of the pan-American Black Movement.[27] Present at this conference was Romero Jorge Rodriguez, the influential leader of the Uruguay-based organization Mundo Afro. Mundo Afro would become an important model and ally for the Afro-Chilean organizations that were about to emerge. In 2000, the organization was generally categorized as part of the *movimiento negro,* or "Black Movement." During the Santiago conference, Rodriguez argued that the term "Black" was a product of colonialist thinking. Activists in the Black Movement, following developments in Brazil (Caldwell 2007, 47), believed that adopting the term *afrodescendiente,* or Afro-descendant, would be an accomplishment. The abolition of slavery had done little for "populations of African origin in the Americas," 92 percent of whom, Rodriguez argued, still lived under the poverty line. Nation-states, in referring to such populations as "Black," simply disguised the history of racism and enslavement that were at the root of these problems. Rodriguez claimed that self-identification as Afro-descendants made that history visible and pointed a way forward for the work that needed to be done. He is often quoted as saying of the conference, "We entered as Blacks and left Afro-descendants" (Rodríguez, 2004).

While similar terminology had some history in parts of Latin America, it generally took hold in the region after the Santiago conference. In my experience, the individuals who identify as Afro-descendant have been primarily activists, like Marta Salgado, who have been exposed to this type of international politics. Yet I also heard many members of Chilean Afro-descendant organizations refer to themselves as Black in various contexts. This usage points to the much longer history of the term negro alluded to earlier, but the term has never been consistently applied. For example, Jack Forbes notes that "The term 'negro' has been applied to Black Africans, Indians of India, Native Americans, Japanese, and slaves of whatever ancestry. 'Black' has been used for all of the above and for non-whites in general" (1993, 2–3).

This broad usage highlights Rodriguez's point that the single term Black has been used to disguise certain historical and social realities that would otherwise lead to challenging nuances in how one understands such varied populations. While this broad use could have negative consequences, activists in the late 1970s and 1980s preferred to identify with Black as a term that both transcended national boundaries and pushed against the idea that they were of a mixed, and therefore tainted, culture (Whitten and Torres 1998, 27–28). Stuart Hall recognized this tension between the historical reality of the varied experiences of African diasporic peoples versus the value of essentializing these experiences as Black to gain recognition within the field of popular culture at a particular moment. Hall went on to argue, however, that this moment had passed; it was time to recognize the number of ways Black popular culture had always been a result of interaction between cultures. "It is to the diversity, not the homogeneity, of black experience that we must now give our undivided attention" (1996, 473).

Hall's argument is well taken, and it reflects how I use the term Blackness as a framing concept. Blackness, defined as the criteria used to identify individuals as Black and the qualities being ascribed to or claimed by those individuals as a result, varies according to time and place. The local organizations that emerged to represent Chile's Black population at the beginning of the twenty-first century mainly focused on a form of Blackness that emphasized their culture as Afro-descendant. This choice reflected the political moment, since the international Black movement had generally embraced the concept of Afro-descendant, and Afro-Chilean organizations like Oro Negro wanted to be a part of that movement for at least two reasons. First, politically, the transnational network of Afro-descendant organizations had experience in dealing with discrimination on a larger scale, meaning that more international pressure could be exerted on the Chilean government. More specifically, however, given that Chilean culture had negated the presence of Blackness for such a long time, engaging with Blackness as Afro-descendant also gave individuals an opportunity both to understand their history better while connecting to other parts of the African diaspora.

Identifying as part of the diaspora offered members of Afro-Chilean organizations access to a historical narrative that, spun positively in this context, stretched back to great civilizations in Africa. As Rodríguez pointed out, these histories have generally been denied to populations when Blackness was framed negatively solely in racial terms, in which phenotype is believed to determine an individual's intellectual and behavioral characteristics. To combat such discrimination, some early twentieth-century scholars, like Melville J. Herskovits, argued for something like the diasporic perspective. They initially crafted a history in which culture flowed from Africa in one direction. As Afro-descendants went through an "acculturation" process in the Americas, they maintained aspects of this African culture over time through "retentions" or as part of a "syncretism" (Yelvington 2001, 228–29; 2011, 65–66). Later scholars, working from a more formulated diasporic point of view, envisioned a circulation of expressive culture that was born out of the experience of the Middle Passage and chattel slavery, perhaps most notably Paul Gilroy's conception of a Black Atlantic (1993) as the cultural space for that interaction. To complement and further nuance the ideas of such cultural interactions, Heidi Feldman more recently offered up the idea of the Black Pacific (2006), a complex of communities along the west coast of the Americas that are geographically more distant from Africa than the Black Atlantic. These ideas illustrate how contemporary scholars now understand the African diaspora as a complex process. Rather than a single transformative experience—one based on the enslavement of Africans, who, transformed by the Middle Passage, created a monolithic diasporic culture—specific characteristics of the diaspora changed over time and in dialogic fashion between Africa, the Americas, and beyond. Its history includes a variety of ethnicities within Africa, with multiple formative experiences shared by the diasporic population as a whole, while still recognizing important differences among various communities based on multiple passages, specific types of enslavement, and varied living conditions.

Feldman also noticed, however, that many people in Black Pacific countries (and she considers Chile one of them) look to Black Atlantic cultures as credible stand-ins for Africa. Using this logic, Black Pacific cultures emphasize their similarities with Black Atlantic cultures to highlight their relationship with African culture. The unfortunate result is a simplified vision of the African diaspora. As Hall suggested, adopting this strategy may be politically expedient, but other factors also play a role. Individuals may assume this stance to understand themselves in the face of limited information about their own history. This choice may also be due to aesthetic preference, or because it resonates with their own cultural experiences of Blackness. In the next chapter, I concentrate on how this recent shift to focusing on Blackness as Afro-descendant in Chile has played out in music-dance, and how this tension between seeking similarities and finding differences within the diaspora has played out in the emergence of the tumbe carnaval. First, however, I describe the founding of the first Chilean Afro-descendant organization and several reasons for why it focused on music-dance within the movement.

Presenting . . . the Afro-Chileans!

In preparing for the 2000 United Nations conference in Santiago, Francisco Estévez, the director of the nongovernmental organization (NGO) Fundación Ideas, was sensitive to the criticisms that Chile's lack of Blackness would result in ignoring Black issues. So, when he encountered Sonia Salgado—the mayor of Camarones, a town near Arica—in a meeting, he was curious about her phenotype. After Salgado confirmed his suspicions that she was of African descent, Estévez visited Arica and invited Salgado and her relatives to attend the conference.

During Estévez's opening remarks at the conference, he spoke of the history and presence of people of African descent in Chile, and as proof, he had the delegation stand up in the hall. They received a thunderous ovation. In an interview I conducted with him on May 16, 2010, Estévez described the experience: "That is the moment—I would say, symbolic—of the Latin American recognition that, in Chile, there was a significant Afro-descendant presence. Historically, yes, the historians and everyone had said that there was an important Black population, but it was thought to be something from the colonial period, ancient, but not something currently present. Today, however, no one can deny that this Black Afro-Chilean population has a presence here in the country."[28]

What Estévez described was a fundamental challenge to the standard thinking on how people of African descent had participated in Chilean history and culture. Afro-descendants in Chile had previously been relegated to a footnote in the history books, to an antiquity that equated an absence. Their appearance at the Santiago conference not only amazed attendees with their existence, but also with what it suggested: that these Afro-descendants had persevered since the colonial era and therefore had participated in the formation of contemporary Chilean society. The following year, Salgado and her sister Marta created Chile's first Afro-descendant NGO, Oro Negro (Black Gold), and they both attended the Durban conference. Afro-Chileans became participants in international networks of Afro-descendant organizations and events. Despite Estévez's assertions, however, as of the beginning of 2019, Chile's national government has yet to officially decree that Afro-Chileans exist.

The Importance of Music-Dance to the Afro-descendant Movement

While Rodriguez was advocating to reframe the Black Movement in Afro-descendant terms at the Santiago conference, his organization, Mundo Afro (Afro World), was illustrating the importance music-dance performance could have for Afro-descendant organizations on Santiago's streets. The group, which sponsors schools, workshops and performances in the Afro-Uruguayan carnival music-dance of *candombe*, had brought their drums to accompany the activists as they marched outside to gain the attention of the international governmental organization and media present at the conference. Estévez observed that Chilean police treated these musical Afro-descendant marchers differently than their Indigenous counterparts. According to Estévez (interview with author, May 16, 2010), while Indigenous activists were direct, yelling slogans that police perceived as threatening, Afro-descendants created circular spaces, guided by a different type of beat that Santiago's law enforcement saw as exotic. Indeed, such circular spaces may even have invited participation, which scholars have often cited as an important feature of Afro-diasporic music.²⁹ Estévez argued that such moments illustrated the importance of music-dance to the newly identified Afro-Chileans.

After the 2000 Santiago conference, Oro Negro focused on growing its membership and establishing its political goals, networking with organizations like Mundo Afro to share information at jointly coordinated workshops. Present at such events was Gustavo del Canto, a Santiago native who, as an undergraduate journalism major, had reported on the Santiago conference for an online newspaper. Based on this experience, he decided to do his senior thesis on Arica's Afro-descendant population and eventually moved to the city to court one of the members of the Salgado extended family. While del Canto does not identify as Black, it became painfully obvious to him and several other younger members of Oro Negro that the organization needed to develop something in relation to music-dance. As he recalled in 2010, "Our idea was to create a comparsa, because it brings people together, it gives you exposure, it supports the movement. At that time, Sonia [Salgado] had very good contacts with Mundo Afro and other Afro-descendant organizations. People would come here [to Arica] and we would go to play at the drop of a hat. That is, the Afro-descendant organizations would come, and there is always a recess in the activities. Okay, no one danced anything, so it was necessary that something be done."

Del Canto's comments suggest that interest in forming the comparsa (a music-dance troupe) was partially motivated by wanting to participate in activities with other Afro-descendant groups. Initially, this motivation seemed to drive much of the music-dance practice because the comparsa would only come together to rehearse before events and trips.

Over time, however, Oro Negro's comparsa began to appear more often, and perhaps most notably, as part of Arica's urban carnival, Con la Fuerza del Sol. The comparsa gave more visibility to the organizations due to the number of people who attend the carnival. The prizes they won positively reinforced the work they were doing. Music-dance gave Afro-descendants the opportunity to invite others to participate in growing awareness for the movement. Observers would express their appreciation of the performance, and that opening permitted members of the comparsa to explain their organization and interests in a nonthreatening manner.

In reflecting on the role of music-dance within the Afro-Chilean movement, I want to highlight two important points. First, I often find that when analyzing music-dance within political movements, there is a temptation to look at them retrospectively as fully formed genres with targeted aims rather than as processes that developed over time to meet emerging needs. The development of the comparsa started with the intention of those involved in Oro Negro to be able to participate with other groups in a communal activity. The comparsa then began to serve the organization in other ways. In hindsight, critiques of such movements as the "invention of tradition" often disqualify performance claims based on questions of self-serving motives, for example, suggesting that the quest for state recognition of Afro-descendants in Chile was at the core of forming the comparsa. As I will describe in chapter 2, however, these performances developed over time in response to other inclinations, the understanding of which requires a more nuanced attitude.

Second, the success of comparsa performances with respect to these motives—whether the desire to interact with international Afro-descendant groups or to inspire advocacy in audience members—are tied to aesthetic force. Del Canto's indication that Oro Negro's members wanted to be able to participate in music-dance with other Afro-descendants suggests that they enjoyed some aspect of these expressions, and, in the quote that opens this chapter, Salgado notes people are attracted to their performances. In my research, I have been particularly interested in the ways in which music-dance performance can persuade both participants and observers through the experience of aesthetics. Music-dance performance involves embodied knowledge; such knowledge is highly specific in sounds, movements, and contexts, while being richly ambiguous in meaning. People initially react to music-dance performances in ways that they already understand as beautiful or important from their past experiences; that initial response is later described in words. When music-dance knowledge is juxtaposed with other types of embodied knowledge, it can create a particularly powerful connection between the two. Could listening and dancing to the Oro Negro's comparsa drums—an exciting experience that connects to Africa even as it contrasts with other experiences of Chilean music—help convince Chilean audiences of the persistence of Afro-descendants in Chile?

In this chapter, I have described the trajectory of the ideas of Blackness in Chile from the arrival of Africans and their categorization into castas through the end of slavery. I have explored the continuing stigmatization of Blackness and its erasure in the national Chilean imaginary, and I have shown how music-dance performances helped contribute to this process. Toward the end of the twentieth century, cosmopolitan ideas about Blackness began to change. These ideas, in coordination with the adoption of the Multicultural Alignment by many Latin American countries including Chile, set the stage for the emergence of Chilean Afro-descendant activist groups. While I explored some of the early rationales for performing music-dance in the wake of this emergence, in chapter 2 I describe in detail the type of music-dance that became central to the movement: the tumbe carnaval. I analyze the way tumbe performers developed signs that connect the tumbe with ideas of what they believe being Afro-descendant means, as well as the life experiences of Arica's Black residents—a process I call styling Blackness as Afro-descendant.

Notes

1. For an overview, see Magnus Mörner's classic text (1967) as well as the more recent summary included in Peter Wade (2010). Kathryn Burns (2011) goes into greater depth on the implications of religion in the casta system.

2. Gómez listed the following castas present in Chile: español, indio, mestizo, cuaterones (mestizo with español), negro, mulato, and zambo. As cited in Hernan Godoy Urzúa (1976, 117–21).

3. For central Chile, the special issue of *Cuadernos de historia* (2006) and Cussen's edited volume (2009) as well as the work of Jean-Paul Zuñiga (2001, 2006) have been enlightening. Specific to Arica, the work of Briones Valentín (2004) and Díaz Ayala, Galdámes Rosas, and Ruz Zagal, eds. (2013) has been important. Directly related to the Afro-descendant movement are the books of Cristian Báez Lazcano (2010), Gustavo del Canto Larios (2003), and Marta Salgado Henríquez (2013).

4. Chile was initially a general captaincy within the viceroyalty of Peru.

5. Such numbers presumably do not include the regional Indigenous peoples. Part of the reason that Arica's Black presence was so high was that it was deemed a malaria-infested region. Africans were assumed to have a higher tolerance for the disease, and local Spaniards preferred to live in neighboring Tacna.

6. An example is the well-known epic poem about the first conflicts between the Spanish and Araucanians (modern-day Mapuche), Alonso de Ercilla's *La Araucana*.

7. As Patrick Barr-Mejel points out, Palacios's depiction was written for a very specific reason. Chile's government at the time gave preference to European immigrants over its own citizens in its settler-colonialist project south of the Bio-Bio River, a territory that the Mapuche people had previously defended from invasion. From his Chilean nativist perspective, Palacios advocated that Chilean citizens be given priority over these foreigners. This position suited other politicians as well, who saw this racially unifying argument as a way to undermine the growing tensions among the classes. The irony here is that Palacios's political aims were damaging to, and indeed exclusive of, the very Indigenous population whose qualities he praised to make his argument.

8. Nevertheless, Palacios still admitted the existence of African blood in the "fewest" of Chile's urban families. Presumably, he recognized this Blackness based on physical characteristics, which he claimed were still visible up to the sixth generation (1918, 57–58). But Palacios asserted that such negative Black qualities were not present in the roto.

9. Barros Arana, *Historia general de Chile,* in volumes 3, 99–100 and 7, 445–49.

10. For more on these patriotic leagues, see González Miranda, Maldonado Prieto, and McGee Deutsch (1993).

11. Turino (2008) defines an indexical cluster as a group of indexical signs that are often found together. Turino uses the term "indexical signs" based on Charles S. Peirce's theories of semiotics. See his articles (1999, 2014) for more in-depth exploration. An indexical sign is one in which the interpretant of the sign-vehicle and its object is through juxtaposition in experience. See chapter 2 for more description of Peirce's work.

12. For a discussion of the unmarked character of Whiteness, see "The Possessive Investment in Whiteness" in George Lipsitz, (1998) 2006.

13. Whiteness, for example, has historically been defined in terms of not being Black, while Black characteristics have historically been negatively defined. See Allende's comment.

14. Allende wrote these words in the 1935 New Year's Day edition of the *Mercurio* newspaper. Reprinted in Varas and González (2009, 185).

15. For an example of research methodology in the practice of proyección folclórica, see Barros (1962).

16. I have placed this initial usage of "authentically" in quotes to question its nature, but, throughout the rest of the book, claims to authenticity and the authentic should be understood as both a way of gaining cultural capital and a value placed on practice emerging from direct experience. See Bendix 1997 and Turino 2008.

17. In my experience, students generally participate in these performances without necessarily discussing the pitfalls or issues associated with representing groups with whom one does not identify. Rapa Nui administratively falls into Chile's central region, and its geographic location is often glossed over in these types of presentations.

18. Exceptions include Rolando Alarcón's 1965 "El Negro Cachimbo," Victor Jara's 1971 Afro-Peruvian recording "A la Molina No Voy Mas," and Inti-Illimani's 1973 Afro-Bolivian influenced recording of "Fiesta de San Benito."

19. An encomienda was an arrangement in which a group of Indigenous peoples were placed in the care of a particular individual. That individual was to "Christianize" these Indigenous people, while they, in return, would provide labor for that individual—primarily serving as a form of Indigenous slavery.

20. This quote, which is often credited to Pinochet himself, is properly attributed to Alfonso Márquez de la Plata. He apparently caused an uproar with this statement, as he said in Temuco, generally considered the Mapuche heartland. The quote can be found in Revista *Hoy*, 13–19/9/1978, p. 29 as cited by Francisco Albizú Labbé (2014).

21. Musicians employed several strategies to make these instruments acceptable again, including performing classical music on them.

22. It is interesting to note the similarities of this shift with the musical shift that Wade observed for Colombia from an Andean to a Caribbean country. See Wade (2000).

23. *Wayno* (or *huayno*) is the most popular and diverse Andean music genre. The harmonies of the wayno move ambiguously between major and minor, and the rhythm, while often grounded in an eighth-and-two-sixteenth note pattern, often includes one-beat measure in keeping with the melody.

24. The "Chicago Boys" refers to a group of Chilean economists, some of whom were trained at the University of Chicago, who tended to espouse the type of free market policies that they would enact during the Pinochet regime (Collier and Sater 2004, 365).

25. "Neoliberal multiculturalism" refers to government policies that are willing to recognize the existence of different ethno-racial groups within a nation-state while focusing primarily on market-driven solutions to address the systemic inequalities that discrimination against these groups has produced. For example, rather than redistribute land, the government offers small business grants to individuals from these groups, often with the intention of promoting tourism and cultural production for consumption.

26. See Paschel (2016, 229–30) for a discussion of the pervasiveness of this concept in scholarship, as well as her strong argument against this blanket characterization.

27. Caldwell (2009, 114, 119n30) describes the questionable circumstances under which Brazil withdrew its invitation to host the regional conference.

28. All translations from the Spanish are the author's.

29. Chernoff, for example, states that "the predominant participatory mode of African music can be said to constitute a formal characteristic that takes precedence over other elements of musical organization" (1991, 1084).

2

TUMBE CARNAVAL
Styling Afro-descendant

THE MEMBERS OF CHILE'S FIRST AFRO-DESCENDANT NONGOVERNMENTAL ORGANIZATION (NGO), Oro Negro, recognized the need, both symbolic and artistic, for the revitalization of the forms of regional music-dance derived from African sources. Although they were aware of the methods and requirements of the proyección folclórica practices described in chapter 1, they did not have the knowledge of specific forms immediately at their disposal. They knew, however, of resources that could help. The Fondo Nacional para el Desarrollo Cultural y las Artes (National Fund for the Development of Culture and the Arts), or FONDART, is a Chilean government program that provides funding for projects that promote the country's arts, culture, and heritage on both the national and regional level. In 2002, Gustavo del Canto, together with a few members of the Letelier Salgado family and a resident Uruguayan, Yoni Olis, put together a regional FONDART project, "Formación de un Grupo de Danzas y Música Negra, para rescatar, mediante la recreación artística, las tradiciones culturales de los afrodescendientes ariqueños" (The Formation of a Black Music and Dances Group, to rescue the cultural traditions of Arica's Afro-descendants via artistic reconstruction).

The group was initially uncertain as to what type of reconstruction it would create. It saw Afro-Peruvian music as a logical starting point, given that Arica was part of Peru until the late nineteenth century and represented a similar population. The award of the FONDART grant gave the group the resources to purchase a variety of instruments, including a guitar, congas, bongó, donkey jawbones, and several *cajónes*.[1] Artists and intellectuals had reconstructed Afro-Peruvian music using this instrumentation over the course of the twentieth century (see Feldman 2006). Playing this type of music, however, required certain skills that the members did not have. It meant depending on musicians from outside the organization, but after a few initial collaborations, the project coordinators found that these musicians' commitment to Oro Negro was limited. Practically speaking, the group needed to find another type of expression.

This chapter focuses on this other expression—the tumbe carnaval. I first explore some of the theoretical resources available for the analysis of tumbe performance, especially dealing with styling and Blackness. I then describe the ethnographic details of the emergence of tumbe carnaval and the details of its performance. I recount how local elders described the tumbe and how Oro Negro members creatively interpreted these descriptions to be able to perform it. This process involved thinking about the past in ways that were consistent with both local and cosmopolitan ways of conceiving Blackness. The music-dance that Oro Negro performed would have to invoke other Afro-descendant performers in the thoughts of those present—a process that I refer to as styling Blackness as Afro-descendant. This process did not stop with the initial tumbe carnaval performance but continued to develop as the number of Afro-descendant organizations and the opportunities to perform grew.

Signifyin' and Signs: Resources for the Analysis of Styling Afro-descendant

My use of "styling Afro-descendant" as a frame of analysis for tumbe carnaval performance has several intellectual points of departure. The political discussion among Latin American Black activists to reframe Blackness as Afro-descendant inspires the "Afro-descendant" category, but I also connect my interest in Afro-descendant style to a line of scholarly activist thinking that has sought out African musical heritage in African American music in the Americas, particularly the United States. In moving beyond the aforementioned scholarship that originally framed Black music as displaying "retentions," US academics, with African American scholars in the vanguard, began to give less weight to observable commonalities with contemporary African musics in favor of grappling with the underlying concepts that were being culturally transmitted.[2] The goal here was to lend credence to the idea of "Black music," a category that was increasingly coming under fire as contrived because many of its musical elements could be found in other cultures.

One particularly influential answer to this critique was Samuel Floyd Jr.'s "master musical trope of Call-Response," which encompassed what he understood were five key elements of African American musical practice (1991, 285):

1. A constant referencing of existing musical material, borrowing and restating it while simultaneously transforming it—a process known as signifyin(g). Here Floyd is adapting Henry Louis Gates's famous theory of signifyin(g) about African American literature to music. For Gates (1988), "Signifyin(g)" is an overarching concept that describes an array of elements in African American narrative practice.
2. A tendency to integrate the audience into a performance by eliciting a response.
3. A framework of continuous self-criticism accompanying performance in its context.
4. An emphasis on competitive values that help performers stay sharp.
5. A complete intertwining of music and dance.

The Call-Response trope relies on specific cultural contexts and knowledge, hence Floyd's references to "cultural memory," a subjective concept that references what members of a culture seem to "know" as true to their experience when encountered, without necessarily having been formally instructed about the topic (1995, 8).[3] Guthrie Ramsey's history of *Race Music* further draws on this idea, as he develops a history of various musical genres in parallel with his personal experiences and ethnographic data about his own family (2003). For Ramsey, the sense of what African American music is emerges from its context and its importance to the African American community, as understood through their own narratives. This cultural memory approach is not limited to African Americans, as musicologist David Brackett points out. Brackett notes how his own White cultural memory has value in describing Black music, so long as it is contextualized in time and place and explores the relationships between the ways in which people identify (2005, 88–89). Paralleling arguments about the social construction of race, these scholars' discussions recognize that Blackness is constructed in music-dance, but that such constructions are part of social realities and have social consequences. When music-dance performances invoke cultural memory, they resonate with these social realities. Cultural memory, therefore, is a criterion for the legitimacy of styling Blackness in a specific way.[4]

The question becomes: how is cultural memory successfully invoked in performance? Building on and generalizing the types of ideas found in Floyd's work, ethnomusicologist Veit Erlmann has argued that Black diasporic musical performance is primarily *phatic*—i.e., focused on how things are being communicated, rather than what is being communicated.[5] Recognizing the similarity of this concept with definitions of style, Erlmann considers performers of Black diasporic music as "communities of style" (2000, 87). To explain the connection between style and experience, I turn to the semiotic work of C. S. Peirce to analyze styling. Peirce argues that humans encounter and think through signs and their relationships.[6] Peirce's work deals with phenomena beyond just language, and ethnomusicologists like Thomas Turino have found it useful. At its most basic, Peirce envisioned a three-part structure for signs: the sign-vehicle, its object, and its interpretant. A sign-vehicle conjures a specific object via an interpretant, the response to the sign. This understanding is much more nuanced than simply saying something stands for something else, because it recognizes that all cases of signification require a translation of some kind into a different medium, often an emotion. A sign-vehicle and an object are related in at least three basic ways: as an icon, an index, and a symbol. Icons function primarily through resemblance, indexes function through a previously experienced juxtaposition, and symbols are linguistically defined. These different sign types are not exclusive of one another but often function simultaneously. For example, songs have lyrics, which use language and so function symbolically, and they are experientially juxtaposed with visuals, sounds, and movement in ways that function indexically. Elements within different facets of performance, whether sonic, visual, or kinesthetic, act as signs for something else, their objects.[7] I base my explanation of a sign-vehicle's dynamics on the ethnographic information at my disposal, justifying why I might refer to things as indexes or symbols during the book. More importantly, this data, the cultural memories of those with whom I worked and the personal experiences gained through participant-observation, provides the interpretant—the feelings or ideas that give the sign-object relationship meaning. The key point here is that styling aims to use potential signs in performance to connect with objects through interpretants that resonate with local cultural memories. With these ideas in mind, I now describe how the genre tumbe carnaval initially emerged and analyze how its performers began to style it as Afro-descendant.

Building the Comparsa: Identifying Genre and Instrumentation

As Oro Negro members discussed the need for a comparsa based on regional forms of music-dance, Gustavo del Canto was already researching Afro-descendants in Arica for his undergraduate journalism thesis. Aware of proyección folclórica methods, del Canto asked about music-dance practices in his interviews with senior members of the Black community in the city and the neighboring Azapa Valley. Del Canto encountered the description of a dance performed by Afro-descendant families during carnival time. Accompanied by a bombo drum, couples would dance together in a circle. Someone would yell, "tumba!" and each person would try to knock over their partner with their hips. The tumbe had not been practiced for several decades, and the elders that described it had been children at the time. Too young to participate, they had only caught glimpses of the dance clandestinely after having been sent to bed. Nevertheless, the features that they described would form the basis for what would become tumba/e carnaval practice: a choreography that references the verb meaning to knock over (*tumbar*), performed during carnival and with the use of a bombo drum.

In Arica, the term bombo generally refers to a bass drum, whether the type used in brass bands, drum kits, or pan-Andean ensembles. The generic nature of the term left room for ambiguity in the interpretation of the type of drum being used. The Uruguayan, Olis, had noticed that the old wooden barrels in the Azapa Valley that had been used for decades to cure olives were being discarded in favor of plastic tubs. Olis, who had casually participated in the Afro-Uruguayan carnival music-dance known as candombe while living in Montevideo, commented to del Canto that the barrels would make good drums. The barrels came in two sizes, so the members of the project initially tried to create two sizes of drums. The larger principal drum they named bombo, and the smaller supporting drum *tambora*. Their first attempts at constructing these drums were disastrous. The barrels were heavy and dense, with skins on both ends, held on and tuned with ropes—all characteristics that made performing with them challenging. Eventually, this bombo design was abandoned for the current one with a single, tacked-on head, similar to Uruguayan candombe drums.

The FONDART grant gave the group the financial resources to experiment with different materials and build relationships with people who could help them. The group discovered an aging percussionist from central Chile,

Kiko Anacona, who had retired to Arica and made a name for himself making professional-grade conga drums. With Kiko's help, they learned how to make drums that were lighter and playable, using metal rims and tuning lugs. As for playing the drums, the group's interviews with the elders suggested using a stick in one hand. Again, they adopted a technique like that used for candombe drums to play the bombo. The tambora, however, was held supported around the neck, horizontal to the ground, so the technique had to be modified to address this orientation.

In del Canto's interviews, the *quijada*, an idiophone made from a donkey's jaw bone, was mentioned more frequently and enthusiastically than the bombo. This instrument is often associated with Afro-Peruvian music and is played in two ways: as a scraper, using a small stick across the teeth, or as a rattle, making the loose teeth chatter with a swift blow to the larger area of the jaw. Oro Negro could only gather a few quijadas, since the number of donkeys in Azapa had greatly decreased by 2002 and the process of making the instrument requires drying the bone out in the sun for the better part of year. The playing technique requires a good amount of dexterity, and one needs to develop a callus on the hand where it strikes the bone. The result was that del Canto was the only person to play the quijada at their first public tumbe carnaval performance.

Building the Comparsa: Formulating the Rhythm and Dance

The group had successfully built a group of instruments, but having them was not enough; one needed to know what to play on those instruments. Unfortunately, not only were there few elders who remembered the expression, but none were musicians who could reproduce exactly what they had heard as children. Del Canto only had one interviewee whom he judged musically skilled, and the interviewee tapped out a rhythm on a tabletop for him. The pattern sounded like the 6/8 bell pattern that Afro-Peruvian and Cuban groups played. Del Canto and others recognized that this rhythm, as well as the other patterns that interviewees verbalized, as one of the generic claves, or guiding rhythmic patterns, played in many different African diasporic genres.

With so little to go on, the group working on the comparsa returned to the fundamental feature of the expression: the attempt to knock over one's partner when people yelled "tumba!" The elders who were interviewed

Example 2.1. 6/8 Cowbell pattern.

would chuckle as they remembered how small but strong women with wide hips and well-endowed bottoms would flatten men with a well-placed thrust. As Claudina Maldonado Sanchez told Cristian Báez Lazcano, "I'll never forget the time when we were dancing a round of tumba carnaval and my husband was dancing with my sister Natalia, when suddenly they said 'Tuumba Carnaval' [sic] and my sister gave him her big ass full on . . . [*laughs*] She hit him with her hip and sent him flying, his head crashing into a table. We had to take him to the clinic in town, because the poor guy ended up pretty bad" (2010, 161).

The drummers working on the comparsa reasoned that the rhythm would have to signal this important characteristic of the dance, so they experimented with several variations that might suggest a buildup to this key moment. Once they were satisfied with this rhythm on the larger bombo drums, they used the smaller tambora drums, together with the quijada player, to provide a supporting pattern.

The dancers, who were being organized by Carolina Letelier Salgado, had similar issues. They discovered only one female interviewee who was willing to demonstrate dances for them. The interviewee, however, had spent years living in Lima, and the researchers questioned if the time she spent there might have "tainted" the information she was providing.[8] In the end, they rehearsed with the steps they had, because the FONDART project they had been awarded required that they had to complete the project within a certain time frame.

The 2003 Pascua de los Negros and its Success

The Oro Negro FONDART project was supposed to be a six-month project, finishing in December 2002. The complexities of the project led to delays, however, and someone had the idea that January 6, locally known as the "Pascua de los Negros" (The Blacks' Christmas), would be a much more meaningful date.[9] The first public performance of tumbe carnaval happened on Sunday, January 5, 2003. The selection of this holiday was serendipitous for local Afro-descendant organizations because it came at a lull in the annual news cycle. National news media continue to cover this now annual event and broadcast cultural information about Afro-descendants at this time. Thus, as often happens with creative projects, external restrictions encouraged inspiration that resulted in a strategically fortuitous result.

Participants recall that the 2003 Pascua de los Negros was a long, tiring trek. The performers started away from the city center, on one of the side streets, led by a flag-bearer waving a black, red, and green flag emblazoned with the words "Oro Negro" and a graphic of a pair of hands playing a drum. The dancers, all women, wore long skirts printed with colorful patterns, headscarves or turbans, short-sleeve blouses with elastic collars that could be worn on or off the shoulder, and large beaded necklaces and hoop earrings. Many of the women gathered the hem of their blouses in a front knot, exposing their midriffs. Next came the percussionists playing the bombo, tamboras, and quijada. Some spectators were a little confused. Wondering if he might have run into one of the turbaned religious dance troupes devoted to a saint, one person asked, "Are you all *gitanos* (Gypsies)?" The dancers asserted that they were reenacting the *comparsas de negros*, or Black dance troupes, that used to perform in the streets at carnival time. Some older residents on the street corners nodded their heads in agreement, saying, "Yes . . . yes! Such folks were here." The performers completed their aim of circling what they understood to be the old Black neighborhood of *Lumbanga* and then got into cars, heading off to celebrate in the neighboring Azapa Valley.

The next day, their picture was displayed prominently on the front page of the city's newspaper, *La Estrella de Arica*. It was the first time in recent history the tumbe carnaval had been performed in public and the first time that Oro Negro had made the front page of the paper. The article estimated the size of the comparsa at some thirty people, with a plentiful group of Afro-descendants following them. Unlike the standard costumes for dancing tumbe that would appear later, the front page photo, labeled "Carnaval de Tumbes," showed a number of female dancers wearing blouses tied at their midriffs, knee-length skirts featuring different floral patterns, and head wraps of various colors. In its coverage of the parade, the article, with its subheadline "Oro Negro Organization celebrates with African dances," described this attire as customary for Afro-descendant women. It also presented several other tropes that would become standard fare in future reports about the comparsa: the traditional practice of the dance in Azapa, the naming of Balthazar as the Black wise man remembered on this holiday, and the location of the Lumbanga neighborhood along the current streets of Lynch, Maipú, San Martín and O'Higgins ("Carnaval de Color en 'Pascua de los Negros'" *Estrella de Arica*, January 6, 2003.).

Unfortunately, other than the names of the quijada and bombo and tambora drums, the article did not give many details of how the music sounded or how the steps were danced on that date. For that, I refer to a January 6, 2009, Pascua de los Negros performance that I documented. I analyze different facets of this 2009 tumbe performance with the concept of styling Afro-descendant in mind, the first of those facets being those related to sound.

Sonic Facets of Style

At the 2009 Pascua de los Negros, the Oro Negro drummers consisted of a güiro player, two cowbell players, and approximately fourteen other members, who had wooden barrel-shaped hide-head drums slung over their shoulders. A few of the drums were smaller, commercially available congas; most of the drums were handcrafted with tacked-on heads. The basic pattern performed on that day consisted of the following:

Example 2.2. Basic rhythmic structure of the Tumbe Carnaval.

There were two drum sizes: the large bombo and a smaller *repique*. The tambora present in the 2003 tumbe performance had disappeared, and the repique had the same construction as the bombo, only smaller. In theory, the bombo drums were tuned lower and the repique higher, but both were played with similar techniques. Bombo players emphasized the fourth beat in each measure in two ways: first, they struck it more forcefully with the stick, and second, the other hand was off the skin. The result was that the skin was permitted to fully resonate, producing what hand drummers often refer to as an "open" tone. This was not the case for the "and of two" beat in the first measure of the repeated pattern, which was muffled by the left hand remaining on the hide head. Nor was it the case with beat two of the second measure of the pattern, which, despite being left open, was not struck with the force of beat four. Note that many drummers doubled the stroke on beat two, as indicated by the parentheses.

The higher-tuned repique used the same stick-hand technique as the bombo, although the left hand did not commonly muffle the skin. The basic pattern I was taught to play was:

Example 2.3. Basic repique pattern.

I was told, however, that the repique had more freedom to play with its basic pattern. One improvised repique figure might be annotated like this:

Example 2.4. Example of a repique variation.

While a bombo player uses the left hand mostly as a time keeper and to muffle the right-hand stroke, the repique player can strike the drum with a left-handed "open" stroke to play more intricate patterns. Repique players use this freedom to signal changes in tempo or signal a break.

The above description is fairly idealized for several reasons. First, while the repique drums were theoretically smaller and thus higher pitched, the truth was that smaller drums were scarce, and since many drums used tacked-on hide heads, tuning could be quite variable, depending partly on the temperature of the skin.[10] Second, at larger events like the Pascua de los Negros, the skill level of the drummers varied widely, affecting how well the rhythmic patterns could be articulated.. While leaders instructed each drummer at some point on the finer points of the rhythm, attention to such aspects as muting the drum head to produce variance in tone—or indeed the fundamental pattern itself—could waver, especially as a performance went on. Some drummers simply defaulted to a basic pattern that reinforced the güiro: long-short-short. Furthermore, drummers sometimes lacked sticks and had to play open-handed, something that they had not been trained to do. Add to this the fact that, occasionally, several drummers performed the repique role, and not necessarily in unison. Despite these complications, the denseness of the sound and the strength of several key drummers, together with the use of several orienting drum phrases, helped the fundamental pattern emerge. For an excerpt of the rhythms being performed, see video 2.1.

Given the preceding patterns, musicians familiar with Afro-descendant musics in the Americas will note that the tumbe carnaval shares several sonic characteristics with those traditions. Many of the tumbe carnaval drummers I initially met, however, did not have much experience performing other kinds of music, so they did not speak to me of these timbral and rhythmic similarities. Nevertheless, certain factors contributed to the resonances that the tumbe carnaval had with other Afro-diasporic genres. First, the Oro Negro comparsa may have been partially inspired by the candombe performances of Mundo Afro, given their presence at the Santiago conference and importance within the Afro-descendant movement. Second, members of the initial group that helped develop the tumbe carnaval comparsa had experience with other types of Afro-diasporic rhythms. Del Canto, for example, had taken some Afro-Cuban percussion lessons in Santiago, while Olis had some experience playing with candombe pickup groups in Uruguay.

Del Canto's and Olis's interests in these rhythms continued after the birth of the tumbe. By 2008–09, they had been performing for several years with a few others from Oro Negro's comparsa in a smaller, more specialized group called Sabor Moreno (Moreno Flavor). The performers in this group wanted to perfect their percussion and dancing skills, so they spent additional time studying both Afro-Cuban and Afro-Peruvian music-dance, in addition to composing new tunes for the tumbe repertoire. At the 2009 government-sponsored event known as Chile+Cultura (which reads in English as "Chile plus culture"), Sabor Moreno performed not only tumbe carnaval, but an Afro-Peruvian *festejo* as well as a Cuban rumba *guaguancó*. The juxtaposition of these genres in performance illustrated how the performers saw the skills required for festejo and rumba as complementary to performing tumbe carnaval. The event also offered audience members the possibility of linking all of these genres and their sonic characteristics indexically, i.e., they could be linked in the audience's minds because they were performed at the same event.

I had played percussion in a salsa band and learned about Afro-Caribbean music, so I made these sonic connections when I first heard tumbe performed. For me, there was an iconicity about it: these signs (certain aesthetic preferences of timbre and rhythmic practice) resembled their object (Afro-Caribbean music). Indeed, my initial response (interpretant) was that I caught myself expecting and applying aesthetic principles that I had learned from Afro-Caribbean music to tumbe carnaval performance. These included wanting to hear more distinction between the different types of drum strokes and expecting variation in the drum voices through more strictly enforced tuning. I had less experience playing conga drums with a stick in hand, but I drew connections with tambora-playing in the Dominican *merengue* and repique-playing in Brazilian samba, which inspired a sense of aesthetic familiarity.

On closer inspection, these similarities in sonic signs manifested themselves in multiple ways. First, there was the voicing, that is, the existence of two differently pitched drums, with the high drum improvising. This arrangement is analogous to the Cuban rumba tradition, for example, in which there are three differently pitched drums, and the player with the highest-pitched drum improvises (Daniel 1995, 81). As another important genre of comparison, in the Uruguayan *tamboril* instrumentation that accompanies candombe, the drum that improvises, while not the highest pitched, is one of the higher drums and is called the repique (Ayestarán 1967, 34).

In both these Cuban and Uruguayan expressions, a fundamental two-measure rhythmic pattern orients the musicians. The Cuban case is perhaps better known, as this type of rhythm, referred to as *clave*, is typical in more internationally widespread types of music like salsa. While the members of these ensembles may not explicitly play the clave pattern, they follow rules of clave practice, consistently performing one of the measures in more syncopated fashion than the other.[11] The tumbe carnaval appears to follow this logic, i.e., the tumbe, like candombe, is arguably played "in clave." Examining the tumbe phrases presented earlier reveals that they have an orientation toward a cyclical timeline: the repique phrases in the examples "squared up" on the second measure, even though this measure tended to be busier. These second measure phrases acted as a response to the first part of the bombo phrase.

Certain playing techniques that affect the sound are also shared between the tumbe, rumba, and candombe. In Uruguayan candombe, the improvising repique drum is played with a stick in one hand and open-handed with the other. The tamboril drums execute breaks, with the drummers hitting the sticks on the sides of the drums. Both the practice of using a stick in one hand and hitting the side of the drum are used in performing the tumbe. In fact, the break I described earlier is also performed in candombe.

Candombe, however, does not generally use additional hand percussion like the quijada and güiro. Sonically, such instruments produce scraper-like sounds. The quijada was historically present in Afro-Peruvian music, but Feldman notes how the Afro-Peruvian revival began to use "non-Peruvian Afro-Latin percussion instruments" like the güiro in the 1950s and 1960s as a way of distinguishing it from Peruvian criollo music (2006, 110, 147).[12] As the quijada did not quite take hold in tumbe performance for the practical reasons mentioned earlier, the güiro, an instrument common in other non-Chilean Afro-Latin music, was substituted—presumably for similarity in timbre. Over time, I witnessed the introduction of other hand percussion, like the cowbell and *chekeré*, to create the multiplicity of timbres that scholars often note as characterizing African and Afro-diasporic music.[13] I have seen this phenomenon also happen recently in several other Andean carnival musical genres that invoke Blackness.[14]

Despite the iconic nature of these signs, I believe that the primary way in which such sonic characteristics might be linked in the experiences of the local Black population would be indexically, through these genres' co-presence at the festivities held by this population. In my early interviews with local elders, they spoke of parties where records were played on Victrolas. Included in the many genres that elders heard this way were Mexican boleros, Peruvian waltzes, and Chilean tonadas, but also included were Cuban congas and Brazilian sambas. These recordings, apparently dating from the 1940s, were part of the elders' experience. They would have shared the soundscape in which the expression that inspired the current "tumbe carnaval" was performed. I found it interesting that when I first asked the elders for lyrics to the tumbe carnaval, they were sung to a melody that sounded vaguely familiar to me. I later discovered a very similar melody in a Cuban popular tune, the "Conga de Santiago."[15]

Such circumstances suggest to me that while the elders might not have been trained to recognize the sonic characteristics that I described, listening to these records would have helped shape their cultural memory. While the elders were not among the musicians that helped create the current version of the tumbe carnaval, they have mostly danced along—in part, I would argue, because of an affinity with their cultural memory.

Instrumental Facets of Style

I have just argued how the sound quality of the instruments used in tumbe carnaval performance are signs for the sounds of other musics in the

Figure 2.1. Comparsa Oro Negro performing tumbe carnaval at the January 6, 2009, Pascua de los Negros celebration. Yoni Olis, center, plays a bombo built by Kiko Anacona, while the drummer behind him plays a bombo with a tacked-on hide head and fabricated from a shaved down barrel. The percussionist on the left (drinking water) holds a güiro. Arica, Chile.

African diaspora, and, consequently, they contributed to styling the tumbe as Afro-diasporic. Instruments are charged with additional potential signification. The handheld Afro-Latin percussion instruments, like the güiro and cowbell added to the tumbe (as in the Afro-Peruvian case), were not only sonically iconic and indexical of the Afro-diasporic genres, they also functioned visually. Feldman not only textually describes the contributions of the Cuban percussionist Guillermo Macario Nicasio to the work of Peru Negro, but she also provides a photograph of him seated and playing bongos, with congas in the background (2006, 149). Similarly, at the Chile+Cultura event previously mentioned, the audience watched Sabor Moreno play the tumbe's bombo, repique, and güiro, while congas, bongos, and cajónes sat next to the musicians.

Nowhere did the visual characteristics of the instrument seem so important as in the case of the drums. The need for the drums to be a barrel held upright, like Cuban congas or the Uruguayan tamboril, seemed to be a particularly important marker of Afro-diasporic style. When I asked Olis about the switch from the original tamboras to repique drums in a September 17, 2009, interview, he stated that he wanted to produce drums that were "more normal, more African, typical, with a skin on one side and underneath to remain 'as is' without a skin, and also, more or less, to respect the barrel and simply, cover it on top. With the reference that I brought with me from Uruguay, that the drums were like that, and why would we keep trying things with the tamboras if in the end, they were pretty uncomfortable."

In part, the change was due to practical matters. There were not many tamboras around; they kept breaking, and they did not function well. Olis's reference to the "African" character of the drum, however, illustrates Feldman's point about the culture of the Black Atlantic standing in for Africa. Context matters, as certain regions of the Black Atlantic hold more signifying weight. In Olis's experience, the Afro-Uruguayan tamboril overshadowed the arguably Afro-Dominican tambora. By 2005, the tamboras had all disappeared, replaced by upright, tamboril-like repiques, so that currently all the Afro-descendant troupes use bombos and repiques.

What should not be overlooked is the local significance of the barrel itself. As Gustavo del Canto explained,

> Using the barrels [in making the drums] really adds a symbolism as well, because the Blacks had also forgotten about Azapa; because at that time, they did not speak of it. Now everyone, [talks about] the Afros... but at that time, nothing had happened. So we always said, just like the barrels. The barrels had been important to the Valley and all, and they were discarded. The plastic arrived: modern, pretty, and displaced them. And people did not use them anymore but left them discarded there. So rescuing, saving the ancient barrels exactly corresponded with the Afro movement. (Interview with author, May 10, 2010)

Del Canto, then, saw metaphorical reasons for using the barrels—a metaphor in Peircian terms being the juxtaposition of signs whose relationship to its object suggests an iconicity between them.[16] In this case, del Canto understood both the Blacks and barrels from Azapa as sharing the quality of being abandoned and forgotten (see fig. 2.1). Del Canto's narrative underscored the local recognition of the olive barrels as part of Afro-descendant culture.[17]

The Challenges of Cultural Memory

Most residents in the Arica region recognize the important indexical relationship between Afro-descendants in the Azapa Valley and olive production. Some, however, take issue with the details of how the olive barrels are styled in tumbe performance. When the explanation "Oro Negro made the drums out of olive barrels" is interpreted as "Afro-descendants used to make drums out of olive barrels," individuals may experience cognitive dissonance with their cultural memory. In a 2005 interview, Pedro Cornejo Albarracín told Cristian Báez:

> I remember that in the old days, they used to make the drums out of plywood and skins of llama or cowhide. We said they were bombos, and the smallest ones were called tamboras. Those bombos had skins on both sides, tightened with twine or a small leather cord. They never made drums with barrels. That is a lie. Who ever said that they made drums from the barrels? Look, since I was a child, I always saw people play bombo, tambora, or at times, a snare and the donkey's jawbone . . . oh, and also the guitar. Of course, when we had family celebrations in the old days, we used the cajón and sometimes, household objects: plates, spoons, ceramic pitchers, and at times, even barrels to make music. Then we would tip them upside down and hit them on the bottom. (Báez Lazcano 2010, 110–11)

The use of barrels as drums in the relatively informal street parade format known as *pasacalle* conflicts with Cornejo's cultural memory.[18] In his experience, on the rare occasion that people used barrels as percussion, they did so without a skin and left them stationary, in keeping with the fact that the barrels were heavy. The reference to the barrels' presence in informal family settings is also important; it indicates the idea that this was how "we" did it. In both del Canto's and Cornejo's descriptions, olive barrels are part of Black Azapeños' experience; what is at play is how the barrels were used musically.

In practice, however, this tension points to a deeper issue: similarities in Afro-descendant and Indigenous performances that complicate their separation into two distinct categories, leading to a sense of discomfort in many individuals. Cornejo's descriptions of the bombo and tambora drums used in family gatherings match those of older types of hide-hide drums (*wankaras*) that musicians used in brass bands and panpipe ensembles. Even though these groups in Arica currently use marching band-type bass and snare drums (also referred to as bombos and *cajas*, respectively), these ensembles are still strongly associated with Indigenous, particularly Aymara, music. The historical use of similar bombos in Afro-descendant and Indigenous communities suggests interaction and overlap in musical practice that might muddle styling Afro-descendant if such drums were used in the comparsa format.

I encountered the tension that such a situation can create during the month preceding the 2009 Bajada de Carnaval Afro.[19] My friend Cristian Báez, the general coordinator of Lumbanga, told me that his organization had some funds that they needed to spend on instruments. By that time, I had come to believe that the bombos that the Afro-descendant elders spoke about were like the ones that panpipe troupes and brass bands used. When Cristian asked for my recommendations for what instruments to buy, I suggested that, following the narratives of some elders, they might want to incorporate some marching-band bombos into their performances. Cristian had been transcribing his interviews for his book and had found Cornejo's description of the drums to coincide with my suggestion. In the spirit of Feldman's Black Pacific, I noted that Cuban comparsa groups use similar bass drums in their performances of the conga rhythm. This later point seemed to assuage any misgivings Cristian had about ordering such drums. As the date for the Bajada drew closer, Cristian told me that Oro Negro members had discovered that Lumbanga had ordered bombos from the leading maker of brass band drums in Arica. One of the founding members of the group had confronted Cristian; he was upset that Lumbanga was mixing "Andean with Afro." Cristian said he silenced the objection with the same fact that Cuban comparsa groups used similar drums.

The new bombos arrived just before the Bajada. Since Lumbanga was committed to using the barrel-shaped bombo drums and existing tumbe rhythms in their performance, I noted that the "Andean" bombos could use a similar rhythm to the one used by their counterparts in Cuba, which, following common clave practice, emphasizes the "and of two," complementing the moment in the tumbe rhythm when it does the same. Despite the flawless execution of this pattern on the new drums on the night of the Bajada, the association of these drums with Indigenous heritage, the attraction to the status of Africanness associated with the barrel drum, or the dissonance with cultural memory of the younger Lumbanga members appear to have been too strong for acceptance. I did not see these drums used again in any performance, and by my 2014 visit, they were nowhere to be seen.

A metaphoric argument could be made here to reconcile two bombo accounts, following the lead of those African American scholars mentioned earlier, such as Floyd, who looked to deeper cultural concepts to explain connections to African musical practices. Both the use of the olive barrels as makeshift drums in family gatherings and their use as material to fabricate comparsa drums illustrate several principles that have been tropes in describing cultural expressions in the African diaspora. These include making use of what is at hand, particularly to encourage larger participation of those present, and signifyin(g) in the reframing of a tool of hard labor as a tool of musical use. Context, of course, is an important consideration here, and the familial character of the setting will be explored further in chapter 3.

Kinesthetic Facets of Style

While instruments work as sonic and visual signs of styling Afro-descendant in various ways, certain facets of dance are equally important in understanding this styling process. While we may associate the comparsas with music, the clear majority of the performers are dancers. In this section, I concentrate on the relationship between dance movement, its perception by observers, and the embodied kinesthetic sense of the performer as signs for styling Afro-descendant.

By 2009, Oro Negro's comparsa had several years' experience participating in Arica's major carnival event, Con la Fuerza del Sol, and their performance reflected their knowledge of this event's practices. Like most of the troupes participating, Oro Negro organized itself into blocs, each with a leader, or *guía*, that would guide the bloc with a whistle. At the 2009 Pascua de los Negros, the main bloc was all young women, who arranged themselves in two parallel rows. They advanced with a basic step: hips swaying as their weight shifted from one foot to another, skirts undulating as they circled their arms. At certain intervals, the guía would hold up her hands with several fingers held up to signal a number. When she sounded her whistle, the bloc would perform a choreographed sequence, often meant to be iconic of the work that Afro-descendants did historically. Sequence number three, for example, consisted of dancers' making a low, sweeping motion with their right hands, mimicking the cutting of sugarcane with a machete, followed by a shoulder shimmy. Other sequences suggested the motions of the *raíma* (olive harvesting) or cotton picking. Yet not all steps referenced agricultural labor. Sequence number four consisted of taking three steps to the right while shimmying the shoulders, then kicking out the left foot while hopping on the right and crossing arms: one-two-three-kick and repeat in the opposite direction. Another sequence had the two leading dancers spin off to the side and head toward the back of the group.

The next couple did the same, and so on, until the lead dancers were back in the front of the group. Alternating between the different choreographies kept the dance interesting for dancers and public alike, and the guía would call on different steps depending on the flow of the procession. For an example, see video 2.2.

As mentioned earlier, the moment of hip contact with the intent of knocking over one's partner is what gives the tumbe its name, yet because of the pasacalle format, it was difficult to reenact this choreography.[20] Instead, an implied hip bump offers a safe, more organized alternative, although the less-informed observer may miss the significance of this more abstract choreography. A special drum break is associated with the hip bump move. Once the dance or drum leader cued the performance of this break, the dancers, in unison, would first thrust out their hips to the right. This motion coincided with the first stroke of the drummers in the break. They then repeated the motion to the opposite side. During this motion, the female dancers would place their fists, still clutching their overskirt, on their waists, emphasizing the hip movement and offering a challenging attitude. In the second half of the phrase, the dancers would step forward and execute a complete turn. Both the musicians and dancers would repeat the entire phrase at least once (if not more). All the drummers performed this break with their sticks on the sides of their drums. The clack of wood on wood and the strongly unified execution of this drum break contrasted sharply with the regular tumbe pattern. Occasionally, drummers executed the notes in parentheses on the drum head with the stick. Watch video 2.3 and see the following example:

Example 2.5. Common Tumbe Carnaval break.

Many scholars have noted the widespread existence throughout Black Atlantic dances of a moment when a male and female dancer make sudden contact in the pelvic area. The most cited examples are the *umbigada* ("bumping bellies") in Brazil, and the *vacunao* (the male's thrust toward the female) in the Cuban rumba guaguancó (McGowan and Pessanha 1991, 25; Daniel 1995, 69). Feldman notes how the intellectual Nicomedes Santa Cruz leaned on the Brazilian *lundu* with its choreography of a "pelvic bump" as a "marker that enabled Afro-Peruvian performers to move toward their African diasporic identity" (2006, 103). Del Canto cites both the Cuban and Brazilian movements in his writing on the tumbe (2003, 36–37), but, with its choreography abstracted to the point of eliminating bodily contact, one can question the value of the dance generally to styling Afro-descendant.

This question can be addressed through the performance facet of body attitude. Citing Thompson (1974, 1–46), dance scholar Yvonne Daniel has explained the importance of the hips and their association with African elements in the Cuban case: "In rumba, the body combines a more elongated 'Spanish' and more flexed 'African' structural orientation to etch a Cuban creole concept of proper body orientation. . . . The vacunao, the heavy emphasis on hip movement, and the undulation display African elements of movement." (1995, 74–75)

What is important to note here is how Daniel describes the hip movement as African in contrast to the elongated body as Spanish. I suspect her writing reflects the explanations of the people she worked with in Cuba and related scholarship, because I heard similar explanations in Arica. During my time there, I realized that the focus on hip movement among tumbe carnaval dancers was an important marker for grouping the tumbe with other Afro-descendant expressions. For example, while growing up in Arica, Sandra Vildoso listened and danced to Afro-Peruvian festejos at family parties. She found that when she learned the tumbe from other dancers in Oro Negro, the steps resonated with her cultural memory: "I think that, in the end, what is Afro is all one. What is recorded most is the movement of the hips, the movement of the shoulders, right? Be it Afro-Cuban, Afro-Brazilian, Afro-Colombian, Peruvian or Bolivian, what they do most, what they display most are the hips and the shoulders. So the steps are very similar" (interview with author, September 15, 2009).

Comparatively, Vildoso described the tumbe in the movement of the hips and shoulders as not as fast or brisk as the festejo, yet the movements were iconic of one another for her—not only as an observer but in her kinesthetic sense as a performer. As Daniel's quote already illustrated, this focus on hip movement also becomes useful for establishing differences with other ways of styling dance, particularly with respect to the ways of styling criollo and indígena that I describe in later chapters.

One incident especially demonstrated to me the importance of hip movement for the dancers. I accompanied the Afro-descendant organization Lumbanga to document their performances at the 2010 Festival of the

Vendimia in Codpa. Lumbanga had faced difficulty in maintaining a steady performing troupe, and at the Codpa festival a new group of young women was making their debut as dancers. They were scheduled for two performances: a preliminary afternoon showing and the featured evening show. After the afternoon show, their choreographer, one of the most experienced female dancers, was furious, complaining, "THEY WERE SO STIFF!" She felt embarrassed and frustrated that the girls had failed to move their hips during the performance. Other members of the group spent the rest of the time before the performance trying to smooth over the verbal lashing that the choreographer had given them. The group focused on moving their hips much more in the evening performance and consequently received many compliments.

A focus on hip motion, however, can be problematic; it emphasizes only one consequence of what is perhaps the broader facet of body attitude. Joanna Bosse provided an example of a similar case when she described how salsa instructors in the United States occasionally get frustrated because the dancers fetishize what they understand as its necessary hip movement. She explained that newcomers to the genre focus only on the hips, without concentrating on the footwork and other parts of body attitude that naturally bring about the hip movement. Bosse analyzed this fetish using the linguistic analogy of dialect, saying that these movements were outside of the newcomers' existing movement dialect (2008, 52). For her informants, what people fetishize is a result of an essentialized difference with their personal embodied experience, something their cultural memory associates with "Latinness."

A parallel might be drawn between hip motion and Blackness for Chilean society, and perhaps Latin American cultures in general. Hip motion as a marker of embodied difference points to the racialized history of these cultures. In his history of Latin American popular dance, John Charles Chasteen observed that "in historical European culture," the hip motion, or "breaking" of the body's vertical line, was "associated almost exclusively with sexual intercourse, and their mere presence in dance was transgressive" (2004, 13). The importance given to this hip movement, therefore, most likely also stems from the long history of tension between two different systems of movement habits (African and European). This tension is a legacy of the overarching history of slavery and colonialism. In a power structure based on racial purity, sexual intercourse between races could either threaten or reinforce that structure, and movements that suggest both intercourse and Blackness in mainstream Latin American society could be understood accordingly. While one can object to sexual innuendo at moments deemed culturally inappropriate, the systemic condemnation of hip movements in dances usually associated with Blackness throughout the Americas points to deeper fears of miscegenation. At the 2010 Codpa performance mentioned earlier, a mischievous, overly enthusiastic, and relatively new member of Lumbanga grabbed the microphone to encourage tumbe performers to seek out partners from the audience. "Black men, listen to me!" he shouted. "Invite the White women to dance . . . so that the White women marry the Black men!" Afterwards, other members of Lumbanga criticized him for his obsessive comments on skin color and sexual innuendo.

Given that most dancers in tumbe comparsa performance are women, one might see possible parallels in other Afro-diasporic musics with the representation of gender. Frances Aparicio points out the existence of "a predominance of the male gaze and masculine desire in Afro-Caribbean music and, in salsa, one that fetishizes the woman's *caderas* (hips) as a signifying locus of (often political) pleasure" (1998, 142). More to the point, the woman in question is usually marked racially as a *mulata*—the offspring of interracial intercourse that is a transgression to the racial power structure. Ironically, Aparicio argues, by focusing on the hips and pelvis as simply dance movement, the sexual violence in which such transgressions were often rooted is erased. The caveat I would add is to emphasize that cultural context is important to understand this movement as transgressive. In chapter 3, some of the female members of the Afro-descendant organizations address this issue.

Whether this hip movement is experientially interpreted as part of Black cultural memory or as an indexical sexual transgression, it has become a significant facet of tumbe carnaval performance. Given the movement's iconic relationship in other Afro-diasporic genres, it has become an important way of styling Afro-descendant. Just as instruments functioned beyond their sonic facets as visual signs, however, the dancing body can begin to raise issues of the gaze beyond movement to the body itself. How the visual facets of costume and the body relate to styling Afro-descendant is the subject of the next two sections.

Costuming as a Facet of Style

Recall that at the initial 2003 Pascua de Negros, the female dancers wore colorful floral print skirts with headwraps and loose shirts, which many tied at the midriff. In 2009, the women were uniformly clad in ankle-length white dresses with solid-colored headbands, matching sashes across the waist, and similarly colored underskirts. A horizontal swath of ruffles and lace trimmed the tops of these dresses, which the women could wear on or off the shoulder. These costumes already pointed to facets that would become fundamental characteristics for styling Afro-descendant: headwraps and fabric colors.

From the beginning, most of the female dancers wore some fabric in their hair, either as a turban or as a wrap around the forehead, keeping the hair off the face. By 2009, the wrappings were the same color as the underskirts, suggesting that some level of thought went into these headdresses. One dancer, describing a new bloc of performers that Oro Negro organized for the 2009 Fuerza de Sol carnival, pointed out that this group wore *turbantes* (turbans) and carried reeds to represent the troupe's African roots. This comment suggests that, within the troupe, there was some association of the turban/headdress with "Africanness." Indeed, scholars Shane White and Graham White stated that "the bandanna is now widely worn in West Africa and widely regarded as a traditional African garment" (1998, 58). Historian John Thornton, however, has argued that this practice must have emerged with the Black Atlantic, given that, at the time of contact, European voyagers made special note of the lack of head covering among Africans (1998, 230–34). Nevertheless, White and White noted that the headwrap proved to be a practical solution to keep hair clear of dust and keep an aesthetically crafted coiffure in place. When I visited several elder Afro-descendant women in Arica as they were doing chores, I noticed that they had their hair wrapped up. Yet this attire suggested that they were not leaving the house, and at my arrival, at least one woman took off her bandanna with a gesture of straightening her hair. This elder generation appears to not have thought a headwrap as suitable for use in public, preferring to have their hair done for that context. A rare drawing from 1869 shows an Afro-descendant woman from Arica with her hair long and loose as she carries a basket on her head (Manuel Fernández Canque 2007, 77). In contrast, some of the contemporary activists did occasionally wear more elegant fabrics as headpieces for more formal appearances, outside of tumbe performances.

The use of the turban in tumbe dance performance therefore could have arisen from an indexical association of such headwraps with their elders doing chores. I suspect, however, that media and staged representations of

Blackness also played an important role. Beginning in the sixteenth century, European portrait paintings included African servants in Moorish costume (Jan P. Nederveen Pieterse 1998, 124–25), establishing an image of Black domestics wearing turbans that the cosmopolitan imagination held into the twentieth century. This representation was also present in morality plays and pageants that became the basis for various religious dances in Latin America (see chap. 5). Of more obvious significance are performances from other groups of the Black Atlantic/Pacific. Photographs of dancers in the Afro-Peruvian revival, for example, show them with their hair wrapped in polka-dot bandannas (Feldman 2006, 60). I witnessed two Afro-Peruvian dancers who performed with Lumbanga at the Bajada de Carnaval Afro in similar costume, and Oro Negro had some five local elders carrying fruit baskets dressed in red polka-dot turbans dance for the larger urban carnival.

The colors of the headwrap fabrics also could hold significance, particularly as related to the entire costume of the dancer. In 2009, most of the costumes were noticeably white—not only the skirts of the female dancers, but also the pants and shirts of the few male dancers. The choice could be contentious; some of Oro Negro's leaders were insistent that white be used because it reflected the narrative that, as slaves, Black women wore clothes made of materials their masters gave them. The materials were primarily either roughly woven cotton or the sacks that held flour, rice, or sugar. In either case, these leaders argued that white was the dominant color, so by the 2005 Pascua de los Negros, the white costumes had appeared. The following year, the whiteness of the costumes had become important enough to become a basis for critique of other groups. In a 2006 interview, Oro Negro's one-time artistic director, Arturo Carrasco, asked, "Who ever heard of Blacks wearing violet?" At Oro Negro's 2009 public presentation in Arica's municipal theater, Marta Salgado emphasized, "White is the color that makes us distinctive." One can find support for such ideas about dress in the work of scholars examining slave dress in the United States.[21] This work, however, also argues that the color white served as a sign of plainness, and these scholars contrast the drabness of daily slave wear in the United States with the African slaves' attempts to complement, modify, or replace this dress with something that would be both more aesthetically pleasing and give them more status. Similarly, a younger generation of performers in Arica wanted to perform in different, more vibrant colors for aesthetic reasons. This argument over fabric color appears to have contributed to at least one group breaking away from Oro Negro because they wanted to perform tumbe carnaval in other ways, particularly in differently colored costumes. The result is that, while white commonly appears in tumbe performance, not all the Afro-descendant comparsas perform in white. More recently, a compromise has been struck in several of the comparsas, in which they wear white on one day and different colors on the other two days of the three-day competitions.

Yet the new color choices were not necessarily random. Marta Salgado stated that when Oro Negro and affiliated groups incorporated other colors, those colors were combinations of the colors of the "African" flag (interview with author, September 5, 2009). The colors Salgado referred to are red, yellow, and green. These colors have consistently appeared on the flag of Ethiopia, one of two African countries that managed to avoid long-term European colonialization. This status inspired many African nations to adopt a similar color scheme upon independence, leading to this trio of colors being referenced as the Pan-African colors (Central Intelligence Agency n.d.). Thus, they have become significant to those wishing to instill pride in their African history, including members of the Rastafarian religion.[22] Oro Negro's and Lumbanga's banners made use of these colors in the Pascua de los Negros in 2009. I noticed that in early television recordings of Oro Negro performances, some performers wore dreadlocks and a knit beret in these colors, a combination commonly associated with Rastafarianism and reggae music. In an interesting connection, directly after mentioning the colors of the African flag in the interview, Salgado told me that Oro Negro's work has led them to build relationships with other groups, such as those that practice capoeira and Rastafarianism in Arica, both of which count Afro-descendants among their members. They have participated in events together, as I witnessed with the local *batucada* group A Cima do Sol at the Arica Cultural Center on July 31, 2009. Salgado claimed that this relationship, this "feeling" (her word), between the groups helped the young people "sentirse afrodescendiente" (feel oneself as Afro-descendant) and instilled in them a consciousness of what they were doing, because, as Salgado remarked, "they also have their origins in Black culture" (Ibid.). I will return to this idea of "feeling Afro-descendant" in chapter 3. What one sees here, however, is once again the metaphorical relationship of various Black Atlantic expressions, in this case from Brazil and Jamaica, with Africanness, and by the indexicality of these performances with tumbe carnaval, a reinforcement of tumbe carnaval as an example of styling Afro-descendant.

It is important to consider the existence of disagreements about the importance of a specific sign, together with the idea that signs can be simultaneously working in different ways. All the performers in Oro Negro might have accepted the idea that Afro-descendants in Arica historically wore white, but they did not all agree that Oro Negro should wear white in performance. This disagreement points to different interpretants, or responses, to the sign at work. The type of sign may have something to suggest here. Most contemporary performers of tumbe carnaval understand the idea of white clothing symbolically, i.e., they read about this idea or heard about it from someone.[23] Arguably, symbolic representations do not make as strong an impression as iconic or indexical associations. They can be strengthened, however, by repetition and multiplicity in other modes. As an example, the colors of the Ethiopian flag were symbolically defined. Their repeated use, however, in Rastafarianism and other contexts built a visual connection with Ethiopia and, by extension, to Africa. Thomas Turino refers to this redundancy of indexes as indexical clustering (2008, 197). Through this clustering, the connection between Africa and the colors red, yellow, and green were strengthened in the thoughts of Oro Negro and Lumbanga performers. Tumbe carnaval performers not only felt confident in their use of the colors in their flags and costumes but were also able to connect with other residents interested in Rastafarianism, thanks to their common use of colors. I will discuss other motivations at play in the interpretants of these signs in the conclusion of this chapter, but first I will discuss visual facets of performance in which race is most clearly implicated: those of the body.

The Body as a Facet of Style

In addition to their potential as a sign for Africanness, the headwraps serve another purpose for some dancers: they support the addition of multiple hair extensions as tight braids. While these extensions were present in 2009, I have noticed a significant increase in the number of female dancers wearing very thin, tightly woven braids since that time. These braids could be all their own hair, added hair extensions, or imitation braids attached to their headwrap. Unlike the relatively recent practice of wearing a bandanna, the use of braiding has a long history in Africa, with cornrows (often using beads as ornaments) particularly associated with Afro-diasporic culture. Scholar Kia Lilly Caldwell (2007, 99–104) has noted how the use of braids among the Black Brazilian women that she worked with could be part of a move to take pride in their natural hair, which tended to be at odds with the more widely accepted standards of beauty across Brazil. Caldwell found that whether this move toward natural hair was influenced by US ideologies of Black Power depended on the woman's age; older generations connected the braids with the rejection of White domination, while younger generations saw the choice of how to wear their hair as empowering. Arica's female Afro-descendant community often included references to the social consequences of how they wore their hair when they described being recognized as Black in Chile. While perhaps not directly identified with Africanness, this hair texture in the Chilean context was often associated with countries considered to be more Black than Chile. As Sandra Vildoso stated, "When I was working in a hospital in Santiago, they asked if I was Colombian, Brazilian, or Peruvian, but never Chilean. So likewise, I had to say to people, 'No. In Chile, there are also *morenitos de pelo crespo* (darker skinned people with curly hair)—like me'" (interview with the author, September 15, 2009). Usually hair with tight curls acted as a sign for Blackness, but the increasing use of thin, tight braids suggests a similar sign at work. Women dancers in carnival troupes in genres associated with Indigeneity wear long, thick braided pigtails, so the type of braid is significant.

Vildoso not only mentions her hair but also references her complexion, employing the diminutive form of *moreno*, a term that will be further discussed in chapter 5. Her use of the word illustrated that, despite the growing acceptance of the "Afro-descendant" concept, other racial terms for referencing skin color continue to be active. After all, Salgado's group, the first Chilean Afro-descendant organization, named itself Oro Negro, literally "Black Gold." Its name both symbolically references the color and uses it visually in the image of jet-black hands in its logo. An indexical relationship is created between the skin color of the hands on Oro Negro's banners and the skin color of its performers.

Part of the issue here is that sometimes people discredit the Afro-descendant organizations for not being dark-skinned enough, suggesting a type of colorism. As described in Hochschild and Weaver, colorism is the perception of and resultant behavior toward individuals solely based on the lightness or darkness of their skin tone, and it can happen across and within perceived racial groups, as has been documented in the United States (2007, 646). In Arica, people may simply associate lighter skin tones with Whiteness, even though these tones might register as dark in other parts of Chile. A long-time resident immigrant whose skin color is darker than many in the Afro-descendant organizations commented to me that one reason she does not participate with the organizations was that "there are more White people than Black in them." The speaker went on to say that, if she were to participate, she would do so with Oro Negro, because it has "more black women, more people who are truly morena." This was in comparison with Lumbanga, the other Afro-descendant group that was dancing that day. Note that Lumbanga's sole banner did not use the word negro (choosing instead the phrase "Organization of Afro-descendants"), but its logo featured a figure with jet-black face, arms, and legs. On that day, a small Cabbage Patch doll with dark-brown skin was perched on the Lumbanga banner's crossbars as well. In contrast to the previous comment, at a meeting I attended, one of Lumbanga's elder founding members complained that Oro Negro's performers were all Whites, and some of the women who participated on behalf of Lumbanga agreed. Such comments seem to mimic what Peter Wade found in Colombia: "Blacks discriminate against blacks: *nosotros mismos nos discriminamos*, we ourselves discriminate against each other" (1993, 319). In Wade's case, however, the reference was still Blackness as bad, and those who thought themselves superior would avoid connections with other Blacks—or at least a certain kind of Black. The valuing of Whiteness is still the norm in Arica, but in this specific frame, that is, associating Blackness with being part of an Afro-descendant organization, darker skin lent authenticity and belonging. I have occasionally noticed the use of self-tanning products among some of the dancers in the comparsas, solely for performances—a problematic practice if one considers the historical use of blackface in entertainment, but as Feldman notes, blackface was also present in the Afro-Peruvian revival (2006, 145–47).

This strong emphasis on skin color was most obvious to me after I noticed that, on many public occasions, the organizations seemed to feature their darkest-skinned members in performance, even if these members were not Chilean. Perhaps more to the point, press camera operators, or at least their editors, seemed to gravitate toward these darker-skinned individuals as subjects. Thus, their images most frequently appeared in the newspapers or television clips, independent of their formal positions within the organizations. The degree of darkness of a person's skin seemed to be related to how newsworthy the story was, or perhaps more bluntly, how authentic a claim that an individual had to styling as Afro-descendant. I noticed that several of the male dancers with the darkest skin color occasionally danced shirtless with white pants, and they inevitably were the ones whose photos appeared in the media. The use of white clothes may inadvertently intensify the perceived contrast between the clothing and the performer's skin color. When anthropologist Sara Busdiecker asked Afro-Bolivians in Tocaña why they wore white clothes when they danced *saya*, she received the answer that it was "eye-catching" (2006, 174). I would note that an Afro-Bolivian comparsa paraded with both Oro Negro and Lumbanga in Arica during 2005 and 2006, so groups in Arica would at least be familiar with this attitude.

What tended to be lacking in performers' understanding of bodily facets of performance were direct connections of these signs to Africa. This lacuna is rooted in the persistent history of skin color and hair type as general markers of Blackness, a strong part of the social construction of race. The strength of their association with Africa, however, has ebbed and flowed, particularly after the abolition of slavery, with these features taking on more localized meanings. Rather than associate a person with dark skin directly with Africa, Chileans associate them with Peruvians, Brazilians, Cubans, or—with increasing migration—Ecuadorians and Haitians. The ambiguity of Blackness is why there is work involved in styling Afro-descendant. Racial markers such as skin color and hair type are necessary but not sufficient conditions for styling Afro-descendant, helping to indicate why the other resources discussed earlier play important roles.

Styling Afro-descendant: Arica's Diasporic Production of Blackness

Throughout this chapter, I have referred several times to Feldman's Black Pacific model—the idea that countries along the Pacific coast look to expressions found in the Black Atlantic as surrogates for their connection with Africa, given their additional distance, both physical and cultural, from the continent. The observations I made in Arica, however, suggested a few amendments to this model. First, as some countries in the Black Pacific become more accepted as having a Black population, then these countries can also function as surrogates. In Arica, such is the case with Peru. One possible correction for this model is to think about a Black Periphery, removing the geographic specificity of the model. Doing so makes explicit the Black Pacific as a center-periphery model, one that relies on centering a cosmopolitan understanding of Blackness in Africa. The center expands and absorbs surrounding countries based on how well they reiterate characteristics of that Blackness. One can understand the Black Atlantic as the expansion of this center, but Gilroy's model is much more nuanced because it recognizes how the countries in the Americas influenced Africa, as well as how Europe contributed culturally to this Blackness. Unfortunately, in its conception, the Black Atlantic does not explore how certain countries have more signifying weight than others. Uruguay and Bolivia, which play important roles in Arica, are generally overshadowed by Cuba and Brazil when Black Atlantic expressions are discussed. Proximity and local history give significance to expressions from other areas of the African diaspora, revealing the local nature of Blackness.

Ironically, what may be more helpful in understanding the Chilean Afro-descendant movement is a greater emphasis on the "diaspora" part of the African diaspora. While the concept of the "African diaspora" has been defined in multiple ways, the version I find most compelling recognizes the decentralizing nature of the process, so that Africa becomes displaced as the sole producer of Blackness. This diasporic focus means that any site where a community of Africans was established becomes a site of production for Blackness; the cultural similarities among these sites result from the replication of the structures of political and cultural capital.[24] Furthermore, these similarities create conditions in which expressions used by one culture prove useful to other cultures with similar issues. Jacqueline Nassy Brown (2005) has called these expressions "diasporic resources."[25] In Brown's model, the production and recognition of Blackness is related to a sense of place that goes in and out of "phase" with national expectations of what constitutes Blackness. The concept of phase here emphasizes how different ideas about Blackness can be created and sustained over time but change in the way they resonate across ethnoracial, national, and diasporic ways of thinking.

One can apply these ideas to the styling of Blackness in the tumbe carnaval in various ways. Following the Black Periphery model, tumbe musicians looked to Black communities in Peru and Uruguay for diasporic resources to stand in for Africa when interpreting the tumbe. Styling Blackness as Afro-descendant using such resources as hide-head drums and turbans was "in phase" with the cosmopolitan ways that Chileans imagined Blackness, and Arica became recognized as site for its production. Yet Gilroy's ideas about the Black Atlantic ask us to consider influences on the diaspora beyond the African ones. For example, while olive cultivation does exist in some parts of Africa, Spanish culture is largely responsible for its presence in Arica. The important role that Afro-descendants have played in Arica's olive production, however, explains why the manifestation of a bombo drum made from an olive barrel was consistent with the cultural memory of many of Arica's residents. Olive cultivation had been a site for the local production of Blackness for many years, but it did not translate well as such on the cosmopolitan level. Afro-descendant activists found some level of recognition through the tumbe carnaval because they styled it in a way that placed Arica's diasporic resources "in phase" with the transnational idea of Blackness as Afro-descendant.

This diasporic perspective advocates that we take the local production of Blackness seriously, and in part 2, I explore other strategies of locally styling Blackness were important earlier but later went out of phase with how Chile understood Blackness on the national level. Before I turn to these other styles, however, I first will examine the impact that styling Blackness as Afro-descendant had on individual lives.

Notes

1. The cajón is a wooden hand drum in the shape of a rectangular prism. The player sits on the drum and plays with their hands between the legs on the thinnest face. See the first video example in chapter 4 and Feldman (2006) for additional descriptions of the instrument and genre.

2. For more on retentions, see discussion in chapter 1, p. 51. For examples of scholarship, see the contributions of Wilson and Maultsby in Jackson's edited volume, *More than Dancing* (1985).

3. Floyd borrows this term from Jason Berry.

4. The concept of "cultural memory" is different from the concept of "ancestral memory" that the Afro-Peruvian artist Victoria Santa Cruz asserted. Santa Cruz believed that "rhythm is innate in all Black people by way of ancestry" (Feldman 2006, 68) and that, by being disciplined and relying on rhythm, they could reawaken the memory of Africa in their bodies. She used this approach to reconstruct the *landó* dance, despite this attitude's resonance with biological determinism. In contrast, "cultural memory" is rooted in a person's lived experience that accounts for that individual's social realities. While I believe that culture can be transmitted through the body, this is a process of enculturation rather than biological determinism.

5. As Monson points out in the introduction to the book in which Erlmann's essay appears, "phatic" is one of linguist Roman Jakobson's six functions of language (Monson 2000, 7, 18).

6. See Peirce's original work in the 1955 collection edited by Buchler. Short's work (2007) was helpful to my understanding of the three-part sign-object-interpretant relationship.

7. The idea of facets comes from Ruth Stone (2005), who uses the term as a metaphor for performances as jewels. Each facet of a jewel presents a different aspect of the same gemstone

and results from the jeweler's careful decision to cut the stone at a certain angle so that the beauty of the stone is enhanced for the observer. So too, facets are the characteristics that performers have used in their attempts to achieve a specific goal.

8. Of course, such an attitude suggests that dances are restricted to state borders—particularly problematic given Arica's fluid culture.

9. In Chile, the word "pascua" can refer to the Christian holidays of both Christmas and Easter. Internationally, the Roman Catholic Church officially recognizes this date as the Epiphany, a reference to the Gospel story of the Magi's visit to the infant Jesus. Popular tradition developed the depiction of one of the Magi as a Black African. The feast was one of the few that recognized the participation of Africans within the Catholic Church, and Africans in several places in the Americas were permitted to hold festivities on this date. In the northern Chilean town of La Tirana, the Pascua de los Negros is a time to sing and dance to the Christ child statue in household crèches. Every religious dance troupe goes to sing at one house that was presumably home to a Black family. Del Canto encountered several interviewees in Arica who mentioned that their families celebrated this date, although it was mostly a time for families to gather together to drink chocolate and eat Christmas bread.

10. The drummers had met before the event in a secluded parking lot to light a small fire of newspaper and kindling to tune the drums. Heating the drum heads caused them to stretch tighter, resulting in a higher pitch.

11. This orienting characteristic of two-measure clave patterns is often described in terms of 3-2 or 2-3. The numbers refer to the idea that one measure contains three notes of the pattern (known as the three-side) and the other measure, only two. The two-side is generally understood to accent more toward the steady pulse, while the three-side less so. See Gerard with Sheller (1988) for more elaboration.

12. I write more about Peruvian criollo music in chapter 4.

13. The patterns I witnessed played on the cowbell mimic those used in the Afro-Peruvian festejo.

14. See chapter 6.

15. There was a recording by the group Kubavana in the 1950s and 1960s. It is unclear, of course, whether the melody was originally shared among various Afro-diasporic populations or learned from recordings.

16. See Turino (2014, 215).

17. Reinforcing these ideas are other narratives told about the fabrication of drums in other parts of the diaspora, including the tamborils of Uruguayan candombe that Ayestarán notes are occasionally made of olive barrels (1967, 26). Such narratives usually praise the resourcefulness of Afro-descendants to create instruments out of what was at hand.

18. *Pasacalle* (literally "passing through the streets") in Arica generally refers to any event in which a group organizes to walk through the central part of the city, either to promote a message or celebrate. They are less formal than *desfiles,* or parades, like those held by the military on Sundays throughout the year.

19. The "Bajada de Carnaval Afro," or the Descending of the Afro-descendant Carnival, is an annual event that was started in response to the participation of Afro-descendant groups in the larger urban carnival, Con la Fuerza del Sol. The Afro-descendant organization Lumbanga sponsors the event, in which all Afro-descendant organizations participate, but it is not competitive like the Fuerza de Sol.

20. Having dancers get knocked over on pavement could injure them, and the flow of the parade itself would be interrupted as those who had fallen tried to get up and incorporate

themselves back into the formation. I saw this choreography performed publicly only once, during a show that the organization Lumbanga presented on stage in Arica's municipal theater.

21. In the US setting, the work of collaborators Shane White and Graham White has demonstrated that "it was clearly intended that slaves wear loose-fitting garments made of the coarsest available cloth" (1998, 9). These scholars primarily stress the degree to which the clothes were tailored and the fine nature of the material from which they were made; both factors distinguished the elite from the working class. A close examination of the quotes that the Whites use, however, reveals that the color white was indicative of these coarse materials—not by design, but rather, as a descriptor of the plain, natural color of the cloth. They cite ex-slave Benjamin Johnson's description of slaves' clothes as made from "ol' plain white cloth" (1995, 168), as well as descriptions of advertisements for slave clothing material and for runaway slaves dressed in "white plain" (1998, 9–10).

22. Rastafarianism had an important influence in reggae music, which holds worldwide popularity, and a kind of symbiosis exists between reggae and Rastafarianism. Listeners of reggae often learn about Rastafarianism to understand the music's lyrics better, since these often reference aspects of the religion. In Chile, the first Chilean reggae group to gain significant popularity, Gondwana, happened to do so around the time that the first Afro-descendant organization emerged. The group recorded a song called "Verde, Amarillo, y Rojo" (Green, Yellow and Red).

23. Some performers might also have indexical and iconic connections gathered from media in which they saw depictions of slaves dressed in white in movies or another media.

24. See the essays "New Ethnicities" and "What is this 'black' in black popular culture?" in Hall (1996), as well as the monographs by Brown (2005) and Rivera-Rideau (2015). For similar treatment of the Chinese diaspora, see Ang (1998).

25. Here I am indebted to Rivera-Rideau's (2015) focus on Brown's (2005) idea of diasporic resources.

3

SELF-UNDERSTANDING AS MOTIVATION FOR STYLING AFRO-DESCENDANT

Toward the end of a year-long stay in Arica, I was riding in a car on the way back from a rehearsal with Lumbanga. The following day, the organization would be filming a series of short television vignettes. Cristian Báez, general coordinator of Lumbanga, had asked me to participate, and we had been preparing several dance scenes, including a version of the tumbe carnaval. People had arrived late, and we had to restructure some performances at the last minute. I was feeling a little frustrated and unprepared, so I sat there, doubting my decision to participate in the first place.

But one woman, whom I will call Silvia, was having different thoughts. Behind the steering wheel, she heaved a great sigh of contentment, smiled, and announced in a cheerful voice, "How good it is to be with my people!" She went on, saying how she enjoyed being relaxed and comfortable around the people of Lumbanga. She joked around, even using double entendre, without having to worry about anyone taking anything the wrong way. She wished they would get together more often. Her comments jolted me out of my inner dialog. Silvia is a smart, stylish working mother. In her dress and manner, she always gave me the impression of a confident, responsible professional, even though I had only seen her within the context of Lumbanga meetings. In our limited interactions, I had not considered her personal challenges with Blackness and the role that dancing tumbe might play in them.

In retrospect, I was frustrated in the car that night because I was judging the rehearsal from a technical perspective. Lumbanga certainly did want to do a good job with the television programs, but there was more important work going on that night. As Cristian once told me, "I think that drum playing is a pretext to be able to get together, to keep ourselves together, and at the same time, by playing the drum and dancing, each time, we feel ourselves becoming more Black" (interview with author, September 12, 2009). Similarly, another member, Azeneth Báez Rios, described her participation in the Afro-descendant organizations as a process that allowed her to accept and own her Blackness: "For many years, I fought to not feel Black, so here [in Lumbanga] I had to assume a Blackness that I had rejected and cried over. But now I realize that it was not because I did not want to be Black. There was an existential question behind it. And that question was: how can I integrate myself to live in a world of difference without being stigmatized?" (interview with author, September 7, 2009).

Music-dance could, in part, provide opportunities over time for group members to value who they were as Black with others whom they understood were also Black, in a space that they understood as safe to explore these ideas. In other words, the organizations gave individuals whom society categorized as Black a way to create positive self-understandings of what that term meant to them.

Up to this point, I have focused on how performers styled the tumbe carnaval as Afro-descendant by examining the associations between the signs and objects present in its performance. I have examined possible associations through meanings rooted in performers' comments, in cosmopolitan understandings of Afro-diasporic performance, and my own ethnographic observations. Interpretants of the sign-objects relationships in tumbe carnaval performances do not just result in word-based explanations. They include feelings and behaviors based on previous life experiences and multiple performance contexts. In chapter 2 I examined how styling Blackness as Afro-descendant could function between the Afro-descendant organizations and the greater Chilean society or transnationally.

This chapter focuses on how tumbe carnaval performance makes its performers "feel more Afro-descendant" about themselves and their fellow performers. First, I describe a few additional situations in which the tumbe carnaval was performed outside of the Pascua de los Negros context. I mentioned a few of these examples in chapter 2, but here I explore how the different contexts of these performances created both fellowship and tension between certain groups of performers. These contexts go beyond the more well-known public performances to include an organization's rehearsals and more intimate spaces. Particularly important was the question of who might be styling Afro-descendant and for what reasons. I discuss some of the benefits of performing tumbe carnaval, concentrating on individuals and groups who identify as Afro-descendant. I will deal with some of the tensions of performing tumbe carnaval for those who do not identify as Afro-descendant in chapter 7. Here my argument is that performing tumbe carnaval has helped certain individuals establish spaces in which they can discuss and create common experiences that result in a feeling of relatedness to other individuals as Afro-descendant.

Tumbe Carnaval Tensions: Different Contexts and Motivations for Performance

By comparing my limited description of the tumbe in 2003 and my more complete description in 2009, one can see changes in the way the tumbe was performed. In part, these changes—such as new performance contexts and the emergence of new performance groups—resulted from the tumbe's success beginning in 2003. With success, however, came tension. While the tumbe carnaval continued to be styled as Afro-descendant, tensions began to appear between performers about the details of the messages that they wanted to convey while performing. These tensions offer insight into the different motivations for styling Afro-descendant.

Oro Negro's comparsa followed the initial success of the Pascua de los Negros with several other pasacalles in 2003, before repeating their Pascua de los Negros event in 2004. Their continuing appearances led to an invitation to participate in the third annual carnaval, Con la Fuerza del Sol. This carnaval had always included competition, and Oro Negro's comparsa took first place in the competition in the category of "Other Ethnic groups." Later that year, they also participated in the last version of another important local carnival event, La Ginga.[1] As the troupe became better known, different civic and private organizations wanted the comparsa to perform at their functions. The goals of these performances were mixed. Sponsors sometimes framed them simply as a novel form of entertainment at private events; other performances were intended to promote local tourism or to act as a government gesture toward multiculturalism. Significantly, some of these performances were paid. Not all of the comparsa performers could rehearse for or perform at these smaller events, so a smaller group of more dedicated and experienced members started to fill this role. Initially, they went under a similar name as the NGO, but eventually they took on the name Sabor Moreno to distance their gigs from the organizations' official activities. The regional office of Chile's Cultural Council often selected Sabor Moreno to perform at festivals like Chile+Cultura. While Sabor Moreno has performed some Afro-conscious pieces like "Negra" by Victoria Santa Cruz, the performers that I spoke to tended to de-emphasize any strong political agenda.[2]

The inherent difficulty here, however, is that performing the tumbe carnaval publicly is rarely without political implications. Often, invitations to government-sponsored events, whether at the local or national level, imply support for the government's neoliberal multiculturalism policy. Such gestures, while intended as welcoming, can ring hollow when not accompanied by a commitment of further resources to support systemic inclusion of Afro-descendants in Chilean society. Compared with these more systemic changes, investment in public displays is relatively inexpensive in the short term, and government officials may be more inclined to sponsor performing groups that are considered less politically demanding. On the other hand, this strategy may be more complicated in the long run, because it can create a public expectation that the government is more heavily invested in Afro-descendant issues than it is prepared to concede.

The distinction between Sabor Moreno and Oro Negro was primarily about a division of artistic labor, but real disagreements among Oro Negro members over political agendas, strategies, aesthetic choices, and personality traits led to several divisions and the formation of new organizations. The first of these new organizations was Lumbanga in 2003, after the inaugural Pascua de Negros. Up to this point, I have mainly discussed Oro Negro, due to its early political and cultural role in developing the Afro-descendant movement. I spent most of my fieldwork time, however, with Lumbanga, a group that has developed its own cultural events. Its leaders are equally as committed to advancing Afro-descendant cultural revival and political goals and have been active in developing economic opportunities for Afro-descendants, particularly the effort to include a count of Afro-descendants in the Chilean census.

Unlike Oro Negro, Lumbanga has generally decided not to participate in the carnival, Con la Fuerza del Sol. While a few performers from other organizations claimed that this decision was because Lumbanga had difficulty in forming a strong performance troupe, Báez argued that the urban carnival was at heart a competition, and while some individual Lumbanga members did participate with other troupes, Báez believed competing as Lumbanga would only fuel any tension with Oro Negro. Thus, Lumbanga created its own event, the Bajada de Carnaval Afro, a carnival celebration focused solely on Afro-descendants. The idea was to place the tumbe in its proper setting, as a local carnival expression within a celebration that included other practices mentioned by their elders: the burying of Ño Carnavalon (the spirit of Carnival), the mourning of his widow (played in drag), and the reading of his last will and testament. Originally, only Lumbanga participated, but over time, the Bajada became an annual community event, with all the major Afro-descendant organizations taking part. Lumbanga's cultivation of relationships with international groups like Saya Afro-Boliviana and the Afro-Peruvian group Poder Negro from neighboring Tacna led to these organizations' participation as well.

While other groups may dismiss Báez's critique, the nature of performing for the carnival Con la Fuerza del Sol has led to further changes in the tumbe carnaval. Having many members as part of the comparsa is a valued characteristic in the event, and to grow, Oro Negro would need to train additional performers. As a result, members of Sabor Moreno held a series of workshops in Arica's Chinchorro district in 2006. During these sessions, conflicts arose between personalities, and the matriarch of the Lares, one of the locally recognized Black families, decided to create a new group, Arica Negro. Given the family's history and its location within Arica, this organization has staked its claims of uniqueness with the tagline "Memories of the Chimba," a reference to a former coastal wetland that used to be home to several Black families. The Sabor Moreno instructors told me that these students had not yet mastered the tumbe the way they were teaching it before the split. Thus, Arica Negro continued to develop their drumming skills under their own intuition, creating their own variation of the tumbe carnaval rhythm that used more open tones on the drum than Oro Negro's version. The group also created new choreographies based on movements associated with coastal labor like fishing and doing laundry. Initially the animosity between Arica Negro and Oro Negro meant that these groups did not perform at the same events. While this tension has largely subsided, the two organizations do compete against one another in the Con la Fuerza del Sol in a new carnival category for Afro-descendant troupes. The diversity in the rhythm's performance is now generally seen as natural and healthy for the genre's growth.

Figure 3.1. Sign for Arica's Slave Heritage Route posted at Plaza Lumbanga, Arica, Chile.

While the tumbe carnaval is most obviously seen in the pasacalle format, as mentioned previously, it can also appear in staged presentations. Oro Negro, Lumbanga, and Arica Negro each have created shows for Arica's municipal theater. The goal of these presentations is to disseminate local Afro-descendant culture to the audience, often coupled with a celebration of an organizational milestone like the anniversary of the group's founding. The presentations have included skits, fashion shows, individual dance numbers, and group performance of the tumbe carnaval. The change from the pasacalle format means that the choreography is often through-composed (as opposed to being called out by a group leader), but the steps that form the basis of the choreography are often the same.[3]

More importantly, variations of these stage-formatted dances are performed at other events that have political or economic significance. For example, in 2005, Lumbanga proposed and received support and funding from the government and the United Nations to create a local site of UNESCO's Slave Route, or *Ruta del Esclavo* (see fig. 3.1). This project is meant to document the international history of the African slave trade by identifying locations that hold special significance for Afro-descendants within this history. Each year, on Chile's National Heritage Day, guided tours are given of the locales in Arica and the surrounding valleys that are meant to narrate the history of slavery in the region. At the end of the tour, a tumbe carnaval performance is offered to participants, together with a sampling of the local produce, cooking, and handicrafts that Lumbanga members in the Azapa Valley produce. The UNESCO Slave Route site eventually also became Chilean National Heritage Route #79, complete with Spanish-English brochures, and tourists can visit the sites by appointment on other days of the year.

The number of events in which the tumbe is used to promote tourism to the Arica-Parinacota region has increased annually. Significantly, no public political action during my time in Arica happened without a tumbe carnaval performance, or at least, a representative form of Afro-descendant music-dance. In 2008, several leaders of Lumbanga and Oro Negro traveled to Santiago to accompany Chilean congressman Antonio Leal as he introduced a bill aimed at officially recognizing the presence of Afro-Chileans. Romero Rodriguez, leader of Mundo Afro, was also present as the group arrived at La Moneda, Chile's presidential palace, to explain the bill to Francisco Vidal, Chile's general secretariat at the time (see fig 3.2).[4] Báez, knowing that he would not be able to bring tumbe carnaval performers to the event, called on some Santiago-based Afro-Peruvian artists to help. There, in the courtyard of La Moneda, government officials were treated to an impromptu performance of festejo, with two dancers and two percussionists, before entering one of the Cabinet offices. One minor government official was particularly interested in the expression and stayed behind to ask several questions about the performance and Arica's Afro-descendant community. He was given a quick explanation of the tumbe. I later discovered he was a member of a local Chilean folkloric dance troupe. Once again, tumbe was juxtaposed with Afro-Peruvian expressions to style as part of the larger Afro-descendant community.

Tumbe carnaval was also present at several protests. When a local Black resident who worked for the municipal government was fired under dubious circumstances, Lumbanga members stood outside government offices with signs questioning the decision. They also brought drums, and the aggrieved party danced in front of news cameras reporting the incident. More importantly, in 2011, members of all the Afro-descendant organizations traveled to Santiago to perform tumbe carnaval in front of La Moneda to bring attention to their desire for inclusion in the 2012 census. Despite years of campaigning and even conducting their own internationally supervised

90 | *Styling Blackness in Chile*

Figure 3.2. Members of Lumbanga and Oro Negro with Antonio Leal (fourth from left, back row) and Romero Rodriguez (second from right, back row) in La Moneda (Chile's presidential palace) to present the draft of the Afro-descendant law to Francisco Vidal (center). Activists pictured include Cristian Báez (far left), Azeneth Báez (third from left, back row), and Marta Salgado (fifth from left, back row). The invited musicians are kneeling in the front row. November 26, 2008. Santiago, Chile.

pilot study, the Alliance of Afro-descendant Organizations was denied its request. The government, however, promised and completed their own pilot study in the years that followed.

Beyond Strategic Essentialism: Reframing Identity as Self-Understanding

The events I described in the previous section might generally be framed in terms of the economic and political motivations for performing tumbe carnaval. Smaller performing groups have emerged to meet the private demand for tumbe performance, while larger performing groups participate in both government-sponsored activities as well as events designed to garner government attention. When I asked Afro-descendant activist leader Azeneth Báez Rios about the motivation behind the dances, she stated:

> More than anything, the dances today are a strategy to reach out, to become known, to reach the Other . . . I show who I am, what I do, why I am doing

this. So that there is an understanding towards this culture from the other side, it's an awareness. That is, as I see it, what the dance provokes, its principal purpose.... [Otherwise,] how do you get them to understand who you are? First, let them get to know you, then form an opinion about you. So they gain an awareness of how they were thinking about you. (Interview with author, September 7, 2009)

Báez Rios was the most explicit about this political use of dance, yet even as she advocated for political action, she recognized that individuals needed cultural expressions like dance before they could do any political work. Because without such expressions, she argued, individuals could not understand who they are. As she put it, "I can't take part in a political action if I don't have a sense of identity. How do I identify myself? I identify myself with these rhythms, these dances, with this group, with these people. So, it's been an important part, I tell you, essential. It shapes the whole—this Afro-descendant movement" (Ibid). Several other Afro-descendant leaders repeated this idea of a need for dances and other cultural expressions for individuals to be able to identify as part of the Afro-descendant movement.

With this concept in mind, I now turn to explore the experiences that have led individual members of the Afro-descendant organizations to style music-dance this way. Note that I am not necessarily focusing on the "creators" of the genre; rather, I care about those individuals who choose to participate in these performances because of the feelings of relatedness with other members that they experience through these performances. As individuals, members may not agree with all the interpretations I have offered of their performances, but their continuing participation indicates that they see some benefit or positive outcome from their participation in tumbe carnaval performances.

Readers will note that, despite its use by activists, I avoid writing literally in terms of an Afro-descendant "identity." I am following the ideas of Rogers Brubaker, who challenged researchers not to settle for overly simplified "strong" or too-vague "weak" understandings of identity. Instead, Brubaker advocated for researchers to replace the term with descriptions of the more specific purposes that using it is meant to accomplish. First, he proposed that scholars adopt the more processual concepts of identifying and categorizing. He then offered the term "self-understanding" to reference the more specific "situated subjectivity" that is sometimes encompassed by the term identity. Highlighted among Brubaker's forms of self-understanding are those that are collective and deal with senses of commonalities, connectedness, or groupness (2004, 37–48). Following his suggestions, I now examine ideas of self-understandings relative to social position that result from participation in the Afro-descendant organizations. The concept of self-understandings emphasizes the experiences that individuals use to comprehend their place in society. By looking at experiences that several members of the Afro-descendant organizations have in common, I hope to create both a dynamic portrait of these members as well as a basis for understanding the motives for styling Afro-descendant.

Self-Understandings Framed by Negative Experiences

Several members of the Afro-descendant organizations that I interviewed spoke of formative experiences in which they were called names by their peers based on their Blackness. They developed certain behaviors based on this treatment. For example, as a child attending a Catholic school in Arica, Marta Salgado was insulted by her classmates with terms like "negra" (Black) and "poto de la olla" (the charred bottom of the pot). She claims that she developed an aggressive personality as a result, responding to the insults with force. She says that this personality has served her well, helping her become a leader. This quality of being self-assured was shared by a young adult activist, Camila Rivera, who stated that this characteristic helped her brush off the names that she was called during her school years. At the same time, Rivera views a quick temper as one of the characteristics of being Afro-descendant, saying "As Afros, we are very unique. We are *gritones* (yellers), good at teasing—we get angry very quickly, veeeeery quickly. You say something or look at me in the wrong way, and I will get angry with you" (interview with author, May 25, 2010). Of course, such characterizations can be problematic, as they have the potential to create or resonate with stereotypes. What is important here is that this attribute is framed as a response to a systemic social issue—the practice of insulting people based on how they are interpreted racially.

Getting angry is not the only response, however. Another alternative is to try to fit in. For Báez Ríos and another Afro-Chilean activist, the insults appeared once they began attending school in the city, after growing up in the rural Valley of Azapa. The insult of "negro azapeño" (Black from Azapa) had not only a connotation of skin color but also of being a country bumpkin, unfamiliar with facets of urban style. Indeed, Báez Ríos's cousins, who had grown up in the city and with whom she lived to attend school there, were the first to chemically straighten her hair so she would not embarrass them. To meet expectations of others, Báez Rios grew accustomed to straightening her hair and dyeing it with blond highlights. She felt she needed to do this to prevent obstacles to her career stating "A person gets used to feeling less Black, because it is a way to defend yourself. As long as you are less Black, better groomed, more professional, you are going to have a decent job. Because if I had been Black, really Black, I would not have been working for a company—I believe not. I am convinced I would not have, because, for them, appearance is worth a lot" (interview with author, September 7, 2009).

Similarly, the Afro-Chilean activist, a generation younger than Báez Rios, also found himself being called names associated with Blackness and rurality ("negro azapeño," "leche de burro") as he began middle school. His initial response was to brag that he had land in Azapa, complete with horses and a donkey, as if to make a show of his wealth. A classmate of his had the last name Corvacho, a name very much associated with Azapa's Black population, and the activist shamefully recalls that, at that time, he would deny having any affiliation with the Corvachos in order to fit in. He avoided having friends meet his darker-skinned grandmother. Such experiences made both the activist and Báez Rios aware of the differences in their social positions between the urban spaces of Arica and the rural spaces of Azapa.

Beyond rurality, occasionally the names or insults made reference to Africa and the Black Atlantic. For example, because Rivera liked to dance salsa and her father played bongo as a hobby, people in Copiapo called her "Celia Cruz," a reference to the famous Afro-Cuban singer. More derogatory was a name she was called in Arica, "Choca-Choca," a moniker that presumably was meant to reference her as a member of some African tribe. Note that this practice of referencing Africa was not meant in a positive way, but rather was aimed at underscoring a connection with incompetence and primitivism. Perhaps the most offensive insult of this type that was reported to me was "Piticus," aimed at comparing a Black male to the extinct hominin "Australopithecus."

In addition to having these discriminatory experiences, some Afrodescendants in Arica also encountered objectification due to their Blackness. For example, Silvia stated that, while working, she had to be cautious about what she said and did. At her job, she found that her colleagues tended to take jokes the wrong way, and, if not careful, she could quickly become fodder for gossip. As an attractive woman with darker skin, she found that her coworkers might interpret her comments in terms of a heightened sexual appetite, a negative stereotype commonly associated with Black women. Likewise, Rivera, who was studying prelaw at the time, sometimes felt that she did not receive the respect she should in her classes. The professor and her fellow students seemed condescending, not taking comments from the *negrita bonita* (pretty little Black girl, Rivera's phrase) seriously.

If these women felt objectified in these more formal situations, then festive, casual situations were no exception—particularly where dancing was concerned. Both Rivera and Silvia complained that others misinterpreted their dance movements. Silvia said that she would never *a perrar* (dance doggy style) at an office party. Rivera explained that once, when she was dancing with a male friend who was also a member of Lumbanga, his wife reminded her to tone it down. The wife pointed out that some of their Indigenous friends were at the party, and these friends were liable to misconstrue their dancing as sexual. Rivera felt like a damper had been placed on the party. When I asked her about it later, she stated: "Generally, when someone enters a new place, they look at you as if to say, 'Hi, pretty little Black girl that dances well and is super cheerful.' And occasionally that can be misinterpreted in other ways. Like—I don't know—that chick is crazy and she likes to have various men . . . I don't know. The point is that that is not the goal. The goal is something else, to have a good time" (interview with author, May 25, 2010).

Both Silvia and Rivera feel these unwanted interpretations were imposed on them for their preferred or habitual way of behaving and how they look. As a result, Silvia felt obliged to alter her behavior at the office, and Rivera at a party. As explained in chapter 2, these interpretations arise from a colonialist view of movement styles. Báez Rios faced these issues even as she walked:

> It has to do with one's ancestry—the movement that one makes, I don't know. For example, personally, many people used to say to me, why do you walk like that? Always . . . it felt very natural to me, but many people told me that I walk with a movement very [*sways*] and that I would raise my gaze [*nose in the air*], that I had a high opinion of myself. Because of the fact that I would be upright and move myself when I walked. But it is something very natural in a woman—being that I did not want to be a Black woman—and I had the movement of a Black woman. (Interview with author, September 7, 2009)

Báez Rios's experience suggests that many Black individuals have the differences between themselves and others—even in movement— brought to their attention. There are two possibilities here. People may be sensing her movement habits as different and out of place with the way they identify her (whether White women should not sway or Black women are not supposed to move in an upright haughty manner). She, however, seems to think that her Blackness is the issue. She walked in a way (i.e., "the movement of a Black woman") in which those around her felt she should not. For Báez Rios "movement of a Black woman" has to do with swaying and elevated posture; I will discuss this body attitude further chapter 4, styling Blackness as criollo.

The unwanted interpretations were not confined solely to the female gender. An athletically built, very dark-skinned Afro-Peruvian resident of Arica, whom I will call Roberto, experienced similar situations. In addition to dancing, often bare chested, in pasacalles, he enjoyed dancing socially at night clubs. After dancing with a woman, men would occasionally comment, with a wink and a nod, that Roberto had conquered the woman, insinuating from his dancing that he planned to take the woman home for the night. Roberto's build and manner had commanded the attention of these men, and it angered him that he could not dance without having these interpretations thrown at him. He would often confront these men, turning their comments back at them with the argument that they were dirty thinkers.

The descriptions above tell of self-understandings emerging from negative experiences shared among several members of the Afro-descendant organizations. They signal a commonality among some members in the organizations, but not all.[5] These experiences reflect the presence of stereotypes about Blackness that frame it as undesirable, as ignorant and incapable, as angry, and as sexually available. Such stereotypes should not be surprising, as they tend to be cosmopolitan and common throughout the diaspora, but I felt it particularly important to acknowledge them in the Chilean context, given that many Chileans do not perceive Chile as a place where such racist behavior occurs. These experiences also help provide the basis for understanding some benefits of participating in Afro-descendant organizations.

Individual Benefits of Participating in Afro-descendant Organizations

When talking with individuals who have performed as part of Afro-descendant organizations, many reminisce fondly about the travel opportunities that performing gave them. The organizations received validation in the form of invitations to perform, most notably in locations outside of

Arica. For some of the members, whether young adults or elders, these trips were the first time that they could travel nationally, such as to Santiago, or internationally, such as to Bolivia or Peru. Participants spent time together rehearsing and traveling for these performances. Such activities resulted in one of the key benefits of the formation of the Afro-descendant organizations, the one that Silvia alluded to in this chapter's opening vignette: the creation of a space in which Black individuals felt they could participate without being subject to the kinds of stereotypes discussed in the previous section. Rivera's earlier quote continued as follows:

> The goal is something else, to have a good time. In Lumbanga, you don't have those prejudices, those hang-ups. There we can enjoy ourselves, talk, we can talk with friends.... As individuals, we Afro-descendants, in other situations, in other environments, we don't feel comfortable. But being in Lumbanga, it's super comfortable and pleasant, despite all the confrontations we have, all the fights, because in all groups there are difficulties. Every group has their difficulties. But I think that these difficulties should be seen from the high road, and as a learning experience. That's what makes us different, how we treat one another.... So in Lumbanga, one finds themselves in family. (Interview with author, May 25, 2010)

Rivera's reference to family can be taken quite literally. Various people told me that they would attend the meetings of the Afro-descendant organizations because of their interest in the organizations' goals and expressions, and then find out that other people at the meeting were relatives. They might not have met before, or they might have been acquaintances but had not realized that they were related until they had discussions within the structure of the organizations. Such separations among relatives were, in part, a result of the additional stigma attached to Blackness during and in the wake of the period in which government control of the region transferred to Chile (in the wake of the War of the Pacific, see chap. 1). To demonstrate the connections among families, during the 2009 Bajada, members of Lumbanga descended on the city in troupes grouped by four family lines: Baluarte, Corvacho, Rios, and Quintana. Each family group performed its own skit at the end of the pasacalle, and family pride inspired an informal competition over the quality of the skits.

Incorporating Tumbe into Traditional Spaces

The previous sections make clear how music-dance as an activity within Afro-descendant organizations helped clarify an individual's self-understanding of who they are as Black. The degree to which this new vision of self-understanding incorporated itself into the community can be seen in how the tumbe carnaval has worked its way into other, more intimate spaces that may be open to the public but which are not the most obvious ones for performance of tumbe carnaval. For example, when I was attending a Cruz de Mayo celebration in 2010 held by the Corvacho family in the Azapa Valley, I was surprised to find members of the recently formed group Comparsa Tumba Carnaval there. They had brought their drums to perform at the party following the traditional procession that marks the end of the novena for the Holy Cross.[6] Combinations of brass bands, panpipe troupes, and even a dance orchestra typically provide the music for this type of yearly celebration. Indeed, a brass band and dance orchestra were the main attractions, but the presence and acceptance of the tumbe carnaval at the event was a novel integration of the genre into what many considered a traditional community celebration sponsored by a single family. Since the family sponsor in this case was locally associated with Blackness, integrating tumbe performance was seen as acceptable.

Of greater impact has been the appearance of tumbe carnaval at funerals. One of the most poignant examples was the funeral of a well-respected Black matriarch in the Azapa Valley, whose son was a member of Lumbanga. At her funeral, I was surprised to hear that this son and several family members of his generation who had been playing drums with Lumbanga performed in front of her casket in the early hours of the morning, after many of those who had come to pay their respects (including myself) had gone home. This practice was repeated at the 2016 funeral of Rosa Rios, Cristian Báez's grandmother and an elder who was particularly beloved in the Afro-descendant community. One can speculate over the rationale behind such performances. Over the last two decades in Azapa, particularly with the arrival of additional Bolivian immigrants, it has become customary for people to perform music for the dead. On November 1, friends and family in the Azapa Valley gather around the gravesides of loved ones to share food, drink, and music.[7] Musicians-for-hire wander the cemetery as family offer them money to play a piece or genre of special meaning to the deceased, and the bands are sure to stop by the graves of their own departed family members to pay tribute. Individual families do this throughout the year on the anniversary of someone's death. Some of the members of Afro-descendant organizations also started to follow this custom. On several occasions, for example, members of Oro Negro gathered around the grave of Kiko Anacona, the drum maker who helped them construct the tumbe drums, to play a song or two for him, and received some press coverage for doing so. The drummers at the Black matriarch's funeral, however, had not been part of those performances and certainly were not seeking press. Instead, as Báez described it: "They waited until everyone had gone—well not everyone—but since the funeral service had ended—onto the intimate. They—bam!—began to play the drums. And they came up with rhythms that were very pretty. They stayed all night. I left; they kept playing. That's how you realize that there are things that no workshop can teach.... That is a response to feeling Black" (interview with author, September 12, 2009).

This event suggests the extent to which tumbe carnaval, particularly for a younger generation of musicians, has become a cultural resource for them to apply on a personal level as well as an organizational level. While it is tempting to simplify the tumbe as styling Afro-descendant for the gaze of Others such as international organizations, the tumbe has, in fact, become more complicated than that. Its appearance in more intimate Afro-descendant spaces means that it has also come to represent the local and even familial. This familial connection becomes particularly important when considering moments of conflict in the Afro-descendant organizations.

Dealing with Division: A Return to Family

Lest this depiction of the comfortable space that Afro-descendant organizations provide individuals seem too idyllic, the fact that these groups have fractured and developed into multiple organizations points to the difficulties involved in coming to common creative visions and managing different personalities. The splits that have occurred have primarily developed around a combination of these two issues. For example, chapter 2 details the tension over the use of white costumes in the carnival Con la Fuerza del Sol. A 2010 split in Oro Negro was catalyzed by a debate over whether dancers must perform in white costumes. Making it quite clear that the dancers needed to respect their Afro-Chilean ancestors, an Oro Negro leader ordered the troupe to dance in white. Many members of the troupe took this as an overly authoritarian move and a slight against one of their Afro-Peruvian artistic directors, who was advocating for a different costume. After that year's carnival, many performers—including several from the original Oro Negro troupe—withdrew to form their own carnival troupe, Comparsa Tumba Carnaval.

Such splits have created additional problems, because they result in a division of talent and resources. In 2009, the number of experienced tumbe carnaval drummers was limited. If a performance opportunity arose for one organization and that organization came up short of the needed number of drummers for an event, an invitation for drummers would go out to other organizations. These other organizations might agree to participate, but if they felt that they were being used or there was tension between the different organizations' leaders, then the performing organization could find itself shorthanded when the other organizations' drummers were told not to cooperate. This situation was especially problematic if the performance opportunity was related to political and economic goals that could theoretically be in the best interest of the entire Afro-Chilean community. For example, in theory, Arica's version of the Slave Heritage Route benefits everyone, as it promotes tourism to the region, while allowing Afro-descendant artisans to sell their goods at stops along the route. Yet some performers saw this route as a project led strictly by Lumbanga and its leaders. Drummers from other organizations were heard to complain, "Why do we have to go drum for Cristian Báez?" In their defense, performers are often not compensated for such performances, and members of the group organizing an event often stand to benefit the most, whether financially or promotionally, although often this benefit is meager.

This discord can be particularly discouraging to the leaders of the Afro-descendant organizations. I had several leaders lament how much more they could accomplish if all the organizations would work together toward a common goal. A few even expressed that they had felt on the edge of depression when attacks became personal, or that they experienced frustration at the lack of support for a specific initiative. When I asked these leaders about how they continued forward in the face of these challenges, they pointed to a sense of familial obligation. Salgado, for example, after mentioning her commitment to the original goals of Oro Negro, stated flatly that she remembered that her family members, the Salgados, Henríquezes, and Leteliers, had started the organization and this labor. Her glance told me that it was understood that she was obligated as a family member to continue her work—although later she told me that she had also taken on other responsibilities to keep herself from being consumed by the challenges facing the Afro-descendant organizations. Báez Rios, now a member of an association called las Hijas de Azapa (in addition to Lumbanga), said she took inspiration from her mother, whom she described as one of a generation of rural Black women who endured hardships with quiet patience and strength. In her mother's case, she had to raise eleven children, occasionally going without food herself so her children could eat. Yet these women were not bitter, Báez Rios fondly remembered, but kind and always happy to greet you. She stated it was for that generation of women, and her mother in particular, that she continues to fight, and their memory gives her fortitude in the face of challenges.

This use of family for inspiration by activists in their political struggles can be interpreted as bringing tumbe carnaval full circle. Anthropologist Krista Van Vleet reminds us: "Rather than being based on some essential biological relationship or on static social structures, relatedness emerges among individuals who have differing life experiences and move within and between communities that are marginal to but not isolated from national discourses or global processes" (2008, 2).

Tumbe carnaval performance was constructed based on interviews with the *abuelos* (literally, grandparents, but more generally, the elders). As described in this chapter, individuals can use tumbe carnaval practice to create a relatedness among themselves as Afro-descendants within organizations. Tumbe performances can index the conversations that were had with these elders or iconically stand for them, while simultaneously producing new experiences among the performers that can be referenced in the future. Individuals can also use the tumbe to reinforce the self-understandings they already have of relatedness through lineage between themselves and their specific family ancestors, as I described with the funeral performances. Given that all performances involve risk, however, tumbe carnaval performances can fail to create this sense of relatedness, as evidenced by organizations splitting apart. When this happens, individuals often look to reinforce their self-understandings of relatedness in other experiences. Some of these experiences are rooted their family's participation in performances that style Blackness in other ways. These are the focus of part 2.

Notes

1. La Ginga was Arica's signature urban carnival from 1982 to 2004. Organized by Carlos Verdugo, this carnival was initially an attempt to mimic the Carnival of Rio de Janeiro, with troupes dancing to recorded samba music. The focus was costumed performers and parade floats referencing popular culture and representing the local neighborhood organizations

known as Junta de Vecinos. Many older residents of Arica remember La Ginga fondly, but many people of Indigenous descent would argue that the carnival Con la Fuerza del Sol is a better representation of Arica.

2. "Negra," a poem by the Afro-Peruvian artist Victoria Santa Cruz, is recited with a cajón accompaniment. The poem's theme is the transformation of the term *negra* from an insult to a badge of pride in the voice of the speaker.

3. Through-composed refers here to choreographies conceived as one piece from beginning to end, in contrast to the parade format, in which modules of steps are called out in the moment at the behest of the dance leader.

4. The bill was delayed in committee and later withdrawn, as activists saw that their proposals could be strengthened.

5. In the 2009 pilot study conducted by the Afro-descendant organizations Lumbanga and Oro Negro under the umbrella of the Alianza Afrodescendiente, 58 percent of respondents felt that they had been discriminated against (Salgado Henríquez 2013, 153).

6. In the Andes, families often erect a cross on a hill or mountain to overlook their land. The *Cruz de Mayo*, or May Cross, is the annual celebration in which that cross is brought down from its perch, prayed in front of for nine days (a novena), and dressed with new decorations or trappings. On the last day, the cross is reinstated to its high location and a large party is held. While the local church recognizes this holiday as May 3, because so many families follow the custom, families spread out their celebrations through July to be able to attend each other's celebrations.

7. This celebration has connections and similarities to what has become known as the Day of the Dead in the United States. In the Catholic Church, this day is the Feast of All Saints.

PART II
OTHER WAYS OF STYLING BLACKNESS

AN INTERLUDE ON THE IMPORTANCE OF STYLING BLACKNESS AND THE AFRICAN DIASPORA

The stigma surrounding Blackness continues to be prevalent in Chilean society, but as I have shown, performance can mediate the way that Black performers feel about themselves. In part 2, I will describe how, for generations, Blackness in Arica has been performed in several ways that continue to be meaningful today. Performers style Blackness as criollo, moreno, and Indigenous depending on how they want to relate to other performers and how they want audiences to understand those relationships. The qualities of each of these styles has helped to shape Arica's impressions of Blackness within specific contexts. By styling Blackness as criollo, performers share a music-dance culture with family members and others on the basis of nationalism. This culture offers participants a way of accepting the presence of Blackness without having to admit it openly to outsiders, what Herzfeld calls cultural intimacy. Residents of all ethnoracial identifications can engage with aesthetic practices that they might recognize as related to Blackness but have been tempered to appeal to criollo nationalism, using the trappings of European cosmopolitanism. In styling Blackness as moreno, Black families participate in heartfelt religious devotions marked by pageantry and orderly conduct, taking pride in their family's reputation within certain dance troupes. Lay and religious leaders from the local elite can look with praise on these decent forms of styling Blackness, even as performers respond to these leaders by introducing aesthetics of coolness and satire, which are resonant with the diaspora. Indigenous performers make use of local versions of the carnivalesque to style Blackness, raising their own station at the expense of historically Black colonial work captains and fellow laborers. Although today this styling of Blackness as indígena is largely propagated systemically, the contemporary presence of mixed heritage performers can create a cognitive dissonance between the satire in the performance and the desire to support all minority groups in the region. Key facets—whether sonic, visual, or kinesthetic—in each of these modes of styling Blackness resonate with the local cultural memory of Black families. Familial connections often underscore how these ways of styling function as identifying and support mechanisms for individuals.

These three ways of styling Blackness complement rather than contradict the more recent Afro-descendant perspective. As described in part 1, styling Blackness as Afro-descendant emphasizes continuity with Africa, often by appealing to contemporary cosmopolitan understandings of what African music-dance is. These understandings emerge not necessarily from direct contact with African expressions but rather through more locally familiar Afro-diasporic expressions. In Brown's terminology (2005), the tumbe carnaval makes creative use of diasporic resources in visual, sonic, and kinesthetic facets of performance that are in synchrony with aspects of elders' cultural memory. By recreating the tumbe, the founders of the first Chilean Afro-descendent activist troupes created spaces where they could relate with others that self-identified as Afro-descendant. They built new organizations that allowed them to interact with an expanded "family" at a new cultural moment.

What was new here was the way local Blackness was styled to make connections to Africa explicit, since these connections now had more political value on an international level. Historically, however, the power structures that shaped the diaspora placed limits on the cultural activities that Afro-descendants could use to respond to their local situations, usually discouraging associations with Africa. The unique nature of the space, of the individuals in power, and of the available cultural resources meant that each site within the African diaspora produced Blackness in its own way. Similarities in these factors led to cultural commonalities between diasporic sites, but, as the number of these similarities has dissipated over space and time, one can define those regions that had a greater association with African Blackness—a Black Center—and those that did not—a Black Periphery. These peripheral regions participated in the diaspora and had a Black presence, even if it was not necessarily styled performatively in ways that reflected the contemporary cosmopolitan associations with the term. Styling as a concept is useful in this regard, as it asks one to think in terms of the locally important relationships performers have with other performers, the amount of agency they have in their performance, and the aesthetic choices they make when responding to these two factors, given specific contexts.

Furthermore, styling can complicate the perceived absence of Blackness in the periphery in ways that theories of assimilation, creolization, or hybridity, might not. Assimilationist theories, for example, have concentrated on the degree to which minority ethnic groups interact with a dominant culture and how these two groups eventually come together to share traits that are considered mainstream. These theories also recognize that such processes can have racial limitations. Largely using the United States as their model, assimilation scholars historically focused on the erasure of the minority group into the mainstream as the completion of a process. Recent attitudes recognize assimilation as only one piece of more complicated immigrant social dynamics that also include features like transnationalism (see Kivisto 2016). Styling recognizes how individuals might opt to perform aspects of assimilation or transnationalism as dependent upon the moment and context rather than as the completion of a process. Theories of creolization, rooted in the Caribbean experience, celebrated cultural mixture as productive of something new that served as a form of local resistance to European colonial power structures. This celebratory attitude toward mixture has made creolization a fertile area of study for those academics interested in local manifestations of globalization, occasionally at the expense of the details of localized power dynamics. Other scholars of creolization have overly concentrated on colonial Black-White relationships in the Caribbean, unable to incorporate additional groups in more recent contexts.[1] Styling accommodates multiple relationships between performers at different moments, making sure that local dynamics are accounted for, while insuring that creolization is not a permanent end goal but rather an emerging product contextualized in time and space. Finally, like creolization, hybridity theory revindicates mixture, but from a slightly different perspective. Hybridity either exists as a constant force for renovating culture in postcolonial spaces or in cultural expressions that complicate power by resisting the "pure" categories of colonialist power structures.[2] Again, those who espouse hybridity may oversimplify the positionality of these expressions, whereas the co-presence of multiple forms of styling permits analysis beyond simple binaries of the colonized-colonizer, but rather a variety of relationships, temporalities, and individuals.

More practically speaking, styling is especially useful in recognizing and explaining how individuals can participate in multiple music-dance forms that engage different aspects of their identity. For individuals whose families have long been locally recognized as Black, the tumbe was simply one more way of styling that Blackness. They continued to dance valses and other types of criollo national music at family gatherings to interact closely

Figure INT.1. Marcos Butrón in multiple modes of styling: from left to right, dancing tumbe with Lumbanga in 2009, rehearsing morenos de paso with the Morenos de Marconi in 2008, and dancing morenada in the Achachis Generacion 90 in 2014.

with or nostalgically remember previous generations. They dedicated themselves to the Virgin through moreno religious dance troupes to engage their spirituality and family pride. They participated in the Andean carnival in troupes that were associated with Indigenous expressions to either connect with another way of identifying themselves or to celebrate and relate with their peers' ways of identifying. Part of what the concept of styling does is to recognize the agency of individual performers to style Blackness as they see fit in a specific context (fig. INT.1).

Even as the concept of styling suggests the possibility of individuals participating in several of these genres, performers can also interpret the styles of Blackness I have described in this book differently. Styling Afro-descendant has found some success but has also created challenges. Initially, tumbe carnaval helped raise awareness about Afro-descendants generally and the political goals of Arica's Afro-descendant organizations specifically. The expression, however, has appealed to many people who do not necessarily identify as Afro-descendant but want to participate in the more publicly open spaces in which troupes perform the tumbe, for example, the Carnaval Andino, regional pasacalles, and events by invitation in other cities. Performing organizations have had to decide whether they want to grow their membership to have a larger impact on their audiences or become more selective. Furthermore, the political successes of the local Afro-descendant activist organizations have meant that more economic and cultural opportunities have become available for Afro-descendants. The appearance of these opportunities has led to benefits for some groups but has also created tension between the organizations. Finally, one of the primary goals of the movement—the Chilean state's official recognition of Afro-descendants—was just beginning to become a reality in early 2019. The lack of recognition up to this point means that the government has not taken steps to identify and recognize systemic racism towards Afro-descendants in Chilean society—a racism that will become more apparent with the growing number of Afro-descendant immigrants.

Notes

1. For a broad discussion of creolization, see Stewart (2007).
2. The first view emerges from García Canclini (1995), while the second argument comes from Bhabha (1994). I see these views as largely complementary.

4

STYLING BLACKNESS AS CRIOLLO

Dancing the Intimate

On July 26, 2009, the Chilean Afro-descendant organization Lumbanga was celebrating its sixth anniversary. Members were gathered outside on the dirt floor patio at a private dwelling in the Azapa Valley, as the lazy afternoon sun shone brightly through the woven reed panels and tarps that defined the porous walls and ceiling of the space. Some people were handing out beers as the *picante de guata* and *picarones* were being prepared.[1] The mood was jovial, casual, and familial. It was an event organized by Lumbanga, for Lumbanga.

The festivities began when Alex Tajadillo, the resident Afro-Peruvian percussionist who usually accompanied Lumbanga performances, launched into a rhythm on his cajón. Lumbanga's president, Azeneth Báez Rios, took the microphone and started reciting the familiar line, "Ritmos de la esclavitud, contra [sic] amarguras y penas" (Rhythms of slavery, opposing bitterness and pain). It was the opening quatrain of Nicomedes Santa Cruz's famous poem "Ritmos Negros del Perú" (Black Rhythms of Peru), a touchstone of the movement committed to reviving Black culture that blossomed in the 1950s in Lima. With the closing of the first ten-line décima, "ritmos del esclavitud," Tajadillo became more active, filling the space with the sound of his slapping on the drum. The triplet figures inspired Báez Rios to start dancing, and there were cries for Camila Rivera, one of Lumbanga's featured dancers, to enter the open central space. She was quickly joined by another young woman, and the two moved sensually through the next verses. Rivera eventually persuaded Marcos Butrón onto the floor; the young man had been resisting the cries from others to start dancing. Tajadillo intensified the rhythm, and soon two young couples were performing rapid figures, shimmying shoulders, and shaking their hips, with smiles on their faces—until Tajadillo's hands landed heavily on his last stroke, bringing their dancing to a close.

After Báez Rios finished, her nephew Diego took the microphone, still accompanied by Tajadillo. He sang a *vals* titled "La Vendedora de Azapa." The vals is a genre that emerged from the European waltz, and Tajadillo's playing switched to emphasize the genre's strong three-beat rhythmic foundation. Tajadillo had composed this vals based on the stories told by elder Rosa Rios, who had accompanied her mother as she made the daylong excursion from the valley into town to sell produce and milk from the donkey she was riding. The vignette described in the song paralleled the costumbrista scenes that Afro-Peruvian artists like Victoria and Nicomedes Santa Cruz had presented on stage. The performance received warm, if not enthusiastic, applause.

Diego then turned to more familiar valses; this time he and Tajadillo were joined by the well-traveled local keyboardist, Segundo Quintana. The set of valses criollos he performed, "Zenobia" and "Nuestro Secreto," are classics in the repertoire. I had seen Diego sing these valses before as part of Lumbanga's stage performances. In this relaxed atmosphere, Rosa and Marcos began to dance together, while Carmen Baluarte invited her father to the floor. It struck me at that moment that there were three generations on the dance floor: the elders (Carmen's father and Rosa), the adult (Carmen), and the young adult (Marcos). In each case, the couples in close hold were the younger generations embracing the oldest—not an intense, "indelicate" embrace, but one with the intimacy of familial respect and affection (see video 4.1). They danced through both valses and stopped when Diego broke out into another song from Peru's Black cultural movement, "Toro Mata," a *landó* that no one danced to, before he ceded the live entertainment portion of the celebration to recorded music.

The relationship between song selection and dance behavior at this celebration was telling. Except for the original composition, the songs performed at the event were all linked to Peru, and Lumbanga members often justified their use of these songs to me by stating that Arica had once been part of that country. The young adult generation, used to dancing tumbe carnaval and shimmying to the cajón for performances, were relatively comfortable dancing to Tajadillo's festejo-like accompaniment of the décima recited by Báez Rios. The valses, however, introduced an intergenerational element, creating an interaction between individuals of various ages. One could argue that the difference in participation was due to tempo, the slower tempo of the vals making it easier for elders to participate. Be that as it may, during my fieldwork experience, I consistently saw the vals associated with intergenerational dancing. In interviews, the elders continually cited valses as music they associated with their parents. These memories informed Lumbanga's performances, since the group tried to reflect the cultural experiences of its elders in its performances. The intimate hold of the vals can act as a metaphor for the way in which the young and middle-aged adults embraced the stories of their elders, just as the elders related the intimate memories of their parents' activities.

Lumbanga, however, was virtually unique in using valses and songs from the Afro-Peruvian movement as a staple in its repertoire. As mentioned in chapter 2, the winners of the government grant that eventually reconstructed the tumbe carnaval initially had considered basing their project on this type of music, but they decided against it because the music required a level of musicianship that was not easily available within the organization and thus limited the number of performers that could be involved. Valses do not translate well into the pasacalle (street parade) format, and Lumbanga only performed them in staged settings.

Besides these practical matters though, the strong association of these valses with Peru can lead to complications for organizations seeking recognition as *Chilean* Afro-descendants. Comments posted under YouTube videos of performances accuse Chileans of stealing Peruvian culture or dismiss Chilean organizations like Lumbanga for simply being Peruvians in disguise. Such accusations, apparently from outsiders unfamiliar with the region and the dynamics of borderlands, can put the local Afro-descendant organizations on the defensive. In seeking government support, they must somehow demonstrate their Chileanness while acknowledging their Peruvian past—the latter previously being a source of embarrassment, if not outright danger.

This local tension between the familiarity with the vals and its association with the Peruvian past dovetails nicely with anthropologist Michael Herzfeld's concept of cultural intimacy (2005: 4–5). Herzfeld was interested in those acts that cultural insiders can understand as a way of identifying with each other (particularly on a national scale) but that might be a source of embarrassment when performed for external audiences. For example, Herzfeld cites the tradition of breaking plates at celebrations, which could be understood as quintessentially Greek while being open to criticism as uncouth and crass. Intimacy, then, was that emotion that many indexically connect with a knowing glance interpreted as "this is what *we* do but not everyone gets it."

In the case of Arica's Afro-descendants, cultural intimacy is significant in at least two ways. Lumbanga's use of the vals references an older form of Peruvian nationalism consistent with the elders' generation or perhaps more appropriately, the elders' parents' generation. This heritage points to the styling of Blackness as criollo. In chapter 1, I described how the term "criollo" was related to the colonial-era ethnoracial casta categories. Over time, criollo came to refer to European-derived expressions reinvented as local; they were respectable but with enough of a touch of the scalawag to mark difference from Europe. Criollo music-dance includes more than just the vals; other forms like *bailes de tierra* (literally, earth dances), a complex of dances that were presumably danced on dirt floors, are also present. These criollo genres played an important role in the elder generation's experiences, but such national music has not always been explicitly understood in terms of its Black contributions. In this chapter, I first describe the relationship between criollo music and Peruvian ways of identifying. I then consider how these attitudes and social relationships played themselves out in Arica, according to the information offered by the elders. Lumbanga and other Afro-descendant organizations used this information to perform these genres in ways that helped them make sense of their Blackness.

Younger generations in these organizations, however, grew up within Chilean state structures. They learned Chilean national forms in school and other cultural contexts. As mentioned in chapter 1, these forms were also referred to as criollo. In fact, due to shared histories of colonization, revolution, and migration, the division between the two states is not as clear as one might think. Valses, mazurkas, and certain types of bailes de tierra are also part of the Chilean criollo repertoire and continue to hold sway as older symbols of nationalism. As mentioned in chapter 1, beginning in the 1970s, the specific forms of cueca and tonada took on associations with the Pinochet dictatorship and the political right. On the one hand, performing these Chilean criollo genres can read as patriotic and demonstrate one's allegiance to Chile, but it can also be a source of potential embarrassment if one is on the political left. In this chapter, I address how members of the Afro-descendant organizations have interacted with these Chilean criollo forms, both individually and as organizations.

While national music like Chilean cueca and Peruvian vals are meant to be exclusive of one another, historically they have not recognized the contributions of people of African descent. By styling Blackness through these genres, the Afro-descendant organizations in Arica can potentially weave their heritage more easily into these narratives. Doing so, however, means coming to terms with cultural intimacy, the feelings associated with cultural knowledge that can be both be embarrassing and unifying. Here I explore this intimacy through the attempts that have been made to style Blackness as criollo.

Lo Criollo in Peruvian and Black Contexts in Early Twentieth-Century Arica

Although I described the origin of the word criollo and its development in chapter 1, the term has its own history in Peru. Lloréns Amico and Chocano Paredes (2009, 37–38) point out that, at the end of the nineteenth century, the term "criollo" basically signified Whiteness. In this formulation, Lima's elite politically appropriated the term as a way of identifying nationally. Lloréns and Chocano argue that socioculturally, however, the situation became more complex at the beginning of the twentieth century, as the criollo became associated with Peruvian coastal culture more generally.[2] Using this culture as a starting point, identifying as criollo referenced the experience of living in racially diverse neighborhoods like *callejones* and *conventillos*.[3] According to Aldo Panfichi, "To be criollo, which did not negate the fact one was Black, Zambo, or Mestizo, meant being 'happy and festive (jaranero),' giving no importance to the consequences of its use within contexts of modernization, industrialization, and new social demands" (2000, 153).

The festivities referred to here are the *jaranas*, recalled as all-night affairs, in which guitars played the main role in accompanying the key genres performed at these parties: valses and *marineras*. Heidi Feldman has described thoughtfully the process of how these genres were transformed over the first part of the twentieth century, which included adding the cajón box drum. Citing Romero (1994), Feldman has pointed out that efforts to separate "White" from "Black" elements in *música criolla* are problematic at best, but that Black musicians were important exponents for this music (2006, 22). She explained how it was the efforts of José Durand and the artists involved in his Pancho Fierro company in the 1950s that first called attention to the contributions of these musicians as rooted in Black music practice, setting the stage for the Afro-Peruvian revival that was to come.

In Arica, the Afro-descendant elder generation's experiences with the *vals criollo* were influenced by these attitudes. The Arica of the past would

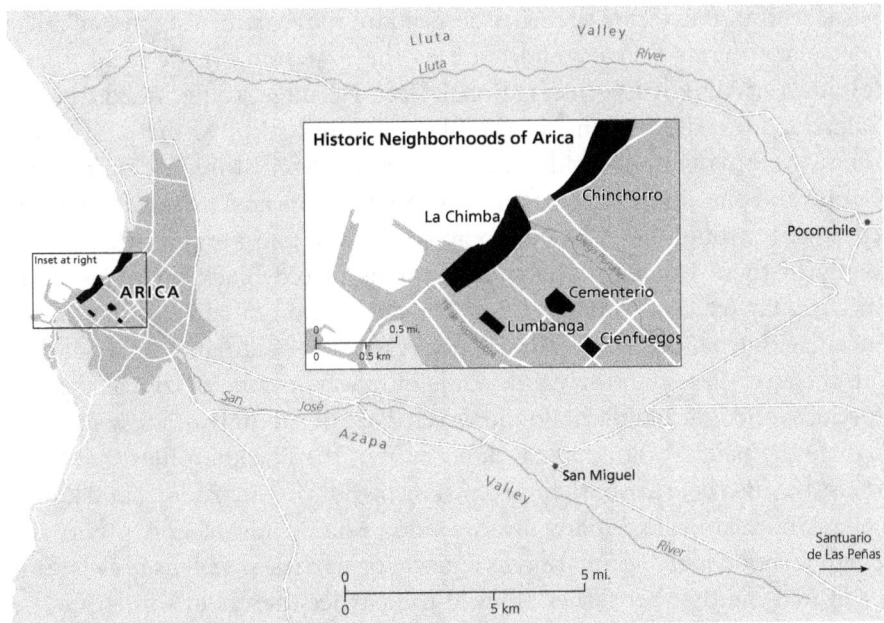

Map 4.1. Arica and its traditionally Black neighborhoods as part of the surrounding valleys. Cartography by University of Oregon InfoGraphics Lab, Department of Geography.

have been part of the older, imagined criollo culture, while at the same time, the traveling back and forth from Arica to Callao during the Chileanization era would have made Arica's residents aware of emerging ways of identifying as criollo in Lima.[4] Cultural intimacy can usefully summarize the tension here resulting from the binary between the political and the sociocultural. At the national level espoused by Lima's elite, Blackness was a source of external embarrassment, even though it was recognizably present in social contexts. While later reformulations of the criollo and, more importantly, the Afro-Peruvian and *indigenismo* movements would mitigate such a national image, this strain of cultural intimacy has not vanished completely from Peruvian nationalism. To better understand this era, I turn to the narratives that the adult and elder generations tell about this time.

When Marta Salgado, president of Oro Negro, recalls her childhood (interview with author September 5, 2009), she thinks of the adobe and cane house in which she grew up. She only now realizes it was part of a Black neighborhood in Arica called Lumbanga. The streets currently named Maipú, General Lagos, San Martín, Gallego, and Blanco Encalada reportedly now mark the borders of what was that neighborhood. Today, because of initiatives by the Afro-descendant movement, a sign in an adjacent plaza marks the neighborhood as the first stop on the local manifestation of UNESCO's international Slave Heritage Route. According to Salgado, a few descendants of the Black families still live there. She says there were many conventillos in the neighborhood, three or four along Maipú and one along San Martín. Since Salgado has now traveled to several countries through her Oro Negro activities, she told me that she noticed many of these conventillos in photographs of old Black neighborhoods in Uruguay (cf. Andrews 2010, 62). The description of conventillos aligns nicely with what Feldman calls callejones in Peru. Feldman points out that "in the Afro-Peruvian revival the callejones were mythologized as the site for authentic Black and criollo music" (2006, 21). Not only did Salgado recognize the neighborhood as Black because of the Black families that lived there, but also because of their professions: tailors, fruit vendors, and liquor sellers. Lumbanga had many taverns along what is now Maipú, giving the neighborhood a bad reputation as a place for parties as well as brawls. Salgado told me that her father enjoyed the parties there, but sometimes he had to escape from altercations.

In general, the Salgado family was musical; she was the only one of her siblings that did not sing. She says she grew up with Peruvian valses because her father loved them. He listened to these valses at home on the Victrola, even though he was a Chilean soldier. She claims that listening to such valses was banned because of Chile's strict prohibitions on Peruvian expressions in anticipation of the plebiscite to decide Arica's sovereignty. Her father was born in Arica in 1913 and, though he grew up during the plebiscite era, he would have been too young to be a soldier during the period, making it is especially interesting that her father would have liked these songs. Salgado explained this fondness saying that, "independent of the Chileanization process, the influence of Peruvian music has remained just the same" (interview with author September 5, 2009).

Salgado's descriptions of Lumbanga coincide with those of historian Alfredo Wormald Cruz. Wormald Cruz stated that the neighborhood was located along the street Maipú and that it consisted mostly of small businesses. He also added that many of the women worked as domestics. In a rather unflattering portrait, Wormald Cruz stated that, at the turn of the century, the inhabitants of this neighborhood were less than enthusiastic about work, preferring to sit on mats in front of their houses to drink wine and play guitar. He wrote that there were famous guitarists and singers at the time; there was even a famous popular poet called "el negro pellejo" (the Black hide), known for his insolence as well as his verse (Wormald Cruz 1963, 174). Unfortunately, Wormald Cruz does not cite his sources for such information, and one is left unsatisfied with his descriptions. Historian Viviana Briones Valentín, however, has searched police records of the time and finds police at the turn of the century being called to the Lumbanga neighborhood for excessive noise, although she does not find mention of the neighborhood until after the colonial era (Briones Valentín 2004).

René Peri Fagerstrom (1984, 34) wrote that Lumbanga existed until the plebiscite era (although Salgado's testimony suggests that at least some families stayed in or returned to the locale). During this era, many of the Black families presumably moved to Peru or to the valleys of Azapa and Lluta to escape persecution by overly zealous Chileans, who assumed that these families would vote in favor of returning Peru to power in the region. Thus, many people today consider the valleys—Azapa, in particular—the cradle of Black culture in the region (and indeed in Chile, in general).

Historically, however, Lumbanga was not the only site in Arica associated with Black families. Salgado suggested to me that several of the families in the Lumbanga neighborhood had been expelled from the region formerly known as La Chimba, a low-lying stretch of land near the beach, but there was fresh water available to grow crops. The area was known for producing different kinds of fruits like tomatoes, figs, and watermelons. The families who lived there had "ranchitos," small plots where they raised these crops and pigs. They also went to the nearby coastline to fish and dig for clams. Some people living there were also known for the handicrafts they made by weaving bulrushes. Due to their proximity to the water, women often took in laundry. Two of Arica's most famous Black residents were siblings who were raised in La Chimba: Rufino "El Negro Rufo" Lanchipa and Rosa Elcira Güisa Lanchipa. Their father had been a fisherman and their mother a laundress. They became well-known for their participation in pre-Pinochet era neighborhood festivities like carnival and the Fiesta de la Primavera (Spring Festival).[5] Güisa was also lauded for her bulrush weaving and was sent to Paris by the Chilean government as a representative artisan. She recalled how her grandmother used to sing her "El Payandé," a piece written as a *habanera* with lyrics that Güisa liked to relate to the Afro-descendant movement, perhaps because the Afro-Peruvian group Peru Negro had recorded it:[6]

Table 4.1. "El Payande" (1892), Luis E. Albertini and Vicente Holguín. Public domain.

¡Ay! Suerte maldita	Oh, the damned luck
llevar cadenas	to wear chains
y ser esclavo,	and be the slave,
y ser esclavo	and be the slave
de un vil señor	of a vile lord

During the 1950s, residents of La Chimba began to leave the area in anticipation of building plans by the Junta de Adelanto de Arica, the now-famous Development Council (Oyanedel 2002). The space is currently home to Arica's casino, a park (*Parque Brasil*), and a satellite campus of a regional university.[7] Many of the families that lived in La Chimba were Black, and when the area was cleared, they scattered to neighborhoods throughout Arica: Chinchorro, Cienfuegos (also known as ex-Chimberos), Cementerio, and Lumbanga (see map 4.1). Again, this dispersal left the Azapa Valley as the primary index for Black culture in the region. Since the valleys were primary loci of agricultural activity in the area, they already had a long history of Black residents.

Francisca Rosa Ríos (referred to as "Abuelita" or "Tía" Rosa) was born and grew up in Azapa, although her Peruvian father and her azapeña mother escaped for a while to the Peruvian port of Callao during the plebiscite era. Her father was a farmer, cultivating many types of vegetables (e.g., yam, squash) as well as cotton. He also grew the most famous crop of the valley—olives. She says they used their own oil to cook with, and she learned to cook at home. During her childhood, Ríos claims she never lacked food, and she was known as a very fine cook; family members were particularly proud of her picarones (interview with author July 26, 2006).

The young Ríos and her mother Natalia traveled regularly to Arica, accompanied by their donkey loaded with agricultural goods. These goods included firewood for cooking and milk from the donkey, which was purported to have medicinal properties. They would make the journey into town and walk through the streets, shouting in a sing-song fashion to offer

Table 4.2. Pregones (street cries) offered by Rosa Ríos, interview with author, July 26, 2006, Azapa Valley, Chile.

Caseriiiiita...	Housewiiiiife...
Caseriiiiita...	Housewiiiiife...
¿Va a comprar naranja?	Are you going to buy oranges?
Traigo lechuga, verduras, de todo...	I'm bringing lettuce, vegetables, everything...

their wares. These shouts are known as *pregones* (street cries), which folklorists and composers have found to be of great inspiration:

After selling their goods in the morning, Ríos and her mother would buy the things needed in the market and return home in the evening. It was an all-day affair.

Apart from this music of everyday life, on special days, such as birthdays or saint name days, school friends might gather to serenade the person of honor. Young women were the most popular target of these music groups, nicknamed the *estudiantinas*, after the serenading university student ensembles common throughout Latin America. The groups came with instruments such as the guitar, clarion, mandolin, violin, accordion and a side drum, and would play songs like "Las Mañanitas," a famous Mexican salutation. Ríos said that her older sisters received these salutations, but not the younger ones. In addition to serenades, friends might come to enliven other celebrations. For example, Ríos's father Juan would not tell (or did not know) his birthday, so the family always celebrated it on June 24, the Feast of St. John the Baptist.[8]

Early on, a cousin from Arica would bring a Victrola; later, her father bought one for his sister. With these machines, the dancing could continue late into the night. The songs heard were primarily valses, said Ríos, but they also included tropical songs like "Ay, Mama Inés," "Se va el caimán," and the conga "Uno, dos, tres . . . que paso más chévere."[9] One should not underestimate the influence of such recordings in the Arica area. "El Chilo" Corvacho had similar memories of growing up in Azapa with Victrola recordings, such as the Mexican vals "La Zandunga" (1937), the Mexican song "La Raspa" (1948), boleros, and the samba "Mama yo quiero" (1940). He told me that his aunt had a collection of some eighty records (interview with author July 26, 2006). Based on the earliest dates of the recordings I found, the abuelos' recollections point to the decades of the 1930s and 1940s.

But Ríos's father Juan also played guitar for his own amusement. The song that she remembered her father playing was the vals called "La Sirena," written by Peruvian Nicanor Casas Aguayo. The lyrics that she remembered speak of a mermaid that curses her luck in seeing herself a captive of the sea. That Ríos would remember this song in particular is interesting within the context of the Afro-descendant movement. One should note that Ríos, like many of the adults I interviewed, was just a young child at the time, and children were sent to bed early. She and her sister would often dance together in their bedroom and peek through the door or window to catch a glimpse of the adults' parties.

These remembrances in conversations and interviews were an important way in which I encountered the vals in Arica. People associated valses with their childhood and often with an older family member. This was even true of the abuelos' generation, who referenced valses among the songs their parents sang. In other words, these songs could be traced as far back as the generation that was born in the first decades of the twentieth century, when the plebiscite question had yet to be resolved. It was not only the generation of abuelos, however, that heard valses growing up. In my interviews, the next generation also spoke of hearing valses during their childhood, often in conjunction with other popular music of the time. These memories suggest that the vals served as an index for elder family members, and they became the inspiration for some performances by the Afro-descendant organizations.

Styling Blackness as Criollo through the Peruvian Vals

As Cristian Báez told me in 2006, Lumbanga cared about constructing an identity of Blackness based on the experiences of their elders. He espoused a belief that he considered to be African: elders were libraries, the sustenance of their community. Lumbanga needed to build on the narratives that their elders told them. The organization demonstrated the value they ascribed to their elders by taking them along when Lumbanga traveled to perform and presenting them on stage, even though they did not dance or sing much during these events. In doing so, Lumbanga's performers recreated the indexicality of their music with the elders.

One of the most obvious ways that Lumbanga relied on the elders' narratives was staging them, describing them in lyrics set within a vals. I already mentioned "La Vendedora de Azapa" in the opening vignette. At a Lumbanga performance in the city of Pica, inland of Iquique, Carmen Baluarte sang the song while a dancer portrayed the vendor by carrying a basket and sashaying across the floor. At other events, the song was simply performed as a musical number. Another original Lumbanga waltz was "Las Lavanderas." It dealt with the female occupation of being a laundress, a theme that folkloric ballets have presented in several other countries, including Peru. I first saw the song publicly performed in May 2010, when I encountered Lumbanga preparing for an appearance at the annual grape harvest festival in the town of Codpa. The singer was accompanied solely by percussion, using not only cajón but the drums used in tumbe, while several female dancers used pieces of cloth to simulate the act of washing clothes. Even though the song was initially composed as a vals, the musicians decided to break into a faster four-beat rhythm between verses, so that the dancers who were portraying the washerwomen could shimmy a little more as they pretended to wring the water out of the clothes. There seems to have been a concern that the slower rhythm was not enough to sustain attention. Indeed, there were a few whistles of disapproval from the crowd as the musicians returned to the slower rhythm, as if to complain, "Boring!"

In rhythm, instrumentation, and movement, the performers of the "Las Lavanderas" began to mix ideas of styling Blackess as criollo with those discussed earlier of styling as Afro-descendant. The faster four-beat rhythms and the emphasis on percussion juxtaposed the vals and tumbe performance, even if these interludes were not tumbe rhythms themselves. The broken body attitude was emphasized more in the faster sections, as opposed to the gentler sashaying of the vals verses. This staged presentation tried to balance the younger generation's desired performance of Blackness with genres that the elder generation could perform.. While both depended on cultural memory for their staging, the vals appeared to be more directly indexed to their elder community members than a more distant connotation of Africa.

This connection emphasizes why Lumbanga felt it had to present valses as staged presentations. Incorporating a closed-position couple dance into the more common pasacalle format is inherently difficult. Lumbanga performed valses only in the final section of their Bajada de Carnaval Afro, when individual groups each made their own presentations on the stage of the outdoor amphitheater in front of the city's ex-Aduana (ex-Customs House) cultural center. Otherwise, they were performed in the stage presentations that were part of FONDART grants or by invitation. One of Lumbanga's most successful vals presentations happened at one of these latter types of performance, which took place in Pica. Lumbanga's show followed a tango club's performance, and the club's dancers, members of an older generation, happily took the floor during the vals performance.

Earlier, I mentioned that the lack of committed performers of harmony instruments had somewhat hindered Oro Negro from performing vals in the FONDART project. Lumbanga did not seem to see this as an issue. While Lumbanga performers were always happy to have Don Segundo accompany them on keyboard, they saw the cajón as fundamentally more important. Diego Báez would often sing the valses without a harmony instrument but never without a cajón. This preference was illustrated when I was asked to participate in some of Lumbanga's events. If Lumbanga's regular cajón player was present, I might play guitar to accompany him. When he was not available, however, I would be asked to play cajón instead of guitar. This preference points to a musicality that was more oriented to rhythm and dance in its approach to the vals, while simultaneously emphasizing the instrument most associated with Blackness in criollo culture.[10]

The aesthetic preference for faster rhythms and percussion accompaniment offers something of an irony here. Lumbanga was attempting to present historical situations that were indexical of their elders' lives in the early twentieth century in Arica. In doing so, they were arguably styling Blackness as criollo, referencing performers like Arturo "Zambo" Cavero and Eva Ayllón, phenotypically Black singers famous for their interpretation of valses. Historically, however, the criollo attitude downplayed its Blackness while recognizing its presence in a culturally intimate way. Thus, although the elders' generation is often understood to be more phenotypically Black, their participation or invocation was not enough for most audience members to accept the vals in the context of a Lumbanga performance. Many audience members' expectations of the local Black experience required more percussion played with a faster beat.

Furthermore, many members of the younger generation had no more than a passing familiarity with the vals. In 2010, Tajadillo was no longer performing with Lumbanga, and the group was training a new generation of percussionists. At a rehearsal, I was asked to show one of their leaders how to play a vals on the cajón. He confessed to me that he had trouble feeling the rhythm, something I found surprising since I knew him to be an excellent carnival dancer. He struggled with the rhythm at first, but he eventually caught on and taught the others. The fact that the new, younger percussionists initially struggled with the vals rhythm suggested to me that they were not as familiar with the vals, in a corporeal sense, as even their only slightly older peers because they were distanced from a Peruvian aesthetic of the criollo. In fact, I found that some of them were quite familiar with other Chilean criollo genres, not surprising given that Arica's borderland status leads to its holding many officially patriotic activities. The Chilean vision of what it means to be criollo, however, has similarities with that of Peru, even though these comparisons are not always made. I now consider these connections and their differences before turning to how members of Arica's Afro-descendant groups have participated in these genres.

Attributes of the Chilean Vision of Criollo

One of the reasons that I could accompany Diego on guitar was that, growing up the son of Chilean immigrants, I heard recorded versions of other types of valses associated with Chilean folk music. I learned to play and sing "Rio Rio," "Mantelito Blanco," and "Si Vas Para Chile," which musicologist Juan Pablo González categorizes as "songs with a vals rhythm" within the larger genre of Chilean popular music, recognizing their circulation as part of commercial production. González (1999) has noted that several types of waltzes have been practiced in Chile, among which was the vals criollo, also called *peruano, norteño,* or *porteño*. The last name listed indicates the way the genre spread, through the network of Pacific ports like Callao, Valparaíso, and Arica. The ports also served as the subject of such valses like the well-known "La Joya del Pacifico," inspired by the city of Valparaíso. González notes, however, "This [type of] vals won a long battle for social legitimacy in Peru that it never managed to win in Chile" (31). Thus, it is vals-rhythm songs rather than valses criollos that, together with tonadas and cuecas, are the basis of Chilean criollo attitudes, often performed by huaso groups and folkloric ballets.

While I was growing up, my immigrant mother played recordings of this music, engaging in a nostalgia for idealized times spent in a now distant countryside with her family during her youth. Initially I associated these recordings with my mother, but after I learned to play guitar, they became indexed with our singing them together. Perhaps more importantly, I indexed these with my maternal grandparents, aunts, and uncle, who would sing along with me during the visits I made to Chile while growing up. They would praise me for learning these songs while living in the United States. My Chilean cousins were bemused, more interested in US or Chilean rock music, and commented how the "gringo" cousin was "more Chilean" than they were for performing these songs. In that space of family gathering, like the Afro-descendants in the opening vignette of this chapter, I indexed these songs in vals rhythm, tonadas, and cuecas with my parents' and, more strongly, my grandparents' generation.

Yet I never associated this repertoire with Blackness. This omission is directly related to how Chilean historiography generally rendered the presence of those of African descent invisible, particularly over the course of the nineteenth and early twentieth centuries. Most recently, musicologist Victor Rondón (2014) went through historical records looking for references to Black musicians. In his sources, he noted the occasional presence of Black musicians from the sixteenth to the nineteenth century, during which time they could attain positions of higher standing via greater skill on instruments. As he has pointed out, these documents illustrate the participation of Black musicians as officially employed musicians, such as organists, and do not reflect if or how Black musical culture had any impact on the music itself.[11] Ethnomusicologist and sociologist of music Christian Spencer Espinoza (2009), on the other hand, has hypothesized how Black laborers must have participated in the social celebrations that gave rise to criollo music-dance forms, particularly highlighting the cueca. The Chilean analog of the urban Peruvian jarana was the *chingana*, a temporary arbor or other type of mobile structure that served food and provided music for dancing. These types of social spaces provided entertainment for the working class, presumably the class that included most of those of African descent. Again, here the argument is one of social presence and not necessarily cultural influence on these genres. The acknowledgment of the presence of Blackness, however, is recent and so limited that it does not lead to any sense of embarrassment or cultural intimacy in Chilean criollo music.

Instead, more recently, a sense of cultural intimacy has formed around this music in relation to Chile's military dictatorship. During this period, criollo genres were given prominence in state events and media; for example, the cueca was declared the national dance in 1979. Despite largely predating Pinochet's rise to power, these genres became associated with the dictatorship. While this perception has slowly changed in the generation since the regime ended, this indexicality can be a sensitive point for those performing cueca, tonada, or more patriotic valses, in slightly different ways based on the perception of whether audiences style progressive or conservative. While all Chileans would understand this music as a display of Chilean nationalism, the connection to the dictatorship and its human rights abuses can function as an unspoken source of embarrassment. Arica lived through this dictatorship, and so such sensitivities are part of its cultural fabric. Its position as the border town with Peru and as home to a military regiment, however, means that shows of Chilean patriotism are also common. As part of Arica's society, members of its Afro-descendant organizations are familiar with these nuances and participate in these activities as well. In the next section, I consider how these members personally relate to the most important of these criollo genres in Chile, the cueca.

Arica's Afro-descendants and Contemporary Participation in Chilean Criollo Forms

Arica's residents are intensely aware of Chilean cueca, because the national cueca competition is held there every year at the *Club de Huasos*. This civic organization, like its counterparts throughout the rest of the country, is known for its attempts to promote certain Central Valley huaso traditions like the rodeo. These goals appear ironic in an arid place like Arica, where cattle raising was never prominent. Several people I spoke with discounted the Club de Huasos as a sort of transplanted institution, the product of retired military personnel who originally had come to Arica as part of their service and then decided to stay. In 2008, Arica's mayor, Waldo Sankán, acknowledged such criticism in a speech he gave to open the club's celebration of the national holidays, saying "And someone might say that we are far from the Central Region, that we are far from the huasos, but the truth is that here we are with them year-round. It is an honor for us that, for forty years, the National Cueca Competition has been held in Arica.... The cueca takes on a special hue in Arica. The truth is that it is a border city with Peru and Bolivia in which we feel very Chilean" (speech, September 18, 2008).

As Sankán pointed out, the Club de Huasos de Arica is particularly famous nationwide for hosting the National Cueca Competition, in which the champions from the regional contests come to compete. Locally, however, the Club de Huasos receives the largest number of visitors during its *ramada*, five days in which the club offers food and drink and hosts carnival-like games, a rodeo, and dances to celebrate the national holidays.

In 2008, I attended the formal opening, in which the mayor and other authorities were present. There was a live group playing cuecas, and dancers performed a folkloric ballet. The following year, however, I attended on another evening when things were not so formal. Cuecas were still being performed that evening, and as a matter of fact, that was one reason I was there. Lumbanga members Báez, Camila Rivera, and others felt as if they needed to dance some cuecas during the celebration of the national holidays. Rivera had danced cueca as part of a folkloric ballet when she had studied at Arica's *liceo artistico* (arts middle school), and she convinced Báez to dance with her. Watching them, what made an impression on me was the way Báez danced with confidence and in his own manner. He occasionally missed the call for changes in position (*vueltas*), responding late, but he was not as jumpy as others around him. I felt he had a certain flair, and I told him as much when he returned to the table. He responded by making one of the few references I ever heard him make to his mother's side of the family, who were from San Felipe, a town in Chile's Central Valley. Báez admired the way an uncle on that side of the family danced cueca. This uncle had told him that he needed to understand the cueca as a courting dance, one in which the man attempted to charm the woman. To do that, the uncle suggested, he needed to find his own personal way of expressing himself through the dance. In response, Báez had developed this way of dancing cueca, which I had just witnessed. I had heard something similar many years earlier from a folkloric dance instructor, who told me that there should be as many ways of dancing cueca as there were Chileans.

Fernando Zavala, another of the male dancers in the Afro-descendant organizations, spent several years formally learning how to dance cueca in preparation for dance competitions. He was aware of his appearance dancing cueca in full regalia, including hat, *chamanto* (dress poncho), and spurs. "There are few Blacks that dance it," he told me, but he felt it was important to know how, particularly when the Afro-descendant organizations went to international events: "One goes to another country—one goes to Bolivia—and it's your turn: 'Let the Chileans dance!' And no one knows how to dance! That's the issue . . . . You go to another country, and shoot, at least leave the name of Chile in good standing. Because they always cry, 'dance cueca, dance cueca'" (interview with author, January 14, 2009).

Because of some of his fellow dancers' ignorance, Zavala has spent some time teaching them how to dance cueca. Part of the problem, Zavala insists, is that the dance is not easy. "Morenada is easy; anyone can dance that. But cueca, it's always, Ay! That's it!" he said with pride (ibid.). Apart from the rhythm of the steps, part of the difficulty comes from having to know the cueca's specific choreographic sequence. Each member of the dancing pair traces out a half-circle, changing places with one another at three specific times during the course of the music. While the musicians often yell *¡Vuelta!* (Turn!) to help the dancers remember when to make the switch, a dancer demonstrates expertise by anticipating and executing the turns smoothly.

On one occasion, I encountered the cueca during a religious celebration, the *Cruz de Mayo* (the May Cross) of the Baluarte family in Azapa. The Baluartes are a well-known Afro-descendant family in the Valley, and the celebration of the Cruz de Mayo is a family affair. Many members of the community are invited, and all are fed, even interlopers like me. After the formal ceremony had finished and we had come down from the mount where the cross had been placed, the secular part of the celebration began. The brass band started with a cueca. Two couples took to the floor, each dancing slightly differently. One man executed the scissor step typical of the cueca from the Central Valley, while the other danced with a type of two-step, what some might argue as more Andean. In my field notes, I wrote that each couple had a dancer who could be identified as Black. In the first couple, it was the woman; in the second, it was the man. The brass band performed the set Andean style—two cuecas in a row followed by a wayno (see chap. 1, note 23). A long-lost Black relative from Peru had come to visit for the occasion, and he was especially pleased to have experienced the cueca, given that a vals often begins the festivities in other May Cross celebrations. While the cueca had the place of honor as the opening of the secular dance, *cumbias* began in earnest afterwards and occupied the rest of the evening.[12]

Each of these experiences illustrates how certain Afro-descendants personally used the cueca to identify nationally as Chilean within certain social contexts. They complicate a simple regional categorization of styling Blackness as criollo as only Peruvian and question ideas that Afro-descendants have not participated in larger Chilean society. Despite the presence of the cueca in many of the lives of these members of Afro-descendant organizations, I never witnessed any of the organizations dance cueca as part of a public performance.[13] I did, however, see one public performance of another genre that fit in both Peruvian and Chilean visions of the criollo: the baile de tierra.

Baile de Tierra: Styling Criollo at a Chilean Independence Day Parade

Chile celebrates its independence on September 18, and, in Arica, a parade is held on that date. Several brigades of troops march in front of local and regional officials. They represent various divisions of the armed forces, some in period costumes. Many civic organizations and schools are also required to parade. The municipality of Arica even presents a sampling of the service vehicles that they own.[14] After the military band kicks off the celebration and everyone sings the national anthem, but before the actual parade begins, a group of costumed huasos, as representatives of Chile's common folk, serenades the authorities. As one might suspect, these people are members of the local Club de Huasos. They make a toast with a horn full of grape-based *chicha* (hard cider), as dozens of huasos and chinas of all ages come before the mayor as well as city and military officials to dance the traditional three *pies* (set of lyrics) of cueca.[15] This serenade has become integral to the parades held both in Santiago and Arica.

In 2009, however, for the first time on Chilean Independence Day, the Afro-descendant group Oro Negro appeared after the huasos to present its greeting to the authorities. Salgado, the organization's president, held Oro Negro's banner high while wearing a special dress in the national colors that she had designed just for the occasion. As might be expected, the troupe paraded into the space in front of the authorities dancing tumbe carnaval. Yet once organized within the space, without warning, they stopped and broke into another rhythm on the same drums:

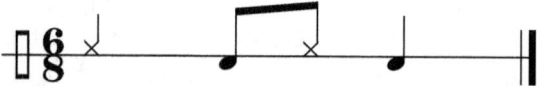

Example 4.1. Baile de tierra rhythm. Upper notes represent sticks struck on wooden side of drum.

Two dancers, one male, one female, each holding a long white handkerchief, came forward to dance as one of the vocalists yelled "Viva Chile!" and began to sing:

Table 4.3. Baile de tierra "Zamacueca de la Libertad," lyrics written by Gustavo del Canto. Used with permission of composer.

|: *Ay, yo tengo un dolor en el alma* *Que llora por su libertad* :|	|: I have a pain in my soul That cries for its freedom :|
Chorus (repeats)	
|: *A la zamacueca negra* *Encontré tranquilidad* *Los tambores son protesta* *Contra el sucio mayoral* :| |: *Yo soy sangre congoleña* *Y mi madre es África* :|	|: To the Zamacueca, Black woman, I've found tranquility The drums are a protest Against the dirty foreman:| |: I am of Congolese blood And my mother is Africa:|
Spoken:	
Pura negra chinchosa *Que el baile de tierra* *es la danza más hermosa* *¡TUMBA!*	Pesky, pure Black woman The *baile de tierra* is the handsomest of dances. TUMBA!

During the verses, the male and female dancers circled each other with their handkerchiefs pulsing up and down. At the chorus, they performed a type of *zapateado*, a livelier section where the male tends to stomp his feet more heavily on the ground. In general, the female dancer tended to keep one hand on her hip, and her hips moved in exaggerated fashion with her steps. The male dancer tended to have a hunched body attitude and almost swayed during the zapateado. Through the last repetition of the chorus, the rhythm slowed, the male dancer dropped to one knee, and the female put her foot on the knee that was off the ground. With the conclusion of the spoken section, the group resumed the rhythm of the tumbe carnaval. After the singer repeatedly sung the word "zamacueca," she broke into the usual tumbe song-chants as several of the dancers performed a staged choreography. When this choreography ended, the couple that had danced the baile de tierra came out again to freely dance tumbe, with the singer shouting out, "Like the rooster!" and, "Like the hen!" The drummer sounded a break, and with that, Oro Negro left the center stage to take its position within the parade that would follow (see video 4.2 for baile de tierra performance).

When I asked Gustavo del Canto about the piece, he said that he had written it himself years ago. The song had been within the early repertoire of Oro Negro, and it appeared as part of a short documentary in 2003. In the film's credits, the piece is listed as the "Zamacueca de la Libertad," but del Canto introduces the piece in the documentary by saying, "We are going to do a dance that is called baile de tierra here. They are dances that originate from the zamacueca and look a little like the Chilean cueca" (ORIGINES Documentary 2003).[16]

The similarity in appearance is not a coincidence. The well-known Argentine music scholar Carlos Vega pointed out that baile de tierra was the generic name for a category of picaresque dances (Vega and Moreno Chá 1986, 93) and the famed Chilean folklorist Margot Loyola remarked that the "of the earth" was meant as a stylistic contrast to those expressions danced in the parlors (*de salon*) of the day (1996, 13). This stylistic reference carries with it insinuations of social class and modernity, as dancing on a dirt floor suggests rurality or popular expressions danced in the chinganas, rather than the elegance required of houses with salons. By such categorizations, the cueca and zamacueca, as well as a number of other genres like the marinera and the *cachimbo*, would all be known as bailes de tierra.[17]

Several facets of this baile de tierra performance style this relationship between it and the other dances. First, it was danced by a couple holding handkerchiefs. Second, the dance included certain choreographic gestures, such as the dancers' pursuit of one another in a circle, the presence of a zapateado section, and a closing flourish in which the couple meets. Finally, the singer's shouts referencing the rooster and the hen invoke a common metaphor for courtship that is used to describe these dances. Such signs are enough for most Chileans to at least see a relationship with the cueca, particularly within this national celebration setting.

Yet there were some noticeable characteristics of this performance that differentiated it from the cueca and other bailes de tierra. The verse-chorus structure does not follow the poetic form of the cueca or the marinera, and the first verse varies from standard couplets and quatrains with octo-syllabic lines. The singer also did not add any of the common stock phrases like "mi vida" or "caramba" that cueca vocalists use to complete a melodic phrase that is longer than the written poetic material. Rather striking to me, however, was the body attitude, hips, and arms that were used in the dance, which contrasted sharply with the unbroken, vertical posture of the huasos that just danced moments before. These facets of the choreography, particularly the up-and-down motion of the handkerchief-wielding arms, hinted at the way Afro-Peruvian performance groups have interpreted the zamacueca (cf. Feldman 2006, 74–76). During the Afro-Peruvian revival, these gestures were symbolically linked to Africa through lyrics that identify the dancers as slaves and of African descent, in contrast to the Peruvian marinera. While I earlier presented some criollo genres that mentioned slavery and the colonial condition, these rarely mention Africa explicitly. These two sets of characteristics (common choreographic figures, handkerchiefs, and shouts, vs. variations in lyric structure and content together with body attitude) highlight the tension within the concept of criollo itself—to present an expression that is familiar and respectable to the elite with just enough of the exotic to differentiate it from other expressions. Finding this balance is difficult, and a performance's success may depend on how it resonates with local cultural memory.

The Place of the Baile de Tierra in Local Cultural Memory

The appearance of the baile de tierra in Oro Negro's repertoire was inspired by the initial fieldwork that del Canto and others conducted among the elders. A year or two later, during one of Lumbanga's roundtable discussions, Guillermina Flores Corvacho also verified the presence of the dance. As was common with elders' experiences of other dances, as a child, she could only witness the baile de tierra by peeking through closed doors. At one point, she referenced the steps performed as being cueca steps, yet she talked about the dance ending in an embrace or with the man dropping to one knee, only to be helped to his feet by the woman afterward. I have not seen these behaviors in cueca performance, but the latter step was present in a dance that I witnessed called the cachimbo. Later she also associated it with a dance form she had seen staged in Tacna, the *tondero*, usually referred to in the literature as a dance from the Peruvian north in the same family. Flores Corvacho described a bent body attitude, and she said that people related the number of *pies* danced to the number of colors on their flag. In other words, the red and white on the Peruvian flag meant that Peruvians would argue in favor of dancing two *pies*, while those siding with Chilean sympathies would dance three.[18]

Flores Corvacho's last comment here points to the difficulties in identifying a dance with a single nation-state. She was clearly describing a moment when people, some of whom identified with Peru and others with Chile, were performing similar dances at the same event, albeit with slight variations in practice. The dancers felt a need to discriminate between origins in performance, and I was told that some people wondered if Flores Corvacho might be confusing local dances with those she had seen in Peru, given that she had lived in both places.

The situation becomes even more complicated when one remembers that the dances took root during the nineteenth century when the region was part of Peru. For example, Loyola points out that "Baile y Tierra" is another name for the dance known as the cachimbo (1994, 29). The dance is considered emblematic of people from a neighboring rival city to the south, Iquique, and its surrounding pampas. The only time I saw the cachimbo danced socially in Arica was during the feast of San Lorenzo, the patron of the town of Tarapacá in the region of the same name. Because of the threat of swine flu in 2009, public officials kept people from traveling to Tarapacá to celebrate the feast. The large number of people residing in Arica who had some connection to Tarapacá held their own celebration. The cachimbo took a place of honor, being danced on the final day first by the sponsors of the fiesta, then next with everyone invited to participate.¹⁹ The rhythm of the cachimbo was the same as the baile de tierra, although this performance was played by a brass band with a military bass drum. The cachimbo's choreography features a series of reverences as well as a section of more intense circling known as the *toreo* (passing of the bull), rather than a zapateado. Loyola's consultants described the dance's character as one of grace, with the ability to dance with a jar on one's head being prized (1994, 71). The body attitude of the cachimbo danced that day, however, was closer to the baile de tierra that Oro Negro danced, with the torso bent at the waist and the wrist snapping the handkerchief close the ground, as if to tag the partner's calves. After reviewing the footage, I was particularly struck by the way in which one of the male cachimbo dancers spread out his arms to sway during the toreo in the same way the male dancer of the baile de tierra had during the zapateado.

Ways of performing the cachimbo can vary dependent on how the performer wants to style, and some individuals will suggest that the cachimbo I witnessed that day was not ideally elegant, not *de salon*. My point is that I saw a performance that was congruent with the stylings that Flores Corvacho remembered. In the context of the Lumbanga roundtable, she was sharing experiences based on Blackness that resonated with her cultural memory. The cultural intimacy of Peruvian criollo nationalism, however, does not speak of this Blackness—thus the need for both Lumbanga and Oro Negro to make these connections explicit in performance. To juxtapose the baile de tierra with the cueca as an expression of Chilean criollo nationalism calls to mind both genres' connections to Peruvianness and Blackness. Although I was unable to discover who had made the decision for Oro Negro to perform the baile de tierra at the Independence Day event, I believe that this decision was informed by the connection that this dance has with the cueca.²⁰ It was similar enough to be recognizable as one of its relatives, and just in case, the vocalist reinforced this connection with the chant of "zamacueca," making it appropriate to dance for the celebration of national independence. Yet it was still different enough in the performance that the Afro-descendant group would not be accused of mimicking the huasos. The question is whether it would be interpreted as too Peruvian in the context of a Chilean national celebration, particularly for Afro-descendant organizations wanting the Chilean government to recognize them. When I returned in 2016, Oro Negro did not perform at the parade. I was told this absence was simply due to lack of organization, but Afro-descendant organizations did not appear the following year either.

The Intimate Vals of Styling Blackness as Criollo

In 2009, after thirteen months of doing fieldwork in Arica, the last night of my stay had arrived. Several members of Lumbanga held a small, informal goodbye for me at Ester Baluarte's house. As refreshments were served, people stopped by to wish me farewell. Báez awarded me a framed certificate of appreciation as the "Gringo Chileno" for the work I had done with them. For entertainment, Baluarte had a young man set up the karaoke machine. Báez Rios and Carmen Baluarte took turns singing valses criollos they selected from a DVD that flashed pictures of Lima on the television screen along with the music. Others joined in if they knew the song, even correcting the melody when the person with the microphone was in doubt. I danced a vals with Rosa Ríos, the matriarch of the Báez Rios family. We swayed from side to side happily, carefully negotiating the space between the coffee table and the entrance to the kitchen. With twinkling eyes and a smile on her face, Ríos softly hummed along or sung a bit of the lyrics. I was smiling widely as well, thoroughly enjoying the sensation of moving to the strong pulse of the music, occasionally throwing in a flashy step for fun. I remember feeling content and appreciative.

While I certainly did not conceive of it as such at the time, the vals we danced could be interpreted as a convergence of the various cultural intimacies that I have discussed in this chapter. With images of Peru on the screen behind us, we danced together on Chilean soil to a rhythm that we each indexed to an older generation, contributing to a common social experience. Styling Blackness as criollo is a way for Afro-descendants to understand themselves through both their past and current experiences of nationalism. Ironically, these criollo spaces have historically emphasized Whiteness, somehow knowing of the presence of Blackness without being willing to acknowledge it. Such an emphasis permits someone like me, a Chilean American whose European roots are marked by name and phenotype, to participate with marginalized groups from a privileged position. Asserting Blackness within this space has the possibility of countering the existing hegemony while co-opting some of its markers, as in the case of the baile de tierra. This path has not been widely exploited, in part because it means explicitly acknowledging the embarrassment of cultural intimacy on all sides.

Notes

1. *Picante de guata* is a spicy stew using the cow's stomach, potatoes, and the *rocoto* pepper as a base. *Picarones* are deep-fried squash fritters in a donut shape.
2. Lima's urban elite envisioned this coastal culture in opposition to the mountain culture that elites in other regions like Cuzco saw as models for national culture. Known as *indigenistas*, these Cuzco intellectuals romanticized mountain culture in terms of Indigenous culture synonymous with the ancient Inca Empire.
3. Both terms refer to difficult housing conditions. Callejones references buildings only separated by narrow alleys, while conventillos are tenement-like buildings.
4. The term Chileanization refers to the policies and practices that the Chilean government implemented to reinforce their sovereignty over the lands previously owned by Bolivia and Peru, especially during the plebiscite era (ca. 1883–1929).
5. The elders all generally remembered Rosa Güisa's and Rufino Lanchipa's participation in these festivities, but exact happenings and dates of the feasts were frequently difficult to pin down. The Fiesta de la Primavera was an annual spring celebration, initially begun by university student associations in the capital in 1913. Such public celebrations were halted with the military coup in 1973. There have been recent attempts to revive the Fiesta in Arica, e.g., in 2013.
6. The *habanera* (literally, the "one from Havana") is a four-beat rhythm with a syncopated second beat, perhaps most famously known for its appearance in Bizet's opera *Carmen*. "El Payande" was originally recorded by a Peruvian duo, Montes y Manrique, in 1911, but the lyrics were adapted from a nineteenth-century Colombian poet Vicente Holguín with music composed by Peruvian Luis Eugenio Albertini (Manuel Acosta Ojeda, http://manuel-acosta-ojeda.blogspot.com/2012/04/la-habanera-o-danza-cancion.html).
7. Currently known as the Campus Velásquez of the Universidad de Tarapacá, it was originally the Arica campus of the Universidad de Chile.
8. Due to its proximity to the winter solstice in the Andes, this feast historically was quite popular. The Indigenous Rights movements have started to emphasize the solistice as the marker of Indigenous New Year celebrations, such as *Machaq Mara* or *Inti Raymi*.
9. "Ay, Mama Inés" and "Uno, dos, tres… que paso más chévere" are both Cuban compositions, and "Se va el caimán" is a Colombian composition.
10. Ironically, the cajón was originally used only to accompany the marinera. Cajón players only started accompanying the vals in the 1950s (see César Santa Cruz Gamarra 1977).
11. Puerto Rican sociologist Angel Quintero Rivera, however, has suggested subtler ways in which Black musical influence can be felt within the confines of more formal criollo culture. He argues that the use of baritone horn in the Puerto Rican danza acts as a "camouflaged drum." The musicians playing these instruments often were free people of color in the artisan class. See Quintero Rivera (1986).
12. Cumbia is a genre with roots in Colombia but has taken root throughout Latin America. It emphasizes a steady upbeat.
13. In an interview, I was told that a "cueca negra" had been danced at one of the early stage presentations (between 2003–06), but I never could locate a recording of it.

14. This parade is a local rendition of the nationally televised military parade in Santiago, which is held on September 19, a day officially commemorating the "Glories of the Armed Forces."

15. The cueca is an energetic but relatively short dance, typically lasting a minute and a half for each *pie* danced. *Pie*, literally "foot," refers to the standard poetic structure of the cueca from the Central region: a quatrain followed by a seguidilla and ending with a couplet. To compensate for the shortness of the dance, usually three *pies* are danced in succession. One can contrast this practice with the Cruz de Mayo in the previous section, in which two *pies* are danced, followed by a wayno.

16. Produced by the Culturas Originarias (Native Cultures) program of the Chilean National Council of Arts and Culture.

17. As described later, the term cachimbo refers to a music-dance genre representative of the Tarapacá region, but it also has other meanings. The Americanism "cachimbo," for example, refers to a crude pipe commonly smoked by elderly Black men and could be used to refer to arrogant Blacks. See Loyola 1994.

18. This session was recorded in 2004, and I thank Lumbanga for giving me a copy. I interviewed Guillermina Flores Corvacho in 2006.

19. As in the earlier case of the cueca I saw at the Cruz de Mayo, it was then followed by a wayno finale (or *remate*).

20. Del Canto stated that probably one member of the comparsa's Board of Directors had suggested performing it at the parade.

5

STYLING MORENO

Taking Pride in Decent Steps

THE PILGRIMAGE TO THE SANCTUARY OF THE VIRGEN del Rosario de las Peñas de Livilcar (or more commonly, La Virgen de las Peñas) takes place twice a year, on the first weekend in October and on December 8.¹ Several thousand pilgrims travel by car or bus to a dirt parking lot that has been coarsely flattened by bulldozer next to a wide, dry river bed. From there, depending on the pilgrim's state of health, time of day, and whether or not the pilgrim has hired a horse or mule, it is another two- to-six-hour trek by foot or animal to the sanctuary. Some choose the lower, cooler, and more tortuous path along the river, while others follow the smoother, more direct, but hotter and hillier path. It is work, but the pilgrims seem content. They are going to see an image of the Virgin Mary that emerged from a crag along the canyon wall. Some pilgrims come to ask a favor, others to repay or thank her for a request already granted. Some simply want to greet the Virgin on her special feast day. Many, no doubt, are there to visit with family and friends—for the camaraderie of the celebration itself. Most of the activities, however, involve those who, in addition to any of the reasons mentioned above, have come to *dance* for the Virgin. The dancers come as part of more than twenty different troupes, each with its own history and each dedicated to its own interpretation of a selected genre within the canon of religious dances, or *bailes religiosos*.²

Bailes religiosos refers to both the category of dances and the troupes who perform them. Over the course of my research, I learned that the dance forms could be grouped loosely into three sets of genres. One set, *folclórico*, consists of dances generally perceived to derive from Bolivian folklore: *diabladas, morenada, tinku, caporal, toba*, and so on. While versions of these dances have longer histories in Bolivia and have been present to some degree in Chile since

Figure 5.1. Sanctuary of *La Virgen de las Peñas*, Livilcar Canyon, Arica-Parinacota Region, Chile.

the War of the Pacific, they began to appear more robustly in Arica in the latter half of the twentieth century with the arrival of Bolivian migrants. A second set, *bailes de salto* (jumping dances), are dances often associated with the pampa of the Atacama Desert, just south of Arica. Many of these genres were initially performed for feast days in that area, particularly the Feast of the Virgen de la Tirana.[3] These include *chunchos* (Indigenous Amazonians), *gitanos* (Gypsies), *pieles rojas* (Redskins) and *morenos de salto* (jumping morenos).[4] In the pampa, the oldest of these dances dates to at least the late nineteenth century, but they began to appear in Arica with miners who migrated from the pampa's nitrate excavation camps as these closed in the early twentieth century.

In this chapter, I focus on the third set of dances under the category of bailes religiosos: those known as *morenos de paso*, that is, the stepping morenos, performed by the reportedly oldest troupes in Arica. The morenos de salto tend to wear turbans suggestive of the Moors who battled the Christians during the Iberian Reconquista, although, unlike other locations in

Latin America, no battle reenactments occur. By contrast, morenos de paso wear elegant suits and step in time to marches, features that are drawn from the dominant religious and military culture. The use of these features suggests that these troupes functioned as a way of earning respect and honor among local elites by emulating their culture. This strategy contrasts significantly with religious dances that seek recognition through the donning of elaborate costumes of an exotic Other to illustrate the world's submission to the faith. I have previously explained how the term "moreno" is often used socially as a euphemism for Blackness in places like Chile and Peru. Here I relate this orientation to a concept found in Andean scholarship: the idea of "decency." Given my interpretation of moreno as a local term that identifies a Black person as decent, I frame this type of performance as one that styles Blackness as moreno.

Here my interpretation of these dances in terms of Blackness does not simply emerge from the name of the expression. While the exact beginnings of the morenos de paso are unclear, what is certain is that families locally recognized as Black have played an important role in this type of performance. Several troupes were founded with Black families acting as their sponsors during the late nineteenth and early twentieth centuries, for example, the Hijos de Azapa with the Baluarte and Zegarra families. Other troupes are associated with neighborhoods in which the concentration of families of African descent was significant at one point, so that key members of these troupes were Black (e.g., the Morenos de Marconi). Participating in religious dancing as a child or young adult is still a common formative experience for many members of these families. Complicating the situation is the large number of participants in these troupes who might identify themselves as Indigenous. Indeed, religious dance in the region is commonly perceived as primarily an Indigenous or mestizo practice. Within the religious dance community, however, the presence of certain Black families and their role in the history of these troupes is well-known, and they are well-respected families, spoken of fondly.

Here I focus on the way cultural memory affirms the importance of these Black families in this expression. As I did with the tumbe in chapter 2 (and less overtly with criollo dances in chapter 4), I discuss visual, kinesthetic, and sonic facets of morenos de paso performance. I explore the ways that this performance resonates with the history of other genres as well as academic writings on aesthetics rooted in the greater African diaspora. Rather than make a direct connection between the morenos de paso with these events and ideas, I juxtapose them to open a space for conversation and future research about a fundamental question: how did the history and the aesthetic preferences of those with African heritage contribute to the morenos de paso expression?

What my observations and these comparisons suggest is that styling Blackness as moreno offers a sense of dignity and pride. This pride can result from earning the respect of others or from a job well done, but it also can manifest itself in terms of outdoing others—perhaps even a response to not having been treated respectfully in the past. Changes in ritual practice and religious perspectives, as well as the new recruits and access to more resources, however, have resulted in stylistic changes. Thus, observers unfamiliar with the history of the morenos de paso may not read contemporary performances in terms of Blackness, which can reinforce the idea that Afro-descendants have not contributed to Chilean culture. My underlying concern here is to argue that the presence of Africans and their descendants should not be overlooked when researching Chilean religious dance expressions; to do so would continue to minimize awareness of their participation in Chilean culture.

Religious Feasts in the Chilean North, La Virgen de las Peñas, and the Morenos de Paso

On the one hand, the celebration of La Virgen de las Peñas is like other patron saint feast day celebrations in the Chilean north. People begin to arrive several days ahead of the official feast day in anticipation of the festivities. They undertake various rituals—some formal (known as *llegadas*), others personal. The celebration begins in earnest on the eve of the feast, known as the *vispera*. Religious dance troupes begin to perform salutations to the saint on this day, one salutation for each time of day: *buenos días* (good morning), *buenas tardes* (good afternoon), and *buenas noches* (good evening). Individuals also visit the saint of their own accord and anxiously wait for the midnight hour, when the lighting of fireworks and the sounding of noisemakers announce the arrival of the saint's feast day. Additional revelry may ensue.[5] The principal mass is held on that day, and the dance troupes salute the saint throughout the day in their best uniforms. Pilgrims experience both melancholy and contentment as the festivities begin to wrap up in the afternoon. Tears are shed as the dancers say goodbye to the saint and prepare to leave. Each troupe's last salutation is known as the *despedida*, or farewell. Dancers who have fulfilled their promises and do not plan to dance again will symbolically turn in their uniforms.[6] Hopefully, the celebration has gone well, and dancers as well as other pilgrims begin to anticipate returning next year.

Yet certain circumstances distinguish La Virgen de las Peñas as unique, at least as far as celebrations in the Chilean north are concerned. First, this Virgin did not begin as the patroness of an individual town; rather, the current mix of church and private buildings sprang up around the Virgin's image.[7] The space is dormant most of the year, and the people who visit come from many surrounding towns. Dance troupes from as far north as the Peruvian town of Ilo arrive to worship at the foot of the Virgin's image. Second, the Virgin is celebrated twice: The Great Feast, related to Our Lady of the Rosary (the first weekend of October) and the Little Feast, associated with the Immaculate Conception (December 8). Presumably, the adjectives great and little here refer to the number of people who attend each feast, since three times as many people visit on the October date. The complete name by which the image is known references the rosary, and the October movable feast is the date that the Vatican recognizes as the feast of the Virgin of the Rosary.

The sanctuary appears to have been in place by 1840, because documents show the church in Arequipa asking for payment of thirty years of past collections in 1870 (Vial 1984, 34). The date is important because it proves the sanctuary was in place before the Chilean government controlled the area. In Juan Van Kessel's book *Aica y la peña sagrada*, Hilario Aica stated the sanctuary was closed for many years by Chilean authorities after they took control of the region. By 1928, however, photographs from *Sucesos* magazine show companies of religious dancers called *morenos*, as well as panpipe groups referred to as *sicuradas*, celebrating the October feast (XXVII, No.1363, November 8, 1928 under "El Santuario de la 'Virgen de las Peñas en Arica'"). In the early twentieth century, sponsors individually organized and paid for such dance troupes as a way of showing their devotion to the Virgin and thanking her for her protection. These sponsors would pay the dancers' expenses to participate in troupes called *compañías*, or companies. The standard length of time for such sponsorship was three years, but these companies could and sometimes did reconstitute themselves with roughly similar membership and even the same sponsor. This revolving system makes it difficult to trace the exact history of the troupes. For example, members of the troupe Los Hijos de Azapa told me their predecessor was the Compañia de Andrés Baluarte, named after the troupe's principal sponsor, a member of a prominent Black family in Azapa.

Despite this heritage, Los Hijos de Azapa do not include the existence of this previous company when officially calculating how long they have existed. Over time, this system of sponsorship changed, such that formal organizations were created to sustain the religious dance troupes and support their members. Instead of sponsorship depending on one individual, the religious dance troupes began to reorganize as *sociedades*, or societies. This change included the creation of governing boards for each society, and dance troupe members now had to pay dues and contribute to the organization. The different societies eventually grouped themselves into associations, according to feast day, and the names of the troupes were inscribed in an association ledger. The founding date listed in the ledger is the official anniversary of the troupe's founding. This date is important because the troupes enter the sanctuary in order of seniority. The Hijos de Azapa celebrated its sixtieth anniversary in 2008, and it holds the first position in the association for the Little Feast.[8] The troupe Morenos de Marconi celebrated its seventieth anniversary in 2006, and it holds the third position in the association of the Great Feast.

My description of morenos de paso performance in this chapter relies primarily on the participation of the Hijos de Azapa at the 2008 Little Feast and the Morenos de Marconi at the 2008 Great Feast. In addition to documenting this participation through recordings, I interviewed several dancers, associates, and musicians who participated in the feasts.[9]

In both the great and little versions of the celebration, the first several troupes are morenos de paso, pointing to the importance of this specific genre in the Chilean Arica-Parinacota and the neighboring Peruvian Tacna-Moquegua regions. I do not know of troupes of morenos de paso south of the region; those that participate in the Virgen de La Tirana hail from Arica. Participants in Las Peñas tell me that the group that travels from Ilo is the northernmost morenos de paso troupe. The participation of Hilario Aica and Bolivian brass bands early on also suggest a familiarity with the celebration in the neighboring regions in Bolivia, at least as far as the areas of Caranagas and its environs. These ideas imply that the morenos de paso troupes have a special connection to this tripartite border region.

Decency and Pride in Styling Moreno

Anthropologist Zoila Mendoza has observed that almost all studies of Andean towns use the concept of "decency" in defining local elites (2000,

115–16), and signs of decency are interpreted through judgments of morality and proper behavior. In discussing ritual dances in Peru, Mendoza describes how, in San Jerónimo, troupes need to adopt costumes and perform music and choreography that style to a high-status group in order to have their dance considered "decent." While I never heard the phrase *gente decente* in Arica, I did notice some tension among troupes of religious dancers and among individual dancers as to what was appropriate behavior in front of the Virgin, paralleling Mendoza's ideas of decency.

In part, this sense of propriety came from formal rules for such celebrations that the troupes enacted when they officially organized into an association in the mid-twentieth century. At first, these rules made explicit the basic concepts for running the festival in a smooth fashion. For example, one rule stated the order in which troupes appeared in front of the Virgin, as having an earlier position in the order was a marker of a longer history and devotion to the Virgin and came with a greater sense of prestige. Beginning in the 1980s, Jesuit priests in Arica took a renewed interest in the religious dance troupes. Older dancers recalled how Fr. José Vial would revise lyrics to be sure that they were consistent with church teachings. New rules requiring mass attendance and increased year-round involvement in church activities followed. These rules governed how much time a troupe could spend in front of the Virgin and stated that an official association committee had to approve any new costumes that troupes wanted to adopt. While one might interpret such actions as the church attempting to impose its authority, the regulations also offered a way to measure piety and modesty, characteristics associated with proper behavior. Some individuals I spoke with noted that the changes in the 1980s were meant to protect the troupes from the Pinochet dictatorship, which frowned on people holding meetings in private homes. Under church guidance and protection, troupe members were less susceptible to accusations of religious nonconformity (i.e., a lack of decency) that could indicate ulterior political motives.

As these rules suggest, a key factor in most value judgments about proper behavior is whether dancers' actions reflected their faith and personal devotion to the Virgin. As Orlando "Nano" Castillo put it: "A good dancer is characterized by that intimate prayer that, at the moment he dances, he has with God and the Virgin. In that moment, you are dancing, and there are many people watching you, because they like to watch the dances, because they are watching the troupes and all that, but in that moment when you are dancing, it is only God, the Virgin, and you. There is no one else" (interview with author, March 17, 2009). By this argument, any aesthetic decision, such as the choice of a specific choreography or a focus on neatness in dress, is therefore an offering to the Virgin herself. Castillo later added, "I dance prettily for her, not because people are watching, but for the Virgin, and because it springs from my heart to dance for her" (ibid.).

While this focus on the Virgin might be the ideal, the dancers are human. Tensions arise between troupes based on whether a costume or choreography calls too much attention to itself—suggesting that a troupe might be more interested in appearances than worship. One leader from a folclórico religious dance troupe explained to me the dilemma he faced. On the one hand, he needed to keep his dancers interested, in particular, the younger generation of dancers who wanted new steps or rhythms. Appealing to young people would attract more dancers to the troupe, and this increased troupe size helps to insure the troupe's longevity and prestige. Novelty also attracts a larger audience in the plaza, a space where the troupes dance once again after their presentation in the sanctuary. Unfortunately, he told me, too large of an audience meant the older generation of religious dancers would complain, saying, "Are we talking about religion or getting attention?" He believed, however, that the real reason they were upset was that fewer people went to see the presumably more spartan troupes, like the morenos de paso, dance in the plaza.

This observation highlights a central tension in religious dance expression. Decency is measured by the sincerity of one's devotion to the Virgin, illustrated by a performance in front of her that is simultaneously aesthetically beautiful without calling too much attention to itself. What is challenging here is that, for many, part of the aesthetic requires having a significant number of dancers in the troupe. A troupe also requires enough dancers to ensure its continuation year after year. Because many of the troupes are associated with certain families, dancers may feel particularly obligated or attached to their troupes, and they want to make sure these troupes are successful. This outwardly focused need to attract potential members to one's own troupe arguably detracts from the internally oriented devotion to the Virgin.

In my fieldwork, I discovered that most of these criticisms were leveled at the folclórico religious dance troupes, due to their colorful costumes and active choreography. Critics may sometimes consider these troupes indecent due to their flamboyance, although certainly the associations with Indigeneity that I discuss in chapter six may come into play. When I consider the facets of morenos de paso performance, however, they too are anything but plain. Rather than pride in dress and steps being a new aesthetic that arrived with the folclórico troupes, I argue that morenos de paso performance demonstrates the longtime presence of a similar aesthetic, built on a strong relationship with decency together with ties to the dancers' own heritages and preferences. These preferences may have addressed the troupes' need to attract new dancers, even as they instilled pride among existing performers. I now describe how the tensions between devotion and pride appear in morenos de paso performance.

Visually Moreno: Impeccable Dress

Morenos de paso performers have historically worn immaculately clean, well-pressed shirts and slacks with matching ties and polished dress shoes. Since all-women troupes were formed, their attire has consisted of knee-length skirts, vests, and sturdy high-heeled shoes. More recently, females participating in previously all-male troupes wear the same traditional uniform as the males. Dancers in all troupes wear a sash with a phrase praising the Virgin (e.g., Viva María) over the shoulder and pinned at the hip to complete the ensemble. On the principal day of the celebration, a troupe's best dress may include matching V-neck sweaters, blazers, and even plumed hats. The attention to the neatness of their dress has earned morenos de paso troupes the nickname of *morenos pitucos*, or the "snobbish morenos." While this term may appear derogatory, most people seemed to think of it merely as a reference to the troupe's dress and not necessarily their social attitude; the term is quite common, perhaps more frequently used than morenos de paso. Oscar Henríquez Apón, a longtime dancer and an associate of both the Morenos de Marconi and Hijos de Azapa, told me that the term was initially used by dancers from the Atacaman pampa (who were more familiar with morenos de salto) to describe the morenos de paso they encountered.

All religious dancers are required to respect their dance attire and keep it clean, in part because a priest blesses these uniforms. However, the morenos de paso, perhaps because their dress resembles professional attire, gave me the impression that they paid special attention to neatness. An early experience that contributed to this opinion was when, during my first trip to Las Peñas, I was awakened before five o'clock in the morning to see the "buenos días" salute of the Morenos de Marconi. It was still pitch-dark, yet my host, dancer Marcos Butrón, was shining his black shoes by candlelight. I was confused: Butrón was running a little late for the time agreed on for the troupe to gather, and he was about to march up a dirt road from the crucifix to the sanctuary. Surely, his shoes would get dusty again by the time he arrived there, and few people would be there to see the troupe at this hour. Nevertheless, Butrón felt it was important to shine his shoes, as well as comb his hair and wear a clean, pressed white shirt. He once told me that, while he was not the most religious man, when it came to the *Virgencita* ("Little Virgin"), he gives it his all. I heard this sentiment repeated many times by different religious dancers as an expression of their devotion.

Bailes de salto and folclórico troupes mostly wear colorful costumes stereotypical of the ethnic groups that they represent; other troupes represent allegories or myths, as in the case of the diablada, in which the costumes are of devils and angels. In contrast, the morenos de paso wear what many might consider urban business attire. However, a comment by Miguel Zegarra Baluarte, longtime associate and former Hijos de Azapa dancer, suggested a different interpretation: "They say that, in the old days, the Spanish performed their ceremonies in uniform, in a blue or black outfit, white shirt, tie—impeccable. From the time of our grandfathers, they keep that tradition" (interview with author, July 25, 2006). Zegarra's comment implies that while the other groups interpreted Indigenous or minority groups, the morenos de paso emulated the group in power, the Spaniards (or perhaps more likely, their descendants). In doing so, the performers aimed at gaining the acceptance and respect of this dominant group on this group's terms. By paying extreme attention to cleanliness in dress—showing that they could keep their dress whites whiter, despite the dust of the interior valleys—the performers could even demonstrate that they were as good as or better than the elite.

Related practices were present in Spain as far back as the fifteenth century. Religious brotherhoods could earn respect through the pomp and lavishness with which they celebrated feasts days, and records indicate Black religious brotherhoods in Andalusia began to be established circa 1401 (Moreno Navarro 1999, 4). One legend recounts that a Black religious brotherhood in Seville put on such a particularly opulent display for the Immaculate Conception in 1653 that two members sold themselves back into slavery to pay for it.[10] In other places in the world, Black freedmen adopted acts of public performance familiar to the dominant group, although they were often criticized for doing so. In Philadelphia in the 1840s, for example, John Fanning Watson complained that Blacks showed "an overweening fondness for display and vainglory—fondly imitating the white in processions and banners, and in the pomp and pageantry of Masonic and Washingtonian societies" (White and White 1998, 87). In the northern US, Whites criticized Blacks for "putting on airs," a phrase that is strikingly close in meaning to the term pituco and suggests that Whites saw Blacks as aspiring beyond their station. Chilean author René Peri Fagerstrom believed that Black people in Chile had a similar aesthetic when he stated, "Where there is Black blood, there is a fondness for titles, for eye-catching uniforms, and for plumes" (1984, 36).

I also discovered that such behavior was not limited to morenos de paso performance but also appeared in other forms of Black religious participation. For example, the people of the Azapa Valley donned their best attire to attend celebrations for the Feast of San Miguel, the patron saint of the valley. Men in the community wore navy-blue suits and felt hats to attend the mass and the procession of the saint that followed. Wearing this attire was so important that individuals wore it even if doing so opened them up to ridicule. Segundo Jorge ("Chilo") Llerena told me the story of one Claudio Lucero, whose feet were so large that he had difficulty finding any shoes that fit him. Nevertheless, on the Feast of San Miguel, he would dress in a white shirt, navy-blue jacket with red carnation in the lapel, tie, and felt hat—and walk barefoot. Lucero's behavior demonstrated the effort that individuals went through to make good impressions, but, despite his effort, he was potentially vulnerable to the same kind of systemic criticism Whites in the US often used to ridicule Blacks as poor imitators of White fashion. After all, Chilo told me the story humorously.

Kinesthetically Moreno: With Swagger in the Step

As I argued in the previous section, pride in being a morenos de paso performer includes more than dressing "decently"—it is dressing especially well, to the extent that some feel threatened and/or criticize the moreno as pituco. Similarly, the dance itself relies on a form of "decent" movement, to which an aesthetic can be applied that is graceful to some, exaggerated to others.

In keeping with the phrase "de paso," the morenos de paso dance utilize a simple pacing step in performance, appearing less like a dance troupe than perhaps a drill team. Each of the salutations they perform follows the same basic formula, although every troupe has its slight variations. After a troupe with its hired band marches up the street that leads to a church, the musicians arrange themselves along the sides of the main floor of the church to make room for the dancers. The troupe then performs an *entrada*, asking the Virgin's permission to enter the church in song. Once the entrada is completed, the band launches into a march, a genre with a straight, steady beat. The dancers sound their *matracas*, or ratchets, succinctly in time with the rhythm. The morenos form two neat columns. The caporal, or captain, stands forward in the space between them, staff in hand. The guía, or guide, on the right side uses his matraca to announce the transitions between the different sections of the salutation. After the troupe genuflects, the guía sounds the matraca to stop the march and begin the actual sung salutation, or *saludo*, which includes the phrases "buenos días," "buenas tardes," or "buenas noches," depending on the time of day. The dancers do not pace during the salutation but stand at attention, although they may use arm motions, such as touching their hand to their heart and then offering it, palm up, to the Virgin. As the morenos sing the two verses, the caporal slowly works his way to the back of the formation. With the salutation complete, the right guía spins the matraca three times as a "ready, set, go" for the march to begin. The caporal, who has worked his way back to the rear of the church, now weaves his way forward in a zigzag pattern toward the Virgin. One could interpret this sequence as a captain inspecting his troops. On reaching the front of the sanctuary, he twirls around twice before genuflecting and making the sign of the cross in front of the Virgin. Seeing this, the right guía spins his matraca to alert the others, and together with the left guía, he marches forward, spins, genuflects, and crosses himself. Like the caporal, each of the guías moves off to their respective sides to let the next pair come forward and do the same. The forward step that the dancers take is not straight ahead but with one foot crossing the other in alternate fashion, so that the columns move toward one another in one step and apart on the next. Throughout the whole process, those dancers who have already reverenced the Virgin work their way to the back of the church, so that by the time those last in the column (often children) finish, the caporal is ready to lead both columns forward again.

If time permits, a troupe may perform additional choreographies.[11] Eventually, however, it must perform the *retirada*, or retreat, from the church. Before doing this, the troupe forms the shape of a cross. Two or more

Figure 5.2. Combined Hijos de Azapa troupe rehearsing in anticipation of its sixtieth anniversary celebration. The veteran caporal kneels at the center with veteran dancers in the inner two columns. The currently active dancers flank them in the outside rows. December 2, 2008. Arica, Chile.

dancers branch off from the two columns to form the cross's arms. Once in formation, the march stops, and the troupe begins to sing its retreat. During the song, the dancers begin to slowly sidestep toward the back of the church. When they finish singing, a march begins, and after another genuflection, the troupe marches backward out the church entrance. The form of entrada-saludo-retirada is repeated in each of the three standard daily salutations.

During my fieldwork in December 2008 at the Little Feast, the Hijos de Azapa was celebrating its sixtieth official anniversary. For the occasion, the troupe invited those dancers who had retired to rejoin them for the last major salutation of the feast and the subsequent dance in the plaza. During that salutation, the younger, currently active dancers marched in, and then stepped aside to let the older dancers through. What surprised me was the way in which the older caporal danced through the troupe. He marched down the gap with crispness, snapping in his turns, leaning back as he moved forward in each of his steps. His long, loosely outstretched arms in line with his baton only added to the effect. Several other of the retired dancers rocked side to side, their shoulder movements exaggerated by the overstated motion of their arms bouncing as a unit with their matracas. In comparison to the younger caporal, the older caporal strutted rather than marched down the aisle. A quick glance at the other retired dancers confirmed that several were doing something similar.

When I asked other dancers about this, they smiled and commented, "That's the old way of dancing." Oscar Henríquez Apón, a retired dancer from another troupe, agreed and made a further observation:

> Each society has its own form of dancing. For example, the Peruvian troupe, the Number One, dance with a movement that is very exaggerated. That's the way they are. So one says that's the way the Peruvians dance. From the way in which they move their body . . . . They drive the rhythm of the body from the beat of the matraca . . . . The Peruvian dances differently than the Chilean. They have the same step, the same rhythm, but they are looser in the body . . . . In the old days, you danced like that. Now the young men are tightening up a bit . . . . Plus, in the old days, the moreno dances were made up of gente morena. And now, it's like the color of skin is changing among the dancers. That's probably because White people have less flexibility in movement than the moreno; that's my opinion. (Interview with author, June 16, 2009)

Henríquez makes two connections with this swaggering, strutting motion: one with Peruvianness, the other with skin color—not Blackness outright, but moreno. Other people made similar statements supporting these connections. For example, Orlando "Nano" Castillo, a lifetime member of the Marconi, believes that the Peruvian moreno de paso troupe dances "closer to the floor," practically dragging their feet (interview with author, March 17, 2009). He describes the Chilean morenos as lifting their feet, as in marching.

As this performative difference seemed to resonate with local cultural memory, I did a closer analysis of the younger and older caporales during sections in the choreography in which they were featured. In these sections, they danced a zigzag path between two rows of troupe members. The younger caporal and guías tended to perform with their shoulders level and square and their centers of gravity directly below them, so that their torsos were almost vertical. Their feet therefore served to transport them while supporting an erect posture. While the feet of the older caporal also transported him from one side to another, he would also push off from his outer foot as he reached the end of his lateral motion. This action left him leaning toward the center of the aisle, giving the impression that his center of gravity was out over his feet. The tilt in his shoulders was much more pronounced, but I would argue that his body attitude derived from his footwork rather than an attempt to exaggerate the motion. The older caporal also did not raise his knees as much as the younger one, which may have contributed to the younger caporal's higher center of gravity and, thus, more erect posture. While both caporales kept time to the straight, steady beat of the matracas during the basic step, the younger caporal would occasionally rush and be momentarily out of sync during his turn. Meanwhile, the way in which the older caporal smartly tapped his inside foot to the ground at the end of a rotation during a turn emphasized how synchronized his movement was with the matraca's beat. These observations help one understand what the descriptions of dance as "looser" and "closer to the floor" mean (compare videos 5.1 and 5.2).

While the specific admiration that many had for the caporal's dancing can be tied to his experience, the shared nature of these movement traits among many of the older generation aligned with Henríquez's ideas about phenotype, which he expressed largely in terms of skin color. The older caporal's skin was darker and more umber-toned than the younger caporal's lighter, tawny-brown undertones. While not necessarily in Henríquez's descriptions, the older caporal's other features, like tightly curled hair, are often associated with Blackness more than the younger caporal's straight, almost spiky hair. Since the social construction of race relies on local interpretation, however, combinations of traits like lanky frames and rounded foreheads with angular jaws that tended to cluster in historically Black families play a role in influencing how a person is read racially. The retired dancers from the older generation tended to share these features like darker skin tone and tighter curled hair more than the current ones. Thus, the comparison between the retired and current Hijos de Azapa at the 2008 Little Feast would seem to resonate with local associations of movement with phenotypical Blackness.

This connection between the older moreno dance style and Blackness again illustrates how aspects of local music-dance expressions might momentarily be in synchronization with Afro-diasporic resources, as Brown (2005) has theorized. These resources can include various aspects of movement, including the type of beat used when dancing and the posture assumed in the dance. For example, one finds similarities in African American stepping traditions. Dance historian Jacqui Malone asserts that, for these expressions, "black Americans demand a steady beat in their dance music" (1996, 33), and, drawing on the work of African American artists as well as art historian Robert Farris Thompson (1974), she argues that the key characteristics of dance in African American vernacular culture are rhythm, control, angularity, and asymmetry (1996, 32–35). The idea of a steady beat becomes particularly powerful when coupled with the idea of control. Rather than being driven by or rushed by the steady pulse, the older caporal appeared at ease, executing his steps in time in apparent effortlessness, or what Thompson refers to as the West African aesthetic of being *cool*. His tilted body attitude created a noticeable angle with the floor, and his tendency to hold his arms and legs to remain straighter than the younger caporal created a greater sense of sharper angles between his limbs and torso as well. The sense that the older caporal's center of gravity was not directly above his feet but rather halfway between the leaning shoulder and his feet created an asymmetry that fits Malone's characterization of African American dance traditions.

Several older scholars have also associated similar movements with common nonverbal behaviors among African Americans. B. Cooke (1972) proposed thinking about the "lowered shoulder" as a *kineme*, Birdwhistell's term for a class of similar movements that tend to preserve their social meaning in different situations within the same culture.[12] Cooke interpreted the lowered-shoulder kineme as part of a series of African American male stances and walks designed to draw attention and admiration, particularly from women. One might therefore interpret the lowered shoulder of the caporal's pacing movement as attention seeking. While religious dancers emphasize the devotional nature of the practice, a standard criticism that dance troupes occasionally level at one another is the desire for attention. One individual who is a carnival dancer told me that young men often participate in dance troupes, religious or otherwise, to meet women. Another troupe leader took a more pragmatic view, saying that the desire to meet a partner might initially draw individuals into participating, but that, through training and fellowship, these individuals learn the true meaning of the dance. The principal argument here is that the caporal's gait is consistent with those aesthetic principles that several scholars have argued reflect diasporic resources, thus offering a moment of possible diasporic synchronicity—in this case, in the service of styling moreno. The marching nature of the dance expression is meant as decent, while the aesthetic of the older generation, whether it is understood as "coolness" or "swagger," suggests a pride in the dance interpretation.

Unfortunately, the scholarly support for these movement characteristics as diasporic can be problematic when it becomes essentialist. Critics of Thompson's work point out that he often is selective with the historical data that he uses to support his claims, that he fails to complicate how these aesthetics may vary over time and space, and that he occasionally errs in interpretation due to a lack of deep ethnographic knowledge of the multiple cultures he works with.[13] As Frank Willet noted about one of Thompson's catalogs, "Thompson does frequently indicate that he is interpreting without supporting fieldwork evidence, but one fears that such interpretations may get to be quoted as documented observations" (1978, 13). Here I offer a set of fieldwork observations whose details seem consistent with Malone's and Thompson's observations, viewing these elements as a palette of oral-kinesthetic resources that can be employed as aesthetic choices within specific contexts. As the younger caporal's and guías' performances suggest (and as I will show later), the appeal of these choices can change. Indeed, one of the key features of the concept of styling is its recognition that individuals can opt to participate in music-dance in multiple ways based on context, including different moments in time.

Motivations for these aesthetic choices are equally complex. The principal orientation in this chapter argues that certain choices emulating religiously devoted, organized marching behavior served to earn respect or decency, based on my ethnographic observation of the way that some dancers comment on other behavior. Another, compatible interpretation with less ethnographic support is also possible: that such movement is a legacy of a satirical take on military-like marching. Again, parallels are found in the broader experience of peoples of African descent. William Piersen has described how US Black militias in the early nineteenth century included performances parodying the officials of White militias (1999, 424). After the US Civil War, such activities continued: "Groups of smartly uniformed blacks, their bodies upright and moving in close formation, marched proudly through formerly white-controlled public space, celebrating their newly gained freedom, marking important symbolic events in the black calendar, and calling for political empowerment. Through parody and ironic reversal they signified against whites, unmasking the masking practices that erased blacks' humanity" (White and White 1998, 149). About these antebellum parades, Piersen remarks, "So many features of the African-American [sic] parades are paralleled elsewhere throughout the Americas that their commonness suggests an African essence to the form" (1999, 418). Again, one needs to avoid Piersen's essentializing move and instead recognize that such similarities in aesthetic choices reveal common, temporally grounded responses to similar forms of treatment within replicated structures of power throughout the Americas.

Sonically Moreno: Of Brass, Marches, and Song

As mentioned in chapter 2, historian Alfredo Wormald Cruz (1963) wrote that bands consisting of only bass drums and matracas (made of donkey jawbones) were present in early twentieth-century Arica, and he associated these bands with carnivals in neighborhoods with a significant Black population. In an interesting parallel, dancers in the moreno troupes with origins in these neighborhoods told me that early on, the only instrumentation the troupes needed to dance was a bass drum and matracas. Few brass players were available in Arica at the time, so such sparse instrumentation probably would have been common in the early part of the twentieth century.

Oral histories suggest that the Morenos de Marconi troupe emerged from such a neighborhood. Many of the long-standing families with members in the Marconi originally came from the district known as La Chimba, a low-lying area along the coast. When city planners decided to build a new casino on the spot, many of the families, as well as the troupe, relocated to the neighborhood of Cienfuegos. Henríquez was born into one of these families and began dancing at the age of seven. Still an associate member of the Morenos de Marconi, he told me that, since 1956, when he entered the troupe, the Marconi has always danced to a brass band (interview with author, June 16, 2009). He had heard that around 1936, when the troupe first formed, the Marconi danced to panpipes. This was primarily due to a shortage of brass players in the area, most of whom were in the military and not always available. Indeed, several interviews revealed that Black individuals with mixed Indigenous ancestry from earlier generations played panpipes for certain morenos de paso troupes. By 1948, however, when Carlos Lavín presented the first musicological study on the Feast of the Virgen de las Peñas, he described at least three morenos de paso troupes, including the Morenos de Marconi, dancing to the sounds of small, makeshift brass bands at the feast in October.[14]

Zegarra Baluarte, former dancer and current associate of the Hijos de Azapa for the December feast, stated that his father told him that they began dancing to pure bombos and matracas (interview with author, July 25, 2006). Later, fifes were included, and finally, brass bands were hired from Bolivia. This point is confirmed in Juan Van Kessel's book by an interviewee referencing the predecessor of the Hijos de Azapa, the Company of Andres Baluarte: "The Company of Baluarte has never had reeds. They only had matracas, and they had something like a fife and drum corps with a cornet, very pretty" (1992, 46). Even with this preference for military band instrumentation, however, the morenos from Azapa still appreciated the panpipe-oriented troupes. According to the same book, the Baluartes often invited the panpipe-oriented Morenos de Ayca, a morenos de paso troupe associated with Bolivian migrant Hilario Aica, to participate in their family May Cross celebrations.

These circumstances might lead one to question whether the use of panpipes in the morenos de paso was an older tradition or perhaps more of a convenient substitution to produce a livelier feast, given the resources and context of a specific troupe. A 1928 issue of *Sucesos* features a photo essay about that year's feast of the Virgen de las Peñas. One photo has a caption explaining that the Morenos de Tacna troupe arrived that year with bass drums (bombos), matracas, and panpipes, but another photo depicts a brass band that had walked for fourteen days from Huachacalle, Bolivia, to participate in the feast. Certainly, at that time, distances and ways of communicating would have made coordinating joint participation of a Bolivian brass band with a morenos troupe in Arica difficult, although at the Virgen de la Tirana, it used to be common practice for musicians to form makeshift bands on site and offer to play for the dance troupes. Later, this would change. Henríquez recalled one year when the Marconi brought a brass band from the interior town of Esquiña, and currently Peruvian bands are commonly employed at the Peñas. It is difficult to tell whether the presence of panpipes within the morenos de paso tradition was something aesthetically inherent to its beginnings or whether it arose from an adaptation to the circumstances. Today, all but one of the morenos de paso dance to brass bands whose standard instrumentation includes an equal number of trumpets and baritone horns (anywhere between three to six of each), one or two sousaphones, cymbals, snare drum, and bass drum. This instrumentation points us to a preference for brass on the part of morenos de paso from Black neighborhoods and areas, but this preference tells us little since it mimics the contemporary dominant preference for most festive performance throughout the Andes.

Interestingly, the expansion of military brass bands in Chile proper hit its stride with the War of the Pacific (1879–83), around the same time as the founding of the Compañia de Morenos No. 1 de la Santísima Virgen de las Peñas in Tacna. The boom was a result of several influences, including the founding of a conservatory in Chile, the arrival of modern wind instruments, and the need to instill wartime patriotism through military music (Gonzalez and Rolle 2005, 273–75). It resulted in the practice of brass bands playing in city plazas for the public's enjoyment. Perhaps the popularity of this emerging pastime contributed to the desire of the morenos de paso to be accompanied by brass bands, although finding a suitable number of musicians in Arica would be a problem for some time.[15]

The music that the morenos de paso use has also undergone variation, but continuity of practice among some of the older troupes does suggest other aesthetic points to consider beyond instrumentation. Historically, their dance music has been marches, which provide the strong binary beat needed for their step. The Morenos de Marconi, one of the oldest troupes, prefers older marches. Not all of these marches have been in use continuously—some have been revived. In 2008, for example, a member of the band Santa Cecilia told me that the Marconi asked the band to transcribe and arrange three marches performed by older musicians that they had recorded on cassettes. This similarity in taste for older marches appears to be shared by the Hijos de Azapa, as well as some of the other troupes with a longer history. For example, I heard one of the moreno de paso troupes from Tacna dancing to "Colonel Bogey's March," more commonly recognized for its affiliation with the 1957 film *The Bridge on the River Kwai*.

The preference for older marches points to the popularity of marches during the nineteenth and early twentieth centuries. At this time, marches were played alongside polkas and waltzes as part of the repertoire of cosmopolitan popular music and were available on commercial recordings. Furthermore, Gonzalez and Rolle state that, together with hymns, marches were important vehicles for "instilling ideas of progress and patriotism in the public" (2005, 278). In this vein, marches would have been of special interest in the Tacna-Arica region during the fifty-year span after the end of the War of the Pacific, as Chile tried to drum up support for its sovereignty of the territory in the presumably imminent plebiscite on the matter. While it is not clear how political the use of marches in the morenos de paso could have been, the association of marches with the military (a respected profession) as well as their popularity within cosmopolitan circles would make marches respectable, decent music for morenos to dance to.

Just as instrumentation and the dance music genres point to respectability, the way the morenos de paso sing to the Virgin also is associated with devotion and decency. Dancers that I spoke with referred to the Marconi's songs as an example of the older way of singing. The troupe does not sing and dance at the same time, so references to songs are focused on the salutations used by the morenos de paso. In the case of the Marconi, these songs are slow, making full use of rubato, or an elastic tempo suited to the musical expression. I would describe them as heterophonic chants that use dramatic, swooping melodic leaps (see ex. 5.1).

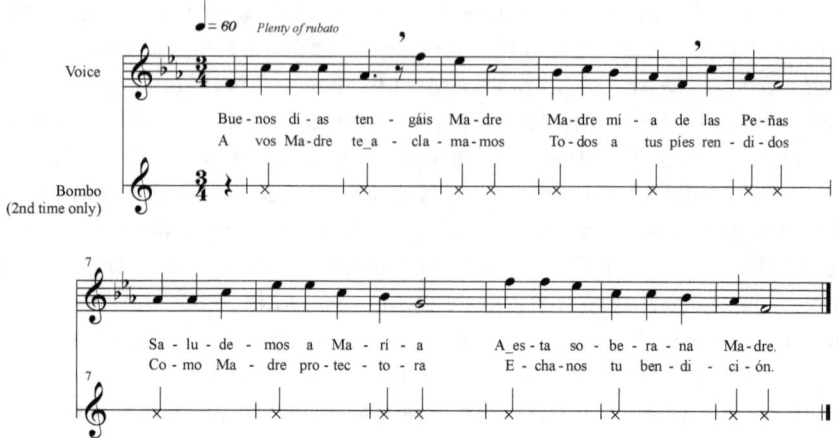

Example 5.1. Saludo of the Morenos de Marconi. Author unknown.
Translation: 1: Good day Mother, my Mother of the Crags. We salute Mary, this sovereign mother. 2: We hail you, Mother, all submissive at your feet. As our mother protector, give us your blessing.

As they sing, the morenos stand still, motioning with their hands and arms as if they are offering their hearts to the Virgin, although on the very last measure they reverse the gesture, indicating the blessing coming from the Virgin to them. The lyrics are similar in theme but not identical to those Carlos Lavín documented from the Marconi in the 1940s.

The aesthetic in this slow, drawn-out singing is consistent with older ideas of penitence and sacrifice associated with the pilgrimage to the Virgin. These slow songs sung at full volume require a lot of air and effort, so that they are not necessarily a respite from the dancing. Previously, individual performers might swoon and require attention, particularly during the last farewell on the final day of the celebration. This aesthetic would have been consistent with demonstrating devotion to the Virgin. Today the church officially frowns on such physical displays of suffering, so they are less common. The volume with which a troupe sings, however, is still valued. The members of the Marconi pride themselves on having maintained some of their salutations for a long time and for being one of the troupes that sings the loudest.[16]

The aesthetic preferences of brass band accompaniment playing older marches complemented by slow, dramatic, and dedicated singing all seems to act as indexes for formality, prestige, and devotion. These feelings are associated with decency, consistent with styling moreno. As has already been suggested, however, these preferences began to subtly change with the arrival and growing presence of the folclórico troupes.

Changes in Appearance, Sound, and Movement

> The moreno dance troupes, the majority of them, arrived from Peru. Many Peruvian troupes come here to the Peñas. And they all have a similar kind of movement. Those troupes from around here don't have it—well, some do. The difference is in the movement of the matraca, in the movement of the body. It is more graceful; they have more grace. From that format, the youth began to move the matraca differently, in a suffering way now, so that the children would see . . . I don't know if they want to dance that way or not, but in a bad way, things change. (Giovanni Gutiérrez, interview with author, December 12, 2008)

The folclórico troupes began to arrive in Arica and at the Peñas in the early 1980s. Many dancers I spoke with pointed to the emergence of the Diablada de Arica as the reason. Although this troupe belongs to the Feast of the Virgin of La Tirana and was inspired by the Diablada de Iquique, people saw members of the group practicing in Arica. The colorful costumes, the novel steps, and the need for a large brass band inspired the formation of similar troupes for Las Peñas. Their appearance coincided with increased visibility and acceptance of carnival dance troupes performing versions of these genres in Arica's carnival, known as La Ginga. Attitudes toward these changes varied. The folclórico troupes created a need for more musicians, leading to the formation of more and larger commercial brass bands. Thus, the morenos de paso now have a fuller sound. This sound came at a greater expense, however, because the larger bands cost more. Somewhat more controversial was the perceived loss of possible future dancers to these newer troupes. For example, when one of the matriarchs of the Afro-descendant families in Arica, Rosa Corvacho, formed a new religious dance troupe, San Geronimo de Lluta, it was not a moreno de paso troupe. Instead, she sponsored a baile folclórico that currently performs three different types of dances during the Little Feast. I was told she did this at the request of a granddaughter, who wanted to dance these types of genres. Many of the group's members have family members who dance in the morenos de paso, and, given that family connections are the most common incentive to join a specific dance troupe, some perceive family members' joining a different troupe from the one their family been a part of for decades as a loss of potential members to their traditional troupe. I also heard older troupe members complaining that young people are joining the folclórico troupes for the wrong reasons—for fun and attention rather than sacrifice and devotion. These complaints do not consider that young people might not otherwise decide to dance or that they perceive the folclórico expressions as those most attractive to the Virgin. Despite these complaints, religious dancers are pleased to have young people joining their ranks.

Nevertheless, to combat this possible loss of dancers to folclórico troupes, some of the younger morenos de paso troupes' choices appear to be an attempt to attract younger dancers. They dance not to marches, but to morenadas, whose strong four-beat pulse easily marks similar time to that of a march.[17] The fact that certain morenos de paso troupes are assuming a rhythm from folclórico troupes shows the strong influence of these rhythms, although the fact that both types of dance share the name moreno might lead some to defend their choice. Similar issues may be at play with the songs these troupes perform. An interesting example is the case of the Marconi. During the 2008–09 religious cycle, the Marconi replaced their traditional entrance song into the church with a popular pan-Andean tune, Ana Cristina Céspedes's "Paloma del Alma Mía" (Dove of My Soul). Since the Virgin is often spoken of metaphorically as a dove, the first verse and chorus of this popular song were appropriate. Members of dance troupes who appreciate pan-Andean groups like the Grupo Proyección, however, would recognize and appreciate the song outside the context of religious dancing.

In addition to incorporating popular tunes, new songs were introduced. Patricio Cortéz told me that the Hijos de Azapa used to sing in the same older style that the Marconi uses for their salutations, but that later they had Hugo Guerrero Honores compose songs for them (interview with author, August 27, 2009). A strong devotee of the Feast of La Tirana and dancer in his own right, Guerrero composed several hymns that are sung by religious dancers throughout the Chilean North. The new entrance song that Guerrero wrote for the Hijos de Azapa incorporated his knowledge of the troupe's history as well as forms common in popular music, such as the verse-chorus format (see example 5.2). The rhythm of the Azapeños's saludo is more regular and faster than that of the Marconi. When singing it, the dancers do not make any of the hand gestures mentioned earlier, although they do keep their eyes fixed on the Virgin's image the entire time. The lyrics of the Marconi salutation focus primarily on greeting the Virgin and asking for her blessing. While the verses of the Hijos de Azapa speak of seeking the Virgin's love, they also remind those present of the history of

Example 5.2. Saludo for the Hijos de Azapa, composed by Hugo Guerrero. Used with permission of his son, Francisco Hugo Guerrero Espinoza.
Translation: Verse One: Temple that still maintains the warmth on your walls that the Baluarte and Zegarra families recorded with love. The songs and dance were the oblation they offered, and, like them, I would say looking for the sign:
Chorus: Good afternoon, little Virgin, Good afternoon, my Lord, I bring you my greetings, together with this song.
Verse Two: Again, among the Crags, in the house of the Lord, the Sons of Azapa return looking for love. Today, as in the past, I will sing to the Virgin that stayed in the crag. Embrace us with your love.

the troupe, in particular by mentioning the family names of Baluarte and Zegarra. The name of the troupe itself is mentioned in the second verse.

Such observations suggest to me that these songs express the troupes' values in new ways. While devotion is still a key trait, instead of focusing on formality and effort, the melodies reference popular music as the lyrics emphasize the troupes' long-standing traditions, the families involved, and the dancers' unique experiences. The rhythms illustrate the influence of the bailes folclóricos as well as the bass drum strokes used by the bailes de salto.[18]

That these markers have become predominant, however, does not mean that the older style has completely lost its importance among younger dancers. As mentioned earlier, dancers recognize the Marconi for holding on to this older style. Despite the lack of a well-defined, upbeat characteristic rhythm and lyrics that are prayerful yet not directly customized to a specific troupe, the chants still hold an appeal, particularly the longer a dancer stays with the troupe. As Manuel Arias, second caporal of the Marconi and a composer for religious dance troupes in his own right, puts it, "It's that when all is taken into account, even with the cadence of these songs, people like it. It's part of their identity. And to want to negate part of your identity is impossible. So, if we were to remove those songs, we would lose everything. We would lose the essence of the troupe" (interview with author, August 26, 2009). In other words, the songs matter, but which markers are important in each situation change. I would note that the Marconi use the same slow singing when they perform their farewell and their salutations. They have another entrance song that they occasionally perform in the same way, but at all the presentations made at a church in 2008, they substituted the previously mentioned "Paloma del Alma Mía." Beyond aesthetics, part of the reason for this change may be practical; the slow songs take a longer time to sing. Given the fact that the troupes now only have twenty minutes for their presentation inside the church, they must be able to perform all three songs plus their choreography within this time frame.

I already observed the phenomenon of change in movement between the older generation of dancers in the Hijos de Azapa and the younger generation. Earlier, I cited Henríquez's implication that this change may be related to the dancers' change in skin color—becoming less moreno, or more White. I would challenge the essentializing character of this statement for several reasons. To begin with, not all dancers with darker phenotypes performed the dance in the same way as the older caporal; given the compliments I heard, one might consider him more as a virtuoso performer. Furthermore, a difference in terms of years of experience may also have played a role. In the past, individuals remained in the role of caporal until they decided to retire, were asked to step down by the troupe's officials, or were voted out by the dancers. In practice, that meant many caporales held their positions for many years. Some troupes still follow this approach. For example, Henríquez could count on one hand the number of caporales and guías in the Marconi in his lifetime. Recently, however, the Hijos de Azapa, like other troupes, put a three-year term on the important positions, so that more people have a chance to participate. This means the younger caporal certainly would have less experience dancing as caporal than his predecessors and will probably not have the opportunity to dance long enough in the position to develop particularly individualistic traits, unless he is given an opportunity later to repeat the role.

Finally, one must consider alternate perspectives in evaluating the dance, particularly from the aesthetic viewpoint of the dancers themselves. Cortéz, the right guía of the Hijos de Azapa, argued that the current style of the troupe is looser than in previous generations, a statement that would seem to challenge Henríquez's claim. Cortéz believed the younger generation had more energy in their step than the older generation. He claimed the older generation danced in a more somber fashion because the age of the average dancer used to be higher than it currently is. Cortéz asserts that he puts all his energy into his step and, in the video of the 2008 Little Feast, one can see him being more energetic than many of his peers. This energy can be seen most clearly in his matraca stroke, and this movement is precisely his second argument. He stated that the older generation of dancers would only produce a small sound with their matraca, while the younger generation tries to make the matraca "jump" in their hands. When I analyzed the video, I noticed that the older generation tended to hold the matraca with their entire left palm facing down and in contact with the matraca's side while turning the ratchet in a tightly controlled motion with the right. The younger generation, however, used only two fingers of the left hand to hold a corner of the matraca while turning. The effect was that the matraca did move significantly more, particularly in Cortéz's hands. These differences suggest a change in aesthetics from "coolness" to "energetic," related to the types of audiences present, the goal of attracting younger dancers, and perhaps even the willingness in the local context to accept such changes.

The Relationships of Styling Moreno

In an interview, Henríquez told me why people do religious dancing, using the phrase "por fe y tradición" (because of faith and tradition). This phrase might apply to any of the religious dance troupes, but he clarified what he meant specifically for the case of the morenos de paso: "the dance is a feeling that touches the moreno people more who are related with this dance . . . and the troupes of morenos are almost all made up of moreno people." Earlier he had explained why: "The moreno de paso is moreno: he [the dancer] arrives to the troupe because there have always been people in his family connected to the troupe. That is an inheritance that we receive from our fathers, grandfathers, great grandfathers. Practically almost all the societies keep going on in that way: the Marconi . . . the Carcamo. It is always by blood and surname" (interview with author, June 16, 2009).

The connection to family was a theme that continued to appear in interviews. It was not just a reason for joining, but also for staying. As Orlando Castillo described it to me in a 2009 interview, "Once you enter into this subject, this environment of the troupes, from my personal point of view, it is very difficult to leave. As I said, it's about tradition. Do you understand? My mom died 13 years ago now. So for me, it's a way of being connected to her at the sanctuary. Do you understand? There is a faith in the Virgin, there is a devotion, a surrender, so it is very hard to leave all that. That's why he who is born a religious dancer, dies a religious dancer" (interview with author, March 17, 2009).

Similarly, Manuel Arias told me, "I think that the Marconi is a way of life for me. To belong to this troupe is a lifestyle. It's something necessary" (interview with author, August 26, 2009). Interestingly, both Arias and Castillo lost their parents, who were also dancers, at a relatively young age. Thus, the troupe became their family. As Marcos Butrón reminded me, "you need to have lots of camaraderie [in a religious dance troupe]. If not, it doesn't work" (interview with author, January 14, 2009). Arias goes so far as to place the treatment between the members as the defining characteristic of being in a troupe:

> If you look at it coldly, a moreno troupe does not have anything more attractive, than say, a salto troupe. Being very [stoic about it]. But if you have a troupe that calls attention to itself because of the number of people, because they work so well together, because they do things so well, maybe that's the way that we win people over. I don't think the songs mark you that much, instead, I tell you, it's the quality of the people that you have in your troupe, and the way in

which you manage to understand the people who love your troupe. (Interview with author, August 26, 2009)

Certainly, having many dancers does attract attention, and the introduction of new types of costumes, movement, and songs (particularly of genres other than what is considered traditional) suggests that the morenos de paso are adjusting their style to reference other, flashier religious dance troupes. This shift in style could be an attempt to keep the troupe attractive to younger family members, recruit members from outside current families, or simply be an influence from the other troupes because of several decades of contact. For many members, however, these stylistic changes are less important than members' treatment of one another.

Throughout Latin America, organizations like the religious dance troupes and Black religious brotherhoods have served historically not only in their devotional capacity, but also to help and support fellow members financially and emotionally. Van Kessel (1973) noted that the press, based largely in Santiago, tended to portray these religious dance troupes as pagan holdovers whose working-class members spent too much of their resources on these activities and were ignorant in the ways of the church. Van Kessel conducted surveys of the troupes of three of the major religious feasts and discovered that the levels of income and religious instruction for the members of these troupes were on par with or more than the average Chilean. His survey suggested that this historical solidarity between troupe members results in real social capital that would be recognized locally as "decent" even if the media did not report it as such nationally.

While these observations did not solely refer to the morenos de paso, they were certainly included in these statistics, and, I would argue, the way in which Blackness plays a role in this expression is particularly relevant. The stigma historically associated with Blackness has often held Black individuals to a higher standard of achievement in society. What I have argued in this chapter is that an earlier generation of morenos de paso established the wearing of especially clean formal outfits, dancing to respectable marches, singing in overly devout fashion, and stepping in a controlled, cool swagger as a stylistic response to the relationships they had to the local elite and other "decent" people and the way they performed their decency. The fact that several other groups of African descendants throughout the Americas have cultural expressions that share these aspects with the morenos de paso points to the idea of diasporic synchronicity with those expressions present in Arica. Going back to post-Reconquest Spain, Blacks performed dances and formed confraternities as efforts to care for one another and earn the respect of broader society. In the United States, antebellum slaves and freedmen, as well as post-emancipation Black populations, performed military drills in formation or paraded in finery, both as expressions of pride and satire (cf. Levine 1977). Even after the War of the Pacific, Chileans saw Blacks in the Arica area as threats, both as Peruvians and soldiers.[19] Given the layering of these histories, I believe it would be logical for Black communities in Arica to style themselves moreno in similar ways as these other groups: as religious and respectable, yet veiled with coolness and satire for those who would know. Circumstances have changed, of course, and as they change, the music-dance of the morenos de paso has every right to change with them. In the wake of the Afro-descendant movement, however, this reading of a moreno styling of Blackness provides an alternate and complementary heritage for descendants of Africans and how they have historically styled their music and dance. One would need to engage in additional, detailed historical and ethnographic research to confirm this styling process, but an investigation of this kind could encourage the wider Chilean public to reconsider the breadth of contributions that people of African descent have made to Chilean culture.

Notes

1. The name translates to "Our Lady of the Rosary of the Crags of Livilcar Canyon." Beginning in 2010, an older group of dancers attempted to establish an additional annual pilgrimage visit on August 15, associated with the Feast of the Assumption. While several celebrations were held, it has not been able to continue.

2. In other regions of the Andes, they might be referred to as *danzas rituals* (ritual dances). See Mendoza (2000).

3. The Virgen de La Tirana, celebrated annually on July 16, is Chile's largest Catholic devotion. The feast centers around a sanctuary constructed for Our Lady of Mount Carmel, the patroness of the Chilean military, located in the small town of La Tirana, in the neighboring Tarapacá region. While the celebration is also a pilgrimage event featuring many religious dance troupes, it differs from Las Peñas in that the sanctuary is in the town square that is easily reachable by vehicle and the celebration receives nationwide media attention.

4. As I discuss in this and later chapters, the imagery of some baile religioso troupes is based on troublesome stereotypes. For example, the gitanos perpetuate visual clichés about Roma people, who are pejoratively referred to as Gypsies. The pieles rojas troupes adapted images of Native Americans from early twentieth-century movie Westerns, hence the problematic name of Redskins.

5. Both church and state officials have prohibited the use of alcohol in the sanctuary city during the celebration, but, historically, the locally made wine, known as *pintatani*, was

part of the festivities. Clandestine drinking does occur, despite the risk of fines and formal punishments.

6. Traditionally, dancers make a three-year commitment to dance if they enter a troupe. Many dancers may, of course, continue to participate, until such time that is no longer possible or desirable. Then they turn in their uniform at the *bajada del altar*, a closing ceremony for a troupe's participation in a specific feast, often a few weeks after the official celebration. Similarly, a ceremony called the *subida del altar* marks the formal beginning of the troupe's preparations for the feast.

7. Multiple origin stories exist for the Virgen de las Peñas. The most well-known tells how the image was once the statue of a church in the province of Carangas in Bolivia. Because of jealousy and audaciousness on the part of the townspeople during the Virgin's feast day, the church caught fire and the Virgin left the town in the form of a dove. The same dove was later seen at the current location of the sanctuary, turning into the embedded stone image when a local healer tried to capture her (Vásquez Benitt 1990). Another story dates the statue back to 1642, when a mule driver on his way to Potosí from Arica spotted a serpent attacking a shepherdess. The driver invoked the name of the Virgin to help her, and a bolt of lightning fell from the sky. Both the shepherdess and the serpent disappeared, leaving the image in their place. Yet another story has the Virgin appearing to a lost shepherdess from Livilcar asking her to build a sanctuary on this spot. When the shepherdess returned with others, they also heard the Virgin's voice (cf. Urzúa Urzúa 1969, 257–58).

8. In the book *Aica y la peña sagrada*, Hilario Aica claims that his company of morenos should have been first but that he was not notified about the meeting in which the order was decided. Since he and Manuel Baluarte were friends, Aica decided not to contest the point.

9. The first position for the Great Feast is held by the Compañía Moreno No. 1 de la Santísima Virgen de las Peñas, a morenos de paso troupe from Tacna, Peru, that celebrated its 120th anniversary in 2008. In both the case of the Morenos de Marconi and that of the Moreno No. 1, I should point out that these anniversaries suggest founding dates that precede the date of the founding of the association.

10. See Mena 1985, 189. For more information on the Black brotherhoods of Andalusia, see Moreno Navarro 1999.

11. Since the number of dance troupes has grown, the association of religious dance troupes has placed a twenty-minute time limit for each group's performance inside the church. Groups with a fewer number of dancers can perform more choreographies since it does not take them as long to cycle through the genuflection of each set of dancers.

12. For further descriptions of Birdwhistell's kineme, see Nöth (1990, 400).

13. See Robertson-DeCarbo (1976), Nzegwu (2001, 399), and Price (2001, 222–24).

14. The others are the Morenos de Tacna and the Morenos de Sama. See Lavín (1948).

15. Díaz Araya (2009) has suggested how the combination of military conscription after the war and the military's implementation of German-style band practices gave people from the interior villages the opportunity to learn to play these instruments; they would later incorporate them into their village celebrations. In interviews, local musicians explained to me that in Arica, the early bands that would play at Las Peñas included members of the local regimental band of the Rancagua division as well as those musicians who had learned how to play in the *salitre* (saltpeter) mining towns. When the salitre mines started to shut down, many of these musicians came to live in Arica. It was not until the 1970s, however, that noticeable quantities of brass band musicians appeared (Rainaldo Santibáñez, interview with author September 14, 2009). Brass bands for hire formed in the 1980s, making it easier to secure enough musicians, albeit for a higher price.

16. Local preference for these aesthetics were also present in similar contexts. When people singled out particularly good singers for the religious ritual of the May Cross to me, they pointed to members of the local Black community. The canticles used for this ritual have similar qualities to the older songs of the morenos.

17. See chapter 6 for a fuller description of the morenada.

18. Most salto troupes use a rhythm called "dos por tres" (literally, two by three), a local reference to groupings of strokes played on the bass drum. In two measures of common or cut time, 2 x 3 means two half notes in the first measure, followed by three consecutive quarter notes in the second measure. This is a common accompaniment for military marches. The Hijos de Azapa song is 3 x 3.

19. In the early 1920s, several magazine covers (particularly the title *Sucesos*) consistently depicted Peruvian soldiers in uniform as Black. See figure 1.2 in chapter 1.

6

STYLING BLACKNESS AS INDÍGENA

Racial Order as Carnivalesque?

ON FEBRUARY 6, 2009, IN ITS EIGHTH YEAR of operation, the Carnaval Andino: Con la Fuerza del Sol celebrated its opening day.[1] City officials sponsoring the Andean carnival (with a byline translated as "With the Strength of the Sun"), estimated that more than 4,500 dancers would participate in the forty-six different dance troupes, with roughly fifteen thousand spectators in attendance each day. These numbers led a few of the more presumptuous announcers in Arica to declare the event to be the third most important carnival in South America, after the ones held in Rio de Janeiro, Brazil, and Oruro, Bolivia.

At six o'clock, with the sun just beginning to ease in intensity and spectators having filled the bleachers along General San Martín Avenue, the Fraternidad Achachis Morenos Generación 90 (The Brotherhood of the Elders and Morenos of the 90s Generation) danced their way into the central performance space in front of the judges' booth. Performing a dance called the morenada, they had already marched past two tall images on either side of the street that represented the shape of a dancing figure backed by the sun. A rainbow checkerboard pattern filled that shape—a pattern that evoked the *wiphala*, a flag often associated with the Aymara people.[2] The same pattern filled the arch that marked the official end of the parade route. As the standard-bearer danced ahead of the group, he wove back and forth across the street while holding the banner high, which was also decorated with wiphalas. The wiphala is designated within Bolivia's constitution as a state emblem, but in this carnival setting, the wiphala flies alongside the Chilean national flag and the Arica municipal flag. The ever-present wiphala demonstrates one way in which local participants and organizers frame the Carnaval Andino as Indigenous.

That afternoon, this framing also happened through language. As the Achachis troupe entered the judging area, one of the announcers, standing on the stage across from the judges' booth, identified the dance troupe and its board of directors. Then, one of the announcers began speaking in the Aymara language, directly followed by phrases in Spanish:

Table 6.1. Announcer's Comments. Translation by author.

Jilatanaka, kullakanaka,	[Aymara] Brothers, sisters,
akhamawa jiwasa andino markata	Here we are, the Andean people.
Walja sumapiniwa phusisipki	They surely sound very beautifully
Walja sumapiniwa thoqosipki	They surely dance very beautifully.
Generación 90 akawa jumanakaxa	"Generation 90" here you are.
Jichha jayp'uxa aka Arica markana	This afternoon here in the town of Arica
Taqi jiwasanakanti	All together we surely,
Walipiniwa, sumapiniwa thoqosipki	Very truly, truly beautifully, dance
Con alegría, con la fuerza	[Spanish] With joy, with strength
Morenos Generación 90	Morenos "Generation 90"
En esta tarde deleitándonos con esos pasos	This afternoon delighting us with those steps
¡Fuerza Moreno!	Take strength, moreno!

Throughout the event, carnival announcers liberally sprinkled short Aymara phrases such as these throughout their descriptions of the troupes. Because few attendees likely understood the Aymara phrases, the announcers also provided Spanish translations.[3] The use of Aymara during the Carnaval Andino was therefore more about framing the event as Indigenous than the direct communication of information to locals or tourists (see video 6.1 to hear announcer's comments).

The passing dance troupe was also generally understood as an Indigenous expression, which was reinforced using Aymara language and designs. As with the other music-dance expressions explored in this book, the reasons for this understanding lie in the political and the performative. Beyond more straightforward markers of Indigeneity, however, a not-so-subtle irony was also at play. The Achachis Generación 90 performed the morenada, a genre that—in addition to its Indigenous connections—invokes the history of Africans in the region. In fact, roughly forty percent of the dance troupes in the 2009 Carnaval Andino performed one of two genres (either morenada or caporales) that, allegorically at least, represent experiences *not* directly related to Indigenous peoples, but to an African slave population—precisely the population whose descendants have been struggling to gain recognition through other dances, like the tumbe carnaval. While two troupes did perform tumbe carnaval that year, this number was small in comparison to the number of troupes that performed the morenada and the caporales, whose appearance in Arica is rooted in Bolivian practice. In other words, two of the major music-dance genres at the event that style Blackness in their performances appear primarily marked as *indígena,* or Indigenous.

In this chapter, I explore this relationship between Blackness and Indigeneity. First, I briefly describe current attitudes toward Indigeneity in the region and their relationship to the Carnaval Andino. I then discuss the historical and theoretical precedents for associating Blackness with Indigeneity. When asked about the visual, sonic, and kinesthetic characteristics of the morenada and caporales, many individuals do see these features as styled to this local narrative of Blackness. I argue, however, that while this styling of Blackness is possible, styling Indigenous is the dominant paradigm. This elevation in the signification of one ethnic group (Indigenous) over another (Black) within a festive atmosphere offers the possibility of understanding these genres through the lens of the carnivalesque, the classic aesthetic proposed by Mikhail Bakhtin. I demonstrate this idea by describing the characteristics of these genres and examining how they style to either Blackness or Indigeneity, with Indigeneity coming to the forefront in the racial order. Thus, the Indigenous styling in these genres contributes to the invisibility of the local Black population, even though individuals from this local Black population participate in these genres. Here I also consider the perspective of these Black individuals, whether they formally participate in Afro-descendant activist organizations or not. These performers can contribute to shifting the style of these music-dance genres toward Blackness, although the degree to which they can be successful is debatable. The result of this analysis offers insight into the complex dynamics between ethnoracial ways of identifying in the region.

Current Attitudes toward Indigeneity in Arica and their Connection to Carnival

Just as Peruvians have often been depicted as Black in the Chilean national imagination, Bolivians have stereotypically been portrayed as Indigenous. During the early twentieth century, when issues over the sovereignty of

Figure 6.1. 1920s *Sucesos* magazine cover depicting Chile as modern White male and Bolivia as Indigenous female. Part of the Alfredo Wormald Cruz Heritage Collection, Main Library, Universidad de Tarapacá. Digitalization courtesy FONDEYCT project 1151514, Luis Galdames, director, assisted by Rodrigo Ruz and Alberto Díaz.

Map 6.1. Arica within the Tripartite Region. Cartography by University of Oregon InfoGraphics Lab, Department of Geography.

Arica were still at play, Chilean political cartoons clearly illustrate Chile as White and a modern male, Peru often as Black and a fearful or overly pretentious male, and Bolivia as an Indigenous and scheming female. Titled "Machiavellianism," the cartoon in figure 6.1 depicts a personification of Bolivia suggesting that she and Chile be friends with the new railroad between Arica and La Paz in the background. Chile responds with "No tricks, understand?" The depiction of Peru as Black was more prevalent in *Sucesos,* appearing at least nine times, while Bolivia's portrayal of Indigeneity appeared in three cartoons.[4]

This stereotype of Bolivians as Indigenous shapes the interpretation of the history of the current carnival troupes in Arica. Several of these dances emerged at the Bolivian feasts of the famous carnival in Oruro and the feast of the Gran Poder in La Paz. While many of these dances are also performed at the Festividad de la Virgen de la Candelaria in Puno, Peru, the history of these dances in Arica is tied to Bolivian migration. Some Bolivian dance troupes occasionally visited northern Chile to perform in the early twentieth century, but the arrival of Bolivian migrants in the 1960s established their regular presence in the region. These migrants wanted to maintain their national cultural practices, but—recognizing local prejudice toward Bolivians—they initially performed their version of carnival in the Azapa Valley, an area adjacent to (but more secluded than) Arica. A generation later, local university students, looking to revindicate their Indigenous heritage, whether Bolivian or Chilean, began to express themselves through dance. They danced local genres like wayno or tarkeada as well as those understood as originating with the Bolivian migrants. Troupes began performing these latter genres within Arica itself in 1983, when an entrepreneur named Carlos Verdugo, who had started an urban, Brazilian-style carnival in Arica called La Ginga, invited them to join in an expansion of the event (see chap. 3, note 1). With their participation in La Ginga, as well as Chile's turn toward multiculturalism through the "Indigenous Law" (see chap. 1), the dance troupes grew in confidence and number. By 2002, a series of conflicts between some of the troupe leaders and La Ginga organizers led to the demise of La Ginga and the emergence of the Carnaval Andino. The fact that many Indigenous activists learned to identify as Indigenous through these carnival dances, coupled with their origins in Bolivian migrants, underscores the idea that, within the Chilean context, to style Bolivian is to style Indigenous. Consequently, Bolivian elements like the wiphala or even the Bolivian national colors are often seen as congruent with the Carnaval Andino.

In contrast to the Chilean perspective of understanding these dances as Indigenous, many Bolivians and Peruvians (and even academics like Abercrombie 1992) identify these folclórico dances as mestizo, that is, a mixture of Indigenous and European influences, even as they are danced by mestizos.[5] This orientation makes these dances available to express nationalism through the ideology of mestizaje.[6] In Peru and Bolivia, music-dance expressions marked as Indigenous, like tarkeadas, are now performed on separate days and/or in separate spaces from the folclórico expressions.[7] Arica's Carnaval Andino differs from those celebrations because, in Arica, all troupes dance together on the same days and in the same spaces, creating an ambiguity that supports the framing of the entire event as Indigenous by the carnival organizers.

Various actors have a stake in these multiple ways of Indigenous framing. Municipal politicians can present the event as an exotic attraction for tourists while also appealing to an important voter base. For the local branch of CONADI (La Corporación Nacional de Desarrollo Indígena, a state organization for Indigenous development), placing the carnival in an Indigenous frame indicates they are supporting local Indigenous activities and assists with garnering greater attention from the government. Finally, some Indigenous leaders I spoke with interpret the event as Indigenous because they see it as a vehicle for "the spirit of carnival," that is, their ancestors' practice of mutual reciprocity. At its simplest, this practice involves sharing, whether it be a drink or a dance; at a more complex level, it is the exchange of gifts or labor with the understanding that these gifts will be returned at another time for each other's mutual benefit.

The point here is that, although Indigenous people in Chile still face prejudice in many facets of daily life, the Carnaval Andino tends to be an acceptable and even desirable space for locals to identify as Indigenous or demonstrate their solidarity with Indigenous people in the region. It may seem even more ironic, then, that some of the most popular dance troupes are allegorical representations of African slavery in the region. To better understand how such expressions came to be, one needs to understand the relationship between these allegories and power relations in the region.

Allegories of Blackness and Connections with Indigeneity

According to scholarly and popular literature as well as the dancers' oral accounts, the morenada and caporales dances are allegorically grounded in the arrival of African slaves to the region, but each emphasizes different aspects of the varying narratives. One Bolivian version of the story explains that Spaniards initially brought African slaves as laborers for the highland mines, only to discover that they were not "naturally" suited to the cold and altitude of those mines.[8] Consequently, the Spaniards sent the Africans to work in the tropical conditions of the lowland Yungas region of Bolivia, an area that even today is often associated with the Afro-Bolivian population. A Peruvian version of the story describes the Spaniards bringing African slaves directly to the warm coastal plantations to replace the Indigenous laborers whom the Spaniards had sent to work in the highland mines (Rodriguez Amado 1995, 72). Both narratives ultimately place the slaves in similar contexts, although the important differences in how they arrived at their destination lead to different allegorical expressions.

In these music-dance scenarios, both African slaves and Indigenous peasants suffered under the harsh labor conditions placed on them. Their supervisors, called *capataces* or caporales, used corporal punishment, whipping the forced laborers when they determined they were not working or behaving properly. According to the narratives, these work captains were Black themselves, but they wore clothes like those of their masters to distinguish themselves from the African workers they supervised. James Lockhart has written that "basic to an understanding of the role of blacks in conquest Peru is an appreciation of their intermediate position between the Spaniards and the Indians: they are not to be thought of as the lowest ranking of the three" (1994, 194). Because Spaniards had a longer period of contact with Africans and because some Black slaves spoke Spanish and were familiar with Spanish customs, Spaniards used Black criollos as intermediaries with the Indigenous peoples, initially as soldiers against them and later as business administrators with them. Judging from the way the Spanish Crown's legislation protecting Indians needed to be repeatedly decreed, one can surmise the amount of abuse to which these Black intermediaries submitted Indigenous peoples. Despite the Crown's attempts to maintain Africans separate from Indigenous people, Bowser has pointed out "the African all too often emulated his Spanish master in cowing and mistreating the Indian" (1974, 150). The result was that "the relationship between the blacks and Indians was, in the main, one of strong mutual hostility, with the blacks occupying a position of much greater power" (Lockhart 1994, 194). While such power was certainly limited, one can understand how such a history might shape a resentful attitude in Indigenous peoples toward Black people generally, an attitude that might later motivate less-than-flattering portraits of the Black condition in popular expressions of music-dance. While such expressions may resonate with mainstream culture, Whitten and Corr remind us that, "when dealing with African American imagery anywhere in the Americas, we certainly must read, reflect, and think about Indigenous American imagery on the same or similar subjects" (1999, 232). Given the local history and meanings currently granted to these dances, I propose to analyze them through a specific lens: understanding how they negotiate local historical and social power structures through the Bakhtinian idea of the carnivalesque.

Racial Order and the Carnivalesque

In his article on carnival music in Haiti (1994), ethnomusicologist Gage Averill critiqued some scholars' unmitigated use of Bakhtin's idea of the carnivalesque without considering the unique historical and social situation. Averill illustrated that in Haiti, carnival was an expression for the masses that made room for the poor and working class to critique those in power but was also under surveillance by the powerful. These elite were aware of the event's potential to undermine their authority, and they took actions accordingly. Similarly, in Arica, the Carnaval Andino is a contested event, in which many of those arguably neglected in daily life take to the streets to become the focus of attention for the day. They are aware that, in doing so, they help create an image of the region that locals can identify with as well as help generate revenue for the city. Unified, they can be a political force to be reckoned with. Politicians know this fact as well and make a point to be present at the event, making campaign promises that might appeal to the participants (and sometimes even participating in it). That said, the city and regional governments control most of the prize money, often grappling with the leaders of troupes over the amount to be given out, and rich individuals in the city sponsor several of the troupes or their activities according to their interests. These dynamics make it clear that carnival is not an isolated event, but rather, as Averill suggests, a specific manifestation of the existing power structure, both in its contestations and reinforcements of that structure.[9]

Nevertheless, Bakhtin's idea of the carnivalesque does offer some tools to think with, particularly in the realm of the aesthetic. For Bakhtin, the carnivalesque is something that draws attention to the material—specifically to the grotesque as associated with the (lower) body. Power is inverted through signs highlighting the commonality of the body, such that even those in power are brought to a recognition of their existence within this corporeal world. This move opposes the intangible ideologies that justify the existing power structure. For Bakhtin, laughter (sparked by carnival humor) provides a pointed yet ambiguous response to the world, momentarily having a degrading effect as it materializes (1984, 20). In his eyes, the power structure can die and be remade in carnival, as society itself is forever in the process of becoming. Of course, here is where the ethnographic corrective becomes important, as history has shown that drastic social change as a result of carnival is limited and, in fact, carnival humor (due to its ambiguity) can actually reinforce the existing hegemony (Dentith 1995, 71–73).

Nevertheless, drawing from Bakhtinian principles can help understand how Blackness is styled as Indigenous regionally. The idea of grotesque realism, with its emphasis on humor, the body, and the material, appears in multiple facets of the two different genres I describe here. After a brief description of the two genres, I focus on specific styling components that appeal to this carnival aesthetic. One result, I argue, is that Indigeneity is foregrounded at the expense of Blackness, which is ridiculed or criticized. Of course, due to the ambiguity of carnival humor, Indigeneity can also be a target of ridicule, and, while a few White characters may occasionally appear as targets of mockery, their relative scarcity means that Whiteness remains at the top of the racial order. Considering the history of the relationship between the Black overseers and the Indigenous workers, this carnival humor functions to raise the position of the Indigenous individual over the Black one. While they may assert their relationship to Indigeneity in one form or another, most contemporary carnival participants do not describe their performance in these hegemonic terms. I believe the current presence of this racial order as systemic, that is, one in which individuals propagate foundational ideas or assumptions through institutions and networks, so that many performers may not even realize their privilege as they continue to keep the traditions of the ancestors (cf. Elias and Feagin 2016).

A subtler version of the grotesque carnival aesthetic is at play in younger participants, as ideas of youthful energy and sensuality have recently come to the fore. Mendoza (2000) noted how youth in San Jerónimo, Peru, during the 1990s gravitated to the *tuntuna* precisely to embrace these values.

The tuntuna is a genre related to caporales. They share a similar rhythm and background narrative, while varying in costume (the tuntuna's use of large ruffled sleeves) and step (more bounce and skip in the tuntuna step). In my fieldwork, I observed similar value placed on energy and sensuality in the caporales as the ones Mendoza described for the tuntuna. The carnivalesque here seems to primarily function in terms of an inversion of power between old and young, while gender roles appear to be reified even as they might be called into question. Racialized stereotypes, however, are also present in these genres, and, once again, I will point out the facets of styling that call attention to the relationships between these performers.

In discussing the genre of the morenos de paso in chapter five, I noted the tendency of Andean scholars to interpret religious dance as primarily an Indigenous expression and, consequently, often neglect the participation of Afro-descendants in this type of music-dance. In this chapter, I revisit this idea from a slightly different perspective. While the styling of Blackness in these expressions seems to be largely systemic and not foremost in many people's minds, Afro-descendants who participate in these troupes often become aware of the signs at play in their performances, either because they are called out as performers or are sensitive to the stereotypes present. After examining the styling of Blackness and the role of Indigeneity in these troupes, I turn to the interpretation of such stylings on the part of Afro-descendant performers and an incident that illustrated a twist on the interpretation of these genres.

Genres That Style Blackness as Indigenous: Morenada and Caporales

While the underlying narrative of both the morenada and the caporales is rooted in the historic presence of slavery in the region, the founding narratives of these dances differ. The morenada is the older of the two genres. Some individuals debate whether the morenada originated in Peru or Bolivia. They may also argue over whether the slaves began the dance as a parody of their masters (a dance that was later adopted by mestizos) or the Aymara began it as a parody of the dance of the Africans.[10] Records show the existence of a troupe of this type in the carnival of Oruro in 1913, with at least one additional troupe forming there in 1924 (A.F.C.O. 2006, 15–17). Several of the people I interviewed told me that the oldest morenada troupe to dance in the city of Arica is the Sagrado Corazón de Jesús, which was known for dancing in celebrations in Charaña, Bolivia (interviews with author, Hector Mamani Huanca September 14, 2009, Juan Carlos Mamani Morales January 27, 2009, Martin Quispe September 18, 2009).[11] It primarily dances on the feast day of its namesake and for the Carnaval Andino. New troupes often form by breaking off from established groups. For example, the morenada Achachis Generación 90 emerged from a schism in the Sagrada Corazón troupe.[12] Several morenadas, such as Papel Pampa, began as groups dancing in a carnival in the Valley of Azapa in the 1980s. As with other genres, several of the troupes share an affiliation or at least admiration for similar troupes in Bolivia, naming themselves after them, as in the case of the morenada Verdaderos Intocables de Arica.[13]

Most people I spoke to in Arica understood the morenada as representative of the march of African slaves during the early colonial period as they traveled back and forth to the great silver mines in Potosí. This explanation fits with the march-like, steady beat to which morenada performers dance. As with the other carnival dance troupes, the morenadas are organized into blocs of characters. Typically, most dancers emulate general characters, although *figuras* (literally, figures, individuals with specialized roles) are present. Some of the characters in the morenada are the *achachis* (the elders or overseers) and *cholas* (or its diminutive, *cholitas*, presumably depictions of the Indigenous women who would follow and cook for the slave caravans). The heart of the troupe are the morenos, who come in several varieties, some of which are associated with royalty: the *reyes morenos* (Black kings) and the *virreys* (viceroys). The latter are among the newest characters and wear long elegant overcoats and sharp fedoras. I will discuss the costumes, sounds, and movements that distinguish the morenos in the following section. Unlike the morenada, whose origins are unclear and hotly debated, the relatively recent emergence of the caporales from Bolivian celebrations has been better documented. Its blocs are made up of characters called caporales and their female counterparts. In the literature, female caporal dancers are occasionally also referred to as *cholitas*, but I did not hear this term in Arica.[14]

In 2012, the Bolivian government officially recognized the fortieth anniversary of the first appearance of a caporales troupe in the celebration of the Señor del Gran Poder in La Paz (Ministerio de Culturas 2012). According to a press release, Victor Estrada Pacheco saw a performance of an Afro-Bolivian dance troupe from the Yungas and was inspired to create the dance, based on the personality of the dance captain there, also known as a caporal. Inspired by the caporal's costume and the rhythm that he danced to, Estrada and his eight other siblings danced as the Caporales Urus del Gran Poder in 1972. In Oruro, the first brotherhood of caporales appeared in 1975, when an older folklore troupe of *negritos* decided to switch to the new genre.[15]

In the region of Arica, troupes of caporales were certainly present by the late 1980s, at least as unassociated ones sponsored for patron saint feasts in smaller towns. With ten troupes of caporales in the 2017 carnival, the genre continues to be the largest category in the event and arguably the most popular. Perhaps one of the reasons that the caporales are so popular is that, as mentioned before, people consider it a "youthful" genre. The dance requires agility on the part of the male caporales, since they need to spin and leap energetically during certain choreographed portions. The female caporal dancers' skirts show off their legs and reveal a bikini bottom when they pivot. Some observers consider that these performance characteristics entail too much energy or too little dignity for older participants, who might more properly dance morenada. There may also be an additional association with class, given that in Bolivia, a significant percentage of caporal performers are university students or young adults from upper-middle-class families (Bastien 2004, 555). Furthermore, as several dancers reminded me, the carnival troupes give participants the opportunity to meet potential partners, of special importance to young adults who may not already be in a romantic relationship.

Whatever the reason, the result is that many caporal dancers are young adults. This means that they have lived much of their lives free of the Pinochet dictatorship and after the passing of the "Indigenous Law" (see chap. 1). Despite the law, these young adults associate Bolivia with Indigeneity and may not be familiar with the foundational narrative of the dance they execute. Other factors may also obfuscate the visual, sonic, or kinesthetic facets that connect the genre to Blackness, which I describe in the following section.

Styling Blackness via Facets of the Carnivalesque

When thinking about the visual aspects of these genres with respect to Blackness, perhaps the most direct and troubling references come from the use of masks. An old photograph shows the use of blackface and masks in the morenada (Beltrán 1956, 15), but in Arica, I did not notice blackface in any of the morenada troupes. Instead, a standard mask with slight

Figure 6.2. Moreno masks used in dancing morenada, Arica, Chile.

variations appeared in those blocs specifically representing the moreno. The masks feature jet-black skin, a similarly colored frizzy wig and beard, bulging eyes, a wide, flattened nose, a wagging tongue with exaggerated bottom lip, and a short pipe.[16] Performers and the popular literature offer explanations that attempt to assign allegorical meanings to these exaggerated features. While the hair, skin, and lips are in line with common methods of caricaturing Black peoples throughout the Americas, morenada performers often explain the overly grotesque nature of the eyes, nose, tongue, and lips common in the morenada as the effects of Black slaves receiving cruel treatment while having to do strenuous labor at high altitudes. According to this interpretation, the eyes come out of their sockets in terror at their treatment, the nostrils flare to try to take in more oxygen in the thinning air, and the mouth and tongue burn for lack of water (Manta 1979, 21–22). In their exaggeration, however, the treatment of such figures does not seek to inspire empathy but rather engage the grotesque—a systemic, ambiguous rendition of phenotype that suggests mockery even as it can be explained as an exaggeration to make a point about the abuse of slaves.

Beyond the masks, early photographs suggest that moreno characters within the morenada wore clothes modeled after the jackets of the colonial aristocrats. This reference could suggest either a slave parody of the masters or an Indigenous parody of the dress the moreno overseers wore to imitate their masters. Over time, these early jackets were reinterpreted to become large, heavy, and covered with lavish sequins. Shapes became exaggerated to produce what some disrespectfully call *trajes de pollo* (chicken suits) or *trajes de torta* (cake suits). Another variation was the *traje de barril* (barrel suit), also glitteringly adorned but explained as suggestive of the barrels that people stomp grapes in to make wine. Bastien (2004) explains that some dancers understand the costumes' ornateness as resulting from the prosperity the slaves gained after they were freed. These costumes, however, have become quite cumbersome, considerably weighing down the dancers and earning the morenada the designation of *danza pesada,* or cumbersome dance.

Traditionally, female chola costumes resonate with ornateness but are markedly Indigenous. Each dancer within a bloc of cholas wears a matching outfit consisting of an elegant felt bowler hat adorned with elaborate metal pins, a finely embroidered shawl, and an ankle-length skirt (*pollera*) that is propped up by numerous petticoats. The chola wears her hair in a single, thick braid, whether of her own hair or as an extension emerging from her hat. The hat, pollera, and braid are common markers of Aymara women in everyday life in the region, but the version of these worn during carnival is much more formal than those used in quotidian dress (one bloc of chola dancers is featured in video 6.1).

Given the expense of purchasing or renting such costumes, some scholars working in the Andes have effectively shown that the morenadas are vehicles through which sponsors and performers can display their wealth—an act that resonates with Indigeneity in the Andes. In Arica, whether you can dance morenada is tied to whether you have the financial means to do so, since one must pay fees to dance with a carnival troupe, which may include costume rentals. The expense of the morenada costume can result in a higher fee for these troupes than some of the other genres, yet this display of wealth through the ornateness of costuming has its logic. As Nico Tassi (2016, 129–30) has explained, the traditional Aymara worldview sees the material and spiritual planes as interconnected. Abundance attracts abundance, and the expense paid during a festival can be understood as an offering that will bring additional prosperity. Recognizing this attempt at economic change, anthropologist David Guss has argued that the current use of the morenada in La Paz is a form of racial displacement in which "native campesinos on the way to becoming middle class mestizos dress up as African slaves who in turn are parodying their masters" (2006, 319).

Such interpretations return the focus to styling Blackness as Indigenous, but the ambiguity of Bakhtinian carnival humor comes into play here. Attention is drawn to the physicality of the material world as it relates to the body. The costume is so lavish that it weighs down the body, emphasized by the grotesque facial distortions seen in the mask. In their ostentatiousness, the ex-slaves have failed in their attempt to gain respectability—a "nouveau riche" joke at Blackness. Yet the humor also correlates to the material wealth of the performer, so that the performers can have a laugh with the audience while reinforcing their status as wealthy in society.

These costumes play an important role in defining choreography, so that the kinesthetic reinforces this carnival humor. The weight and shape of the costume can restrict certain movements like raising the knee or arms. The morenada dance is a pacing step—one step per beat—which can symbolize either the slow, steady march to the mines in shackles or the rhythmic stomping of the grapes. Just as the performers' costumes should reflect the narratives to which they belong, a dancer's individual steps as well as the overall choreography of a bloc of dancers should also reflect these narratives. Simply put, good performers dance in character (see video 6.2 for example of dancers masked as morenos).

The sonic facets of the morenada reinforce this allegory of Blackness. Its fundamental rhythm is a steady, heavy four-beat rhythm played on the bass drums that brass bands use. Musically, the similarity of morenadas with marches is evident and suggests a parallel with the way that the pride and decency of the morenos de paso is interpreted as snobbish. The key variation from the march is found in a common bombo phrase:

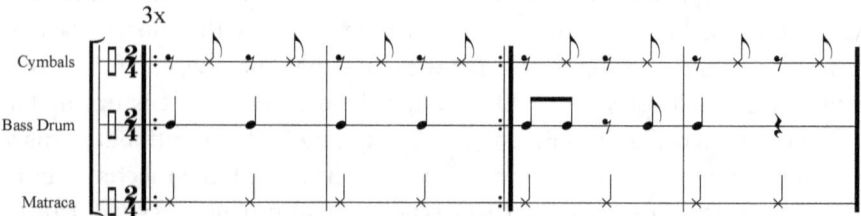

Example 6.1. Basic rhythmic pattern of the morenada.

The bombo rhythm is reinforced using matracas. Both the morenos and cholas play the fancy noisemakers, which come in an amazing variety of shapes—such as buses, machine guns, or monuments—using wood, metal, or even armadillo shells as a resonator. These shapes can act as signs of a shared profession between the dancers (e.g., bus drivers), of characters (e.g., mobsters carry machine guns), or places (e.g., the Arch of Tacna). Matraca players keep the steady four-beat rhythm, occasionally spinning the ratchet around for an extended note. The use of the ratchets contributes significantly to the aural texture of the morenada and is an essential marker of the genre. Virtually everyone I spoke to who mentioned the ratchets explained that the sound imitated the clanking of the chains that Blacks wore during slavery. This narrative was so prevalent that people offered it up in conversations without me asking about it. Later, however, I saw a 1990s VHS recording of a morenada troupe dancing in the Gran Poder celebration in La Paz in which the announcer declared that the slaves used the matracas to keep time on their march to the mines in Potosí.[17] Since their legs were chained together, they needed to synchronize their steps to not trip over one another. The sound of the matraca, rather than being iconic of the sound of the chains, instead was indexical of slavery, because it acted as a timekeeper for marching. This explanation suggests that narratives have varied over time and, given the prevalent use of matracas in various types of morenos in the region, perhaps according to context. What is clear here, however, is the matraca's sonic reference to Blackness remains strong, even while the visual lavishness of the matraca continues its ambivalent nature in carnival humor.

Performance facets of the caporales expression vary from the morenada expression, although aspects of the underlying narratives resonate with one another. Everyone I spoke with who knew about the dance narrative understood the caporal character as enslaved but also serving as an overseer for his master. The character is supposed to be arrogant and proud, aware of his position over his fellow slaves. Presumably to imitate the costume of this master, the men's costumes were flashy and elegant, incorporating a tighter fitting costume with puffed sleeves and a handheld plumed hat with folded brim on one side. In addition to their jingle-covered knee-high boots, they carried a whip as a symbol of their power. Juan Carlos Mamani Morales, an experienced caporales dancer, told me that the ornateness of the costumes had increased over time, suggesting similar values at play to those in morenada costumes.

The female dress adds an additional layer of the carnivalesque to the event: the grotesque as sexual. Meanings that I heard ascribed to the female

Figure 6.3. Female and male caporal dancers at the 2010 Vendimia Festival in Codpa, Arica-Parinacota region, Chile.

character were that she was also a servant or slave. The female dancer wears a brimmed hat adorned with sequins, hair in two long braids, puffed sleeves on a fitted bodice, a pleated hip-length skirt, a matching bikini bottom, tights, and heels. As mentioned in the morenada, the term cholita in combination with hat and braids often registers as Indigenous. Given the founding narrative of the caporales as a dance based on observation of Black dancers from the Yungas, however, the situation is more ambiguous, since, in the Yunga context, cholita can suggest a woman of African and Aymara descent. This ethnoracial ambiguity was not part of the explanations that I was given for the character, who instead was described as dancing delicately and sensually to distract the caporal. This distraction would dissipate his anger at misbehaving male slaves so that he would not strike them so harshly. Yet the fact that all the male dancers are caporales problematizes this narrative in that there are no slaves to strike. The shortness of the skirts is significant.[18] During a more intense dancing sequence, when the dancers spin or quickly rotate the entire body, the short skirts rise to become parallel to the ground, exposing the dancers' bikini bottoms, which explains why they were color-coordinated. I was advised not to take photographs or shoot from camera angles that were low to the ground, in case mothers or other family members walking alongside the troupes might see my perspective as too overtly voyeuristic and worthy of reproach (see video 6.3 for an example of female caporal dancers).

The combination of movement with the revealing costume highlights the erotic element of the grotesque in carnival humor. The revelation of the bikini bottom is socially meant to appeal to the heterosexual male's "lower body," as Bakhtin frames it, a concept meant to range from the libidinal to the scatological. From this perspective of base instinct, this attraction could have a class-leveling effect, with elite and working-class males alike exchanging knowing glances, aware of the possibility of being tempted. Ambiguity comes into play as the young women, on the one hand, are interpreted as the object of the male gaze, but also, as the narrative suggests, are aware of their power to seduce.[19] An additional layer of complexity appears once one considers the ethnoracial position of the characters. With the caporal as Black and the women ambiguously read as Black or Indigenous, stereotypes of racial mixture, the voracity of the Black male sexual appetite, and the sexual vulnerability/availability of Indigenous women within society are reinforced, even as they are inverted via voyeurism.[20] These ideas can also be applied to other female performers, such as the female figuras dancing individually or in small groups within the morenada.

The swishing of the skirts goes in time with the double beat of the bass drum. The source of this double beat may be a reference to the tuntuna or *tundiqui*. These dances, which some authors ascribe as part of an Afro-Bolivian ceremony (Godinez Quinteros 1996, 63–65), had been represented in other genres that predated the caporales:

Example 6.2. Basic bass drum pattern for caporales.

Some confusion arose later, however, when pan-Andean folkloric music groups (like Los Kjarkas) referred to the rhythm as *saya* when composing for such troupes. Due to Los Kjarkas's popularity, the use of this term became widespread. This angered the Afro-Bolivian activists who understood saya as a markedly different music-dance genre that had become a symbol of their movement beginning in the 1970s. The Afro-Bolivian saya features a lead singer that first sings a verse couplet, which is repeated in tandem with another singer, before the chorus, or saya, is sung by the group. A rhythm created by interlocking patterns played on three types of drums and a scraper accompanies the singers and the dancers (Templeman 1998). To better distinguish between the genres, many people now call the rhythm of the caporales dance *saya caporal* or, more simply, caporal.

The male caporal dancers stomp their feet in time with the double strokes of the bass drum, causing the jingles to sound with the same duple rhythm. Daniel Barria explained to me that this sound also is supposed to be associated with chains, "from when they would strike the Blacks" (interview with author, May 13, 2010). The imagery here mimics the significance given to the sound of the matraca in the morenada.

Sonically, caporal troupes have brass band accompaniment, and Chilean brass band musicians find the caporales rhythm extremely accommodating. Arrangers in Arica were quite adept at taking the latest cumbia, salsa, or even pop hits and fitting them into a caporal format, much to the chagrin of more traditionalist Peruvian or Bolivian brass band musicians that also performed at the event. This tendency seems to reinforce other ways of styling Blackness, given that cumbia and salsa are examples of Afro-diasporic genres, and their use could fit Feldman's model of the Black Pacific. These genres can invoke the carnivalesque in terms of their associated dance movements—which can be interpreted again as a recognition of sexuality. These hip gestures occasionally appear during interludes in the main choreography, when the basic caporal rhythm might be interrupted as part of the show in front of the judges.

A variation of this corporeality occurs with the male caporal dancer in terms of his show of strength and perhaps even virility. Beyond the basic requirement of sounding the jingles to the beat of the bass drum, the male caporal dancer skips or leaps. Male caporal dancers often raise the knees and reach arms upward during their choreography, emphasizing their verticality. They advance by skipping forward, again with raised knees, sometimes lifting their ankles to tap them with one of their hands. These movements give the caporales dance a much lighter feel than the "heaviness" of the morenada, whose dancers are often laden down with costumes or heavier props. I would also point out that, unlike the morenada dancers, the caporales often perform an intense choreographed sequence, then strike a pose to wait for applause. The bravado illustrated in this action, consistent with the character, again calls attention to the youthful energy and agility needed to accomplish these moves. In Bakhtinian terms, beauty is placed before age and physical power is placed before the social and political. In both the strength of the morenada and the agility of the male caporal dancer, physicality is associated with Black males—a characteristic in synchronicity with other parts of the African diaspora, such as the United States in which the association of Blackness and sports has been naturalized, a combination of the link between slavery with physical labor and the limited public spaces in which Black men have been given opportunities to excel (see video 6.4 for example of male caporal dancers).

Styling Blackness as Indigenous

The narratives and performance facets described in the previous section suggest a styling of Blackness within the aesthetics of the carnivalesque. The ambiguous nature of the carnivalesque means that Blackness might be performed as mockery but also as an embarrassment to those in power. That same ambiguity, however, allows for multiple interpretations. As I suggested in the opening of the chapter, Indigeneity is marked to such an extent throughout the event that Blackness is styled as Indigenous. In addition to the previously mentioned visual and sonic facets that mark the carnival itself as Indigenous, such as the wiphala and the use of the Aymara language, I now consider the extent to which the genres themselves perform Indigeneity.

As mentioned, female characters appear marked as Indigenous in both genres. The cholas in the morenada are more clearly identifiable as Aymara through dress, given their bowler hats, shawls, and pollera. More ambiguously, with their hats and braids, the female figures in the morenada and the female blocs in the caporales also imply Indigeneity, but their short skirts and low-cut bodices have all the youthful interracial sexual implications of the carnivalesque I described earlier.

Through my ethnographic work, I discovered subtler ways in which the genres could be marked as Indigenous for the performer. For example, brass band musicians explained to me that the morenada was one of the genres in which a musician needed to "ponerse la pluma" (put on the feather), or play in a more Indigenous way. Paulina Luza, one of the few but growing number of female brass players, told me that some baritone horn players play their phrases to "give it swing, delay a bit, so that it sounds as if . . . as if you wait but stay in time" (interview with author, August 27, 2009). Later she placed the responsibility for not sounding square on the bass drum player. As she described it, being square was staying too "on time," and the bass drum player must give it that "touch," like the tension between the need to "keep time" while playing "behind the beat."

The morenada is also special for the freedom that it affords the baritone horns to improvise parts. In other Andean brass band genres, usually the trumpets play the melody, the baritones answer, and then the trumpets enter once again (with the baritones playing a corresponding harmony). But, as Luza describes it, "in the morenada, one plays short melodic figures, so one has the liberty to invent things inside the chord. When they are in the bare parts, that's when they stick in something to play. But not many do it." In other words, "swing" and "improvisation" are what is needed for musicians "to put on the feather," or style Indigenous. Ironically, these same characteristics are markers of Blackness in many African diasporic contexts. In Arica, however, a specific way of swinging and improvising in morenada reads Indigenous among the brass band musicians.

Choreography is also important, because it allows Arica's troupes to style themselves in relation to Bolivian troupes. As previously discussed, both morenada and caporales troupes in Arica often want to establish associations with certain troupes in Bolivia, either informally, by simply naming themselves after these troupes, or more formally, by seeking recognition from these troupes as being a branch of the original. In performance, they attempt to duplicate the choreographies of their favorite troupe, because many Bolivian troupes have developed routines that allow spectators to distinguish one troupe from another. These choreographies are often learned by watching DVDs of the Bolivian troupes' performances in the carnival events called entradas. It strikes me that troupe founders and leaders decide whether to attempt making these associations, and some of these connections to Bolivia may be sought after for nationalistic or family reasons. Given the general association of Bolivianness with Indigeneity in

Chile, however, one could argue that this type of association authenticates a troupe as more Indigenous.

In fact, this practice seemed to become more overt among caporales troupes during my fieldwork, as I saw with several new caporales troupes that were formed. While introducing themselves at events preceding their debut in the Carnaval Andino, some of these troupes even mentioned that they had named themselves after a Bolivian troupe out of admiration and respect for that troupe, but without formal ties with them. The overt nature of this styling, however, seems to be something relatively recent, something that older caporales find discomforting. In an interview with me, Juan Carlos Mamani Morales argued that people have been dancing caporales in Chile for twenty years now, and Chilean dancers were already putting their own stamp on the genre. Despite having danced in Oruro's carnival, Mamani Morales was not interested in looking for inspiration from Bolivian troupes.

What is more problematic for Mamani Morales, however, is that the youth do not see this desire for association with the Bolivian troupes as a way to get in touch with their Indigenous roots. He thought the youth limited their discourse strictly to whose dance moves were better, with no discussion of how these dance practices relate to Aymara worldview. Mamani Morales is of the generation who learned to identify with his Indigenous heritage through dance. Born in Putre, his family has a long history in the Chilean highlands. As a child, he was exposed to local dances such as wayno, *takirari*, and tarkeada. At the age of twelve, he came by himself to Arica to continue his studies. He lost touch with his Indigenous side until he entered college. There he started listening to Andean music and began to associate with Indigenous activists and the sons of Bolivian immigrants. He danced not only wayno and takirari but also caporales. In the caporales, he met his partner. For him, dance was therefore about relationships, particularly a relationship with the Aymara world. He dances not to compete, but with the "spirit of carnaval" in mind. This spirit "begins with a ceremony and finishes in a place where there is some type of ritual related to the Aymara world" (interview with author, January 27, 2009). He criticized those people who do not understand this idea, saying:

> Not to be racist, but there is a certain way of seeing things, and that makes it such that things do not come out the same [in all *caporal* troupes]. They are just not all equal. For an Andean person, there are certain things that go unsaid, because they are implicit, and one notices that in certain attitudes

and the way things are done. Groups that are not Andean, in those groups, one feels like something is missing . . . in the way they spend time with each other, the way they share a meal or have fun. Do you understand? That type of thing. Obviously, everyone can dance. But in the way we spend time with one another. In the Andean world, every once in a while, they'll play a wayno, but in the other groups, they do not even remember the wayno. Things like that. (Ibid.)

Mamani Morales's perspective as stated in the quote above suggests that one can style Bolivian in dancing the caporales, but to truly style Indigenous, one needs to associate with the behavior of Indigenous peoples in ways beyond dance.

In Mamani Morales's case, he saw the caporales expression as a vehicle for identifying with his Indigenous self. Despite the markers linking the morenada and caporales to Indigeneity, however, not all performers identify as Indigenous, even if they recognize the expression in which they participate as such. Many performers dance with a troupe because they are invited by extended family, classmates, or coworkers, regardless of how they identify ethnoracially. There is prestige in having a larger dance bloc or troupe, and although some troupes in the past may have limited participation only to those of Bolivian or Indigenous descent, that restriction is not common practice now. Over time, participants learn the widespread narratives associated with their dance (if they were unaware of these allegories when they first began their dance career), and as individuals, they may use of these narratives to explain their participation in the troupes.

In the case of those expressions that point to Blackness, I initially was surprised to find people who identify as Afro-descendants proudly participating in the Fuerza del Sol with troupes whose characteristics may be interpreted as insulting to them, particularly since they had the option to dance with troupes that were explicitly Afro-descendant. I explore their perspective in the following section.

Afro-descendant Participation in "Indigenous" Carnival Genres

In 2009, Gabriel Huanca Baluarte was the president of the caporal troupe known as San Pedro de Totora, which was the oldest group of caporales in the region still dancing. Since this role was largely administrative, he also participated in the Carnaval Andino as a dancer in a morenada. He was a tall, strong man—he reminded me physically of the boxer Muhammad Ali.

Given his physical features, most people in the US would categorize him as African American, yet in the region of Arica, particularly in the Azapa Valley, people recognized his mixed heritage of Indigenous and Afro-descendant. At the Baluarte family's well-known Cruz de Mayo celebration in 2009, Huanca explained to me that members of Lumbanga sometimes chastised him for not leaning toward his "Afro" side. He countered that he has two lines of heritage and why should he favor one line at the expense of the other?

Huanca told me that he had always felt more drawn to his Indigenous side. This conversation started when he had introduced me to his brother, explaining that I had come to work with Lumbanga.[21] His brother exclaimed that I should talk to him, who had always been in touch with his "Afro" side, and not Gabriel, who was always involved with Indigenous practices. To prove his point, Gabriel's brother shimmied his hips, kicking up a bit of the dirt and reinforcing the jokester image that his family placed on him. When I asked him if he had ever participated with any of the Afro-descendant organizations, he said no; he later admitted that he had learned to make *zampoñas* (panpipes) from his grandfather. Tellingly, both brothers had also danced in the Morenos de Andres Baluarte religious dance troupe while growing up. In other words, the family had raised the siblings so that they participated in activities associated with both Afro-descendant and Indigenous peoples.

Huanca's participation in the caporales and morenada troupes, however, was not simply a way that he could identify with his Indigenous side. To a certain extent, he also saw himself as someone empowered to make sure that the representations within these dances were properly understood. He had traveled and participated in the Carnaval de Oruro, and as I understand it, he had taken part in a workshop on the meaning of the caporales expression. On several occasions, he reminded me that the Afro-Bolivian saya was something quite different from the rhythm that the caporal danced and offered me literature on the subject.

In an interview with me in 2010, Huanca's nephew, Daniel Barria Huanca, nicknamed "Zambo," initially followed his uncle's lead in telling me that his participation in the San Pedro de Totora caporales troupe was an expression of his Indigenous heritage. As a child, Barria would spend his summers with his uncle and cousins when his father and mother would go on vacation to the South. At first, he resisted joining the troupe, but his uncles paid for Barria's costume and fees to dance at age twelve. He liked it, stayed with it, and excelled. Eventually, he became the first guía, or the second-in-command dancer, leading on the right corner of the male part of the troupe.

When responding to criticism from other family members and friends who asked him how he could dance something Bolivian and by extension "Indian," Barria defended himself using his other heritage. Yes, he would say, it is a Bolivian and Indigenous dance, but it represents who I am. Barria commented that the music was slave music; it had passed through slavery, and since he was a moreno, it had his blood in it. It was "Afro," and he was Afro. He told me these comments would make his detractors take pause, especially because he participated actively in Lumbanga—unlike his uncle, for whom Afro-descendant organizations were not available during his formative years.

Other Afro-descendants who did not identify as Indigenous also used the narratives connecting the dances with the history of Africans in Bolivia to justify their participation. For example, Camila Rivera, another active member of Lumbanga, danced with the group Kusi Jatha for the 2010 carnival after being invited to join the group by a friend. She enjoyed herself, noting differences in the degree of spectacle and attention as well as the competitive nature of the event compared to others, like the Bajada de Carnaval Afro that she had participated in. In a 2010 interview, she told me that it was very clear to her that the caporales were marked as Indigenous and Andean. However, she also said, "The caporal is a character of the Afro-Bolivian saya, so I say, no, if the caporal comes out of an Afro-Bolivian foundation, the Afro-Bolivian saya comes from the Blacks of the Yungas, then I am also dancing something that is partly Black. . . . I use the context of the Yungas, of the Afro-Bolivian saya as a personal thing, as a way of not denying my roots. I searched for that context. And from that, I justify it. It's something very personal" (interview with author, May 25, 2010). Rivera also admitted that, while she knew about the male caporal character, she did not have much context for the female character—the part that she danced. She only knew that she had to be "sensual," "delicate," and very "feminine," and she claimed that her bloc was well-known for these characteristics.

In chapter 3, I quoted Rivera's concern that others might construe her as crazy and a man-eater because of the way she dances. In that instance, Lumbanga provided a space free of such misunderstandings. One can see parallels with her participation in Kusi Jatha, which Rivera described as a group where she made good friends with whom she shared and enjoyed time. Presumably within this group, she also was not worried about these types of prejudices.

While Barria's and Rivera's stories relate to caporales, the background narratives of slavery are used to justify participation in other dances as well. Lola, a woman who was not a member of any of the Afro-descendant groups but had a long history of dancing in Andean carnival dances, stated that all these genres—marinera, cumbia, morenada—came from the time of slavery, so they were in her blood—*la raza negra* (the Black race).[22] For both Barria and Rivera, the narrative of the caporales as derived from an Afro-Bolivian expression gave them the confidence and rationale in which to ground their participation and performances in the caporales. As Rivera pointed out, however, this is a personal perspective and does not affect the greater incentive to style the caporales as Indigenous within the context of the Carnaval Andino. Might there be a situation in which the audience might call this styling of Blackness into question?

A Shift in Style: Calling Attention to a Different Blackness

It was the second night of the Carnaval Andino 2009 and the caporales San Pedro de Totora were worried. While they had scored well the first night of competition, the Reales Brillantes troupe had done much better and led the pack. San Pedro de Totora knew that they needed to adjust their choreography to distinguish themselves in front of the judges. As a result, on that second night, after the male caporal dancers entered the judges' area, they split into two parallel sections, allowing the female dancers to pass in between.

Once the troupe filled the area, the dancers in the center parted to leave a circular open space. The band played a break in the music that the troupe punctuated with a cheer. After a short interlude, the band interrupted the regular double beat of the bombo drum to insert a different song with a different rhythm. This allowed a man and a woman to dance solo to this new rhythm. One announcer recognized the new song and tried to sing along. The group Sayanta, from Oruro, Bolivia, had made the song famous, and its lyrics translate as, "The Black woman will be in the coffee fields dancing the saya. How good she is!"[23] The female dancer that night may not have been identifiably Black, but the male dancer was a well-known member of the Bravo family—one of those family names locally recognized as Afro-descendant. They danced in the center circle: the woman waving the edge of her purple, calf-length dress up and down as the man, knees bent, alternately outstretched his arms. Both circled around each other as they spun frequently. As they danced, the other announcer reprimanded the audience with a line from a prepared script, "And you? Why do you confuse the saya with the caporal? The saya comes from the Yungas region and is an Afro-Bolivian mix in memory of those who came from that continent." After performing several more repetitions of the song's chorus, the band and the dancers stopped.

After the two dancers exited the area, another single male dancer came forward with a whip in one hand and an electric-blue, particularly large hat (the same as those used by the caporal in the negritos) in the other hand. He imitated a vicious slave captain's behavior by thrashing the whip violently to the ground. On behalf of the troupe, the announcer admitted, "Yes, it is true. I am the caporal, the headman of the plantation, he who marked the rhythm of the slaves." The band played a break and the rest of the troupe sprang back into action (see video 6.5 to watch this interlude).

I cannot say whose decision it was to perform this vignette in San Pedro's choreography. The troupe must have felt that their choreography accomplished its goal that evening, however, because the following night they repeated the same choreography. They earned a consistent score, and although they did not catch the Reales, they finished in a respectable second place. One must avoid reading too much into the troupe's decision that night. San Pedro could simply have been trying to demonstrate its knowledge of the narrative behind the dance and perhaps earn additional points from the judges for doing their research. From my perspective, however, what they accomplished that night was a shift in style that temporarily took the audience away from those features that make the caporales an example of Indigenous style by referencing another set of performers, Afro-descendant ones. Note that the short vignette had little to do with Afro-Bolivian saya in the formal, generic sense: costumes, rhythm, instrumentation, step—all of that was a mismatch. Yet I suspect the direct show of aggressiveness toward Afro-descendant characters broke the carnivalesque frame. The shift in style called attention to the markers of Blackness that had been previously eclipsed by other references to Indigenous performance.

Styling Blackness and the Carnivalesque Racial Order

I began this chapter explaining that a discourse of Indigeneity, particularly in terms of Aymara culture, has dominated the way in which organizers and performers have framed music-dance in the Carnaval Andino. This discourse means that spectators often understand performances as related to Indigenous peoples and that performers are prone to style themselves in this way. Indeed, I did not discuss the many Carnaval Andino troupes that dance allegories related to Indigenous people, like tinkus and tobas.

Amid these other troupes, however, there are narratives and performance characteristics that reference alternate relationships, particularly with Blackness. Throughout this chapter, I have described the tension between Indigeneity and Blackness in two music-dance genres. Analyzing these genres through the lens of the carnivalesque, one finds that the historic racial structure of power could be partially inverted if those who identify as Indigenous could degrade the Blacks of the distant past via humor related to the body and the material—laughing at phenotype, sexuality, and wealth.

By now, of course, much of this humor is systemic, propagated by the structures of tradition, with few individuals reflecting on the racial ideas that were part of their foundation. Participation in a genre is often based on ideas of age and the relationships one has with friends and family, although a performer's self-identification as Indigenous does come into play. Attending to the involvement of Afro-descendants in the carnival, however, can be instructive; it brings attention to the case when the Blackness being styled becomes self-referential. The last vignette about the 2009 San Pedro de Totora performance demonstrates how thinking about these performances in terms of style, that is, how these performances relate to the two populations, can be productive. By making the narrative of Blackness in the caporales explicit, those performers who might identify as Black asked performers and spectators alike to recall the role in which a Black population played in the production of the expression. Yet the implicit suggestion was for the audience to consider Black participation in the history of the larger Andean region, with the added possibility of considering an actual Black presence in Arica among them today. I believe that the fact that this Blackness appeared in a situation that was otherwise marked as Indigenous is suggestive of the larger history of Afro-descendants in Chile and the Americas.

Notes

1. In Aymara, "con la fuerza del sol" is sometimes translated as *intin ch'amampi*, and some people will use this phrase to refer to the same carnival. Caution is necessary, however, because in the early years of the Carnaval Andino, another carnival called Intin Ch'amampi was held as an alternative to the one sponsored by the city. Eventually the two merged to become the current Carnaval Andino.

2. Wiphala is the word for flag in the Aymara language.

3. Although efforts are underway to revive the Aymara language, the actual number of fluent speakers among locals in the region is minimal.

4. Other representations are also present in these publications. Chile, while White, may be depicted as a roto (see chap. 1), unshaven and in more rural clothing. Peru can be found as having a split personality, between *cholos* (interpreted as rural Indigenous people attempting to act as city dwellers) and unsophisticated Black vagabonds. Of course, individual personalities, whether politicians or military generals, are caricatured in more formal dress.

5. The demarcation is the same and related to that described in chapter 5—dances presumably derived from or part of folklore.

6. See chapter 1.

7. In Oruro, the performance of these dances happens during an event called Anata, after the Aymara word for carnival. This event is separate from the actual celebration of carnival in the troupes' home communities.

8. Buisson-Wolff (1964, 163) has suggested that mine owners in colonial Bolivia made this argument to the Spanish Crown in response to its attempts to legislate the substitution of cheap Indigenous labor with more expensive African slaves. She also noted the important presence of African slaves in lower altitudes, where more Spaniards owned land and could produce crops to support the populations living in the mine cities.

9. The call to ground carnival studies in ethnography and to complicate simple binary Marxist interpretations of power in carnival is, of course, not limited to Averill. For a spectrum of academic perspectives on carnival, see *Carnival Art, Culture and Politics: Performing Life*, Micaeline Crichlow, ed. Routledge: New York. 2012.

10. As mentioned previously, this term reflects use in the literature rather than local use in Arica.

11. According to a description on the 2012 Con la Fuerza del Sol website, they started in the Aguas Calientes sulfur mines found in the highland district of General Lagos in 1938. Over time, the troupe arrived in Arica.

12. Likewise, members of Achachis broke off to form the morenada Los Fanáticos (c. 2007). Other morenadas include the San Pedro de Totora, Papel Pampa, Los Intocables, La Poderosa Azapa and Residentes Bolivianos.

13. Named after the morenada Verdadero Intocables that dance in La Paz for the celebration of El Señor del Gran Poder.

14. I did occasionally hear the term *chinas*, often explained as a Quechua term for servant but also found as a caste in some regions of Latin America. In Chile, china is also associated with the rural female peasant.

15. Negritos is another Bolivian religious-carnival genre that I documented in Arica within a more religious context. It would later appear in the Carnaval Andino in 2013–15, but for length is omitted here. For more information, see Wolf 2013.

16. There is clearly an association of Blacks with pipe smoking in Latin America, although I am uncertain why. The Americanism cachimbo, for example, refers to a crude pipe commonly smoked by elderly Black men and could be used to refer to arrogant Blacks. As mentioned earlier, it is also the name of a music-dance genre representative of the Tarapaca region. See Loyola 1994.

17. The Señor del Gran Poder (Lord of Great Power) is one of the three major celebrations that incorporate these types of dances in Bolivia, the other two being the Carnival of Oruro and the Feast of the Virgin of Urkupiña. See Guss (2006).

18. Female caporales performers in associated religious dance troupes within Chile (i.e., from the folclórico troupes discussed in chap. 5) have altered the female costume by adding numerous layers of underskirts to prevent such revealing situations and cover the dancer's legs to the knees. People were clearly aware of this phenomenon, although most people I spoke with did not directly discuss it.

19. Recently, some young women have begun dressing in the male costume as new characters called *machas*. I use the distinction between male and female caporales dancers here more as a reference to costume. I was not aware of any males dancing in the female caporales costumes, although recently cross-dressing cholas have been appearing in the morenadas that dance in La Paz. This practice has precedent. When no women were present in the comparsas, all such characters were played by men.

20. The women might also be read as Black, however, as mentioned earlier, the common ratio of Black males to females in the colonial era suggests otherwise.

21. Cristian Báez of Lumbanga had introduced me to Gabriel Huanca, hence the rationale behind Huanca's introduction.

22. This woman's perspective was like that of Victoria Santa Cruz and her concept of ancestral memory. See chapter 2, note 4.

23. *La negra estará, en el cafetal, bailando la saya, ¡qué buena que está!*

7

A QUESTION OF SUCCESS

Carnivalization and the Future of Styling

In 2016, I decided to drop in on a cajón workshop being held as part of a neighborhood cultural festival in Arica. After the Peruvian guest instructor finished teaching a few different rhythms, an informal jam session began. Despite having recognized many of the attendees as members of the Afro-descendant comparsas that participate in the Carnaval Andino, I was surprised to hear them informally launch into the singing of several tumbes, some of which I had heard in 2009. One of the players grabbed a shekere (large gourd rattle) to thicken the sonic texture, and, when the guest instructor counted off, the drummers played a rhythmic figure in unison. At that cue, a female attendee, who had been drumming, decided to jump up and begin dancing. One of the cajón players began a solo, following the dancer, so that his accents coincided with the end of her movement phrases. After she sat down, that lead drummer played a call, and the jam session concluded with an orchestrated break that was familiar to many of the drummers there.

This tumbe performance caught me off guard for various reasons. First, the instrumentation was different from what I expected given my earlier experiences, even though familiar aesthetics were at play. I knew that the tumbe rhythm could be performed on cajón, but I had not expected everyone there to feel so comfortable doing so. I later learned that this had become a common practice outside of the comparsa setting. Secondly, while the practice of a lead drummer following a dancer is found in various parts of the diaspora, I had only seen Sabor Moreno perform the tumbe in this fashion on YouTube. The fact that the practice arose spontaneously during a jam session and conversations afterward suggested to me that this aesthetic had become part of the general fabric of tumbe performance in Arica, again pointing to changes that the tumbe carnaval has undergone since I had first witnessed its performance in 2006.

In this final chapter, I examine the changes that styling Blackness as Afro-descendant through the tumbe carnaval has undergone and those social changes that the tumbe has helped bring about. Tumbe performance has contributed to Arica's Afro-descendants gaining recognition, both in terms of regional culture and politics. Similar spaces are just beginning to open up on the national level, and the state has made some moves to recognize Afro-descendant culture. Continued pressure from both the regional and international levels on the central government may result in further resources being ceded to Chilean Afro-descendant communities. These gains, however, bring new challenges, as the tumbe carnaval becomes accessible to a wider group of Chileans. Questions arise as to the value of sharing culture under the multicultural alignment and the ability of the tumbe or other forms of styling Blackness to continue to create opportunities for Afro-descendants. In the wake of these current developments, I conclude by considering the impact a discussion of styling Blackness can have on the understanding of Chilean culture and the African diaspora in general.

Government Interest in the Tumbe: Supporting Local Development and Cultural Heritage

As a unique cultural expression within Chile, the tumbe carnaval fits perfectly into what Paschel (2016) referred to as the "multicultural alignment" in Latin American politics (see introduction). This orientation ascribes specific protections and rights to communities based on cultural difference. Somewhat paradoxically, government structures designed to support national culture can bolster a community's claims of difference, leading to the securing of such protections and rights. This process often results from the state's interest in economic "development," which it associates with the promotion of tourism to a specific region through culture, but it can also reflect a community's growing political awareness, which helps it take advantage of the state's cultural programs.

For example, in chapter 2, I mentioned how the original tumbe pasacalle in 2003 was made possible in part by a government grant known as a FONDART.[1] Several of these grants have the specific goal of promoting cultural development with an eye toward the formation of a region's identity and its local cultures, particularly for Indigenous peoples.[2] In the region of Arica-Parinacota, individuals and groups have won FONDARTs based on Afro-descendant cultural expressions, reflecting local recognition of this population's presence. The grants in the "Regional Cultural Advancement" category have generally marked the emergence of new groups performing tumbe carnaval. After splitting off from Oro Negro, the group Lumbanga used a 2003 grant to purchase instruments and travel to Santiago to perform. Gustavo del Canto won a 2006 grant to found a cultural school, which would teach and recruit new tumbe carnaval performers for the troupe that Oro Negro sponsored in Arica's annual urban carnival. These students, however, eventually separated from Oro Negro to become Arica Negro. Finally, another Santiago migrant, Pedro Méndez, helped win a grant to take tumbe carnaval into the schools. He was supported by the most recent group to break off from Oro Negro—the Comparsa Tumba Carnaval—a group whose membership included some of the performers from the original 2003 project. While personal tensions between individuals created divisions among the different groups, the FONDARTs enabled the spread of tumbe carnaval practice to a larger number of people, as each new group sought new members. The repeated willingness of the regional Council for Culture and the Arts to fund a variety of people and groups performing tumbe resonated with these FONDARTs' goal of the advancement of the tumbe as a regional expression. This goal is associated with ideas of economic development, as a unique cultural expression is believed to attract tourism to the region.

One might question whether the propagation of tumbe performance reflected a growth in the actual number of people identifying themselves as Afro-descendant. While the government did not conceive of "Regional Cultural Advancement" grants for this purpose, Afro-descendant political activists have put other FONDART grants—those aimed at the "Conservation and Advancement of Intangible Cultural Heritage"—to this use. Lumbanga designed its 2006 project to raise awareness about Afro-Chilean intangible heritage as a way to get local individuals who might identify as Afro-descendant to understand the meaning of this ethnoracial term. Doing so would mean that these individuals would likely register as such in an upcoming census. The project involved the creation of radio and television programs, the distribution of a limited run of newspapers, and a show at the municipal theater. While the Chilean government has yet to put a question on the national census that allows Afro-descendants to identify, it did recognize members of the Afro-descendant senior citizen club Julia Corvacho as Living Human Treasures (*Tesoros Humanos Vivos*) in 2011. The tagline for the Living Human Treasure project is "Bearers of Intangible Cultural Heritage."

The preceding examples illustrate the Afro-descendants' organizations' strategic use of existing grants. This continued use has slowly led to structural changes. While not a direct result of the growing number of Afro-descendant performances in the region, several people who identify as Afro-descendant have been appointed to leadership posts in the regional government. In 2015, José Barraza, who identifies as Afro-descendant, was named the new director of the regional Council of Culture and the Arts, and one of the council members during that year was an Afro-descendant leader within the Tumba Carnaval organization, Arturo Carrasco. In 2016, the council created a new trajectory within the FONDART system, unique to the Arica-Parinacota: a line dedicated to Afro-descendant projects. Applicants had to identify as Afro-descendant or be sponsored by an Afro-descendant organization. Theoretically, the creation of this line recognizes the importance of the Afro-descendant population to the region and means that at least one Afro-descendant project will be sponsored annually.

In 2013, Chilean president Michelle Bachelet proposed that the national Council of Culture and the Arts should be elevated to a cabinet-level ministry that also recognized the multicultural nature of the state. The government sent representatives to all the regions of Chile for a prior consultation about any structural blueprints or questions that Indigenous groups might have for a new Ministry of Cultures, Arts, and Heritage. In the case of the Arica-Parinacota region, the representative also invited the Afro-descendant organizations to participate. This action led to an interesting paradox, because the government had yet to approve a law officially recognizing Afro-descendants, unlike the case of the Indigenous groups consulted.[3] As director José Barraza pointed out to me in a 2016 interview, however, the inclusion of Afro-descendants in the consultation suggested that the government was treating Afro-descendants as a "tribal people," a legal designation that holds equivalent human rights status as Indigenous peoples under the International Labor Organization's Convention 169 on Indigenous and Tribal Peoples, originally established in 1989. Chile signed the convention in 2008. The convention requires consultation with these groups prior to the passing of any legislation or administrative changes that affect them. Barraza believed that the regional Council of Culture and the

Arts played an important role in making Afro-descendant organizations part of this consultation. The council's long-term history of programming and working with Afro-descendant performing groups helped make the Afro-descendant community visible in the region and on the national level. Of course, Barraza was quick to recognize the sustained work of the Afro-descendant organizations themselves in "knocking on doors and being found."

The "Carnivalization" of the Afro-descendant Comparsas

Not all the events the council has planned with Afro-descendant organizations, however, have been well attended. Since 2014, the regional Council of Culture and the Arts has supported an event in Arica known as the *Semana Afro* ("Afro Week"). The weeklong celebration features workshops and lectures on Afro-descendant performance, history, and political issues, closing with a concert by a well-known musical artist. During the planning for the 2016 version, I witnessed Afro-descendant activists critique various aspects of this event; organizers and outsiders alike complained that members of the Afro-descendant organizations tended to participate in the activities oriented toward performance and be absent from those focused on history and politics. Critics attributed this phenomenon to the "carnivalization" of Afro-descendant culture. In this context, "carnivalization" refers to the negative consequences of the changes the tumbe carnaval has undergone in becoming a fixture within the municipally sponsored Carnaval Andino. The carnival gives the different troupes their highest level of visibility within Arica as they perform before tourists, residents, politicians, and judges, but, as the critics suggest, this visibility has a price. From their perspective, carnival participation can trivialize the tumbe as purely entertainment rather than a tool for cultural revitalization. Tumbe performers within the Carnaval Andino might worry more about success in this event rather than the political goals associated with the Chilean Afro-descendant movement. Here I describe the characteristics of carnival participation that have opened up the tumbe carnaval groups to these criticisms. These characteristics point to a performance orientation that continues to style Blackness as Afro-descendant, but that does not place as much importance on resonating with cultural memory of the local Afro-descendant community.

The presence of judges at the carnival reminds everyone that the event is a competition with much to be gained. Winning not only gives the troupe members a sense of pride, it also gives them the resources to offset some of the expenses of participating. Even if they do not win, the members' friends and neighbors learn to identify them as dancers within a troupe or music-dance genre. The popularity of the troupes and the carnival itself means that the politicians in Arica have also taken notice. The local authorities participate in the opening ceremonies of the carnival and are sometimes even convinced to come down from the judges' platform and dance with various groups. The carnival troupe organizers have some political clout, for while the troupes do not endorse specific candidates, people running for city council may make promises designed to appease dancers' desires, as expressed by these organizers. For example, in the 2016 elections, several city council candidates promised to advocate for building a special parade route and structure, like Rio de Janeiro's Sambadrome, to support the carnival.

Given these stakes, the troupes generally aim to create a spectacle within their allotted time in front of the judges. One of the ways to accomplish this goal is by having many dancers. As Hector Mamani Huanca put it, "small groups have a hard time. The large groups have a lot of support" (interview with author, September 14, 2009). When the carnival troupes first formed, however, many faced a problem: the number of people who could identify with a specific village or expression was limited. For example, given that migrant Bolivians started many of the folclórico troupes, they initially only wanted other Bolivians to participate. Over time, the troupes loosened this requirement, particularly as the members began to intermarry with locals and their children became old enough to dance. These children wanted their friends to join, and soon the troupes, while representing Indigenous culture in the eyes of many, became organizations with many members who did not identify as Indigenous. All of this happened during the Carnaval Andino's antecedent, La Ginga. The growth of the Andean troupes signaled the end of the city-sponsored Ginga, as the troupes gained the political and social clout to shape the urban carnival more toward their liking. This transformation eventually resulted in the current manifestation of the Carnaval Andino.

The growth of the troupes resulted in other transformations as well. People made distinctions between those troupes that have more Indigenous members and those that do not. People who identify as Indigenous tend to feel more comfortable within troupes with more Indigenous members. Earlier, I recounted how Juan Carlos Mamani Morales alluded to a spirit of fellowship and sharing that he experienced differently in troupes with more Indigenous members. That sharing recognizes the spirit of carnival rituals connected to Andean villages. Sharing means not preventing anyone from participating, yet that participation should come with a sense of enjoyment in the dance coupled with participation from the crowd. The problem with the competition, Mamani complained, is that the troupes worry too much about the choreography and individuals lose the spirit of dancing with all their soul.

The tumbe carnaval groups have undergone similar processes, especially after a 2010 split among several of the Afro-descendant activist groups. The split meant that three separate troupes (Arica Negro, Oro Negro, and Tumba Carnaval) now participated within the urban carnival space, and organizers could create a new Afro-descendant category of competition for 2011. The troupe Tumba Carnaval took many of Oro Negro's performers in the separation and recruited heavily for the following year. It saw itself as free to pursue its own artistic goals and innovated its choreography, costume, and music performance. The carnival judges responded positively to these innovations, awarding Tumba Carnaval first place for four consecutive years. Oro Negro, in the meantime, worked hard to rebuild and sought out new members. Thus, all the groups grew. While every troupe always had members who did not necessarily identify as Afro-descendant, the rapid growth led to an apparent decline in the ratio of members who identify as Afro-descendant to those who do not. The increase in membership also led to complaints about the loss of a sense of intimacy within the groups. With increased membership came an increase in tension among members in the groups, and some people reported that Afro-descendant families began to leave the troupes to avoid such tension.

The competitive aspect also appears to have sped up the tempo of the rhythm, unintentionally excluding another group: senior citizens. In 2016, various experienced performers complained that there was no variation in the tempo—everything was played fast—perhaps to show virtuosity. One drummer remarked, however, that this increased tempo resulted in the exodus of older dancers from the carnival troupes. Those that remained, he said, could only carry a banner or dance along with a basic step.

More experienced members discovered that the new, particularly younger members joined the troupe without a sense of the spirit of the dance. As Paula Gallardo explained, "When the carnival arrived, we realized that not everyone understood the dance: that it is about happiness; about not showing tiredness; that if the costume fits badly, that it doesn't matter—because if I am happy, the people will not notice. So we were left thinking, 'What are we going to do? We can't continue to accept people if they do not understand this'" (interview with author, September 20, 2016). Even more disconcerting for these experienced performers was the fact that some of the newer members did not even know the origin of the dance they were performing, saying only that they were dancing "Afro." Troupe members found it particularly embarrassing when these members could not answer journalists' questions about the tumbe.

The Tumba Carnaval organization decided to create a setting called *la escuelita* (the little school). Aspiring members were required to participate in the training that the escuelita provided, and not everyone who attended the escuelita would be allowed to enter the comparsa. The criteria for selection, however, still seem to be largely performance-based, that is, whether the dancer could properly execute the steps with the desired attitude, as opposed to familiarity with other aspects of local Afro-descendant culture. Not every instructor within the escuelita explained the dance within its cultural and political context. Given this focus on performance, I now turn to look at how the process of styling Blackness as Afro-descendant has continued since the 2009 tumbe carnaval performance.

More Recent Ways of Styling Blackness as Afro-descendant

In the 2009 carnival, the troupes did not have many songs to perform. The only melody I heard performed at the 2009 Pascua de Negros revolved around lyrics that a member of Oro Negro, Francisco "Pancho" Piñones Chávez wrote. The song is "Tiempos de Guarapo:"

Table 7.1. "Tiempos de Guarapo" lyrics, written by Francisco Piñones Chávez. Used with permission of composer.

Eran los tiempos de guarapo	It was the season for the sap
de azúcar caña	of the sugarcane
Azapa grande	in the town of San Miguel of Azapa
Y mi abuela me decía	And my grandmother said to me
"Papito lindo, mamita linda,	"Dear little man, dear little lady,
esos sí eran carnavales."	surely those were carnivals."

In describing his composition, Piñones told me that other original songs had existed but were too long. The singers would sing one verse and then lose enthusiasm. He thought they needed something shorter and catchier to keep up the singing energy. Piñones was a practitioner of capoeira, the Brazilian martial art, and he particularly enjoyed a capoeira song that spoke of the time of the ancestors. To produce the lyrics, he combined this idea with information gleaned from del Canto's book and his own observation that elders always seem to think of the past fondly. It became so successful that I still heard it sung in 2016 at the event described in the opening vignette. Keeping older songs like this one alive is what characterizes the Oro Negro troupe.

By 2016, however, an urgency to expand the repertoire had also developed. The somewhat-neglected original lyrics of the tumbe carnaval (those that had been collected from elders but had only been sung and danced in a circle on stage) made their way into the comparsa format. Both the *copla,* or couplet, format of the collected tumbe verses and the continued use of "Tiempos de Guarapo" underscore Piñones's point that a short lyric helps the current musicians remember the words. While the copla is a Spanish poetic form, the use of shorter, repeated verses has parallels in other types of participatory music-dance in the African diaspora. Some younger tumbe musicians apparently have adopted the practice of using excerpts of known tunes as repeated phrases into tumbe performance. Puerto Rican songs seem to be favored, although performers do not necessarily recognize them as such. For example, *plena* is a Puerto Rican national genre with a couplet structure performed on hand-frame drums called *panderetas*. At the 2016 cajón workshop, I heard the chorus of the well-known plena "Mañana por la mañana," performed as a tumbe. In addition to these couplet choruses sung in unison, one comparsa member took the first line of "Quítate de la vía, Perico," a guaracha made famous by the Puerto Rican group Cortijo y su Combo, and continuously repeated the second line, "que ahí viene el tren," creating an underlying ostinato for a lead vocalist or drummer. This type of dynamic is a diasporic resource that can be found across the Americas, and several genres have incorporated this ostinato-led device into their performances at later points in their development, including Puerto Rican plenas.[4] This "call-and-response" device increases the intensity of a performance, making it attractive to tumbe performers.

The use of lyrics from plenas and certain guarachas suggests that the influence of Puerto Rico appears to have become stronger in the last few years—especially the expression most commonly associated with Puerto Ricans of

African descent, the bomba. As one tumba performer explained to me, two aspects of bomba practice worked their way into the performance of Sabor Moreno: the use of the *cuá* and the interaction between a solo dancer and the lead drum.[5] The cuá is a rhythmic pattern played with sticks on wood (traditionally the side of the drum), but the term can also refer to a separate instrument itself, usually a small barrel or piece of wood that the sticks strike. Sabor Moreno has begun incorporating this sound via a mounted hollowed-out piece of wood, playing a steady eighth-and-two-sixteenth notes pattern. This pattern reinforces the rhythm played on the shekeres and güiros but with a different timbre. The most influential aspect of Sabor Moreno's tumbe performances has been the interaction between the dancer and the drummer (which some tumbe performers call a *contrapunto*). I witnessed this interaction in several contexts, both at the event in the opening vignette and in staged performances. This is considered fundamental practice during bomba performances but did not become part of tumbe performance generally until at least 2010.

Some of the new tumbe music sampled songs referencing divine spirits (known as *orishas/orixas*) from Afro-Cuban Santería or Afro-Brazilian Candomblé, together with their associated popular practices. For example, one of the tumbes uses a phrase from a Cuban *montuno* that declares, "con los santos no se juegan" (you don't play with the saints). Another is taken from a merengue that asks, "Yemayá, quítame lo malo y tíralo al mar" (Yemayá, remove evil from me and throw it to the sea). The reference here is to the Yoruba goddess associated with motherhood and the ocean. In several places in the diaspora, particularly Brazil, participants send offerings out onto the ocean on February 2, asking for good fortune from this goddess. Through migration, this practice has been adopted in other regions, for example, in Uruguay (see Andrews 2010, 173). In Arica, at least by 2013, some members of the Comparsa Tumba Carnaval and the Julia Corvacho senior citizen circle began to publicly celebrate a ceremony in which participants dress in white and throw flowers into the ocean while musicians and dancers perform tumbe on the beach. Anyone was welcome to participate. The key sign-object relationship here seems to be with the ocean, which plays an important role in the life of many families in Arica, particularly those who make their living from the sea. Some have commented that this event has become a unifying one, with performers from the various carnival troupes coming together and no group specifically in charge. Styling Blackness as Afro-descendant through a ceremony to Yemayá mimics ceremonies throughout the Black Atlantic, particularly Brazil and Cuba.

Such practices illustrate that styling Blackness as Afro-descendant through the tumbe carnaval continues to emerge, even as it draws on different sources. While I have focused here on the ways that the carnival troupes have styled Blackness as Afro-descendant by referring to the Black Atlantic (or Black Center from a Black Periphery perspective), an undercurrent of tumbe performance does exist that occasionally gives precedent to the local. In 2017, for example, the Comparsa Tumba Carnaval's presentation in front of the judges featured the Ño Carnavalon, the figure within local tradition that is unearthed and comes to life to oversee each year's carnival celebration, only to be buried again at the end of the week.[6] Despite this specific use of a local reference, leaders of Afro-descendant organizations who complain about the "carnivalization" of the tumbe continue to worry about uses of diasporic resources in performance for entertainment. When performers do not mitigate these uses by local cultural memory, there may be damage to the political efficacy of the tumbe. Voicing a similar sentiment, Piñones stated,

> I think that one can retrieve something from somewhere else, but—I don't know—just one part, not just show up and install it as is. I think part of it has to spring up from right here. Perhaps you can have some type of influence, but it shouldn't be noticeable, because if it is, people also begin to question what you are doing. Someday someone will come from Santiago, from somewhere else, looking for knowledge, and it could be that they doubt that this is from here because they have seen it somewhere else. You have to be careful with that, I think. (interview with author, September 20, 2016)

The question becomes how these recent changes to the tumbe in the carnival context affect the understanding of Blackness in Chile.

Questions of Black Participation and Political Orientation in the Tumbe

Beyond the structural changes that tumbe carnaval has helped create in regional cultural policy, tumbe performance and activist efforts have also led to changes in social policy. In 2010, the municipality of Arica established its own Oficina Comunal Afrodescendiente (Community Afro-descendant Office), designed specifically to orient the local Afro-descendant community to the city services available to them both as local residents and as Afro-descendants (see fig. 7.1). While the government still does not allow individuals to identify as Afro-descendant on the national census, Chile's National Institute of Statistics (INE) did conduct a pilot study of the local Afro-descendant population in 2013.

Despite these gains, questions have begun to surface as to whether tumbe performance will continue to have the same effect in the wake of the carnivalization process. Some Afro-descendant political activists claim that the tremendous growth in the number of tumbe performers, many of whom do not identify as Afro-descendant and are ignorant of the tumbe's origins, will lead to the loss of control over their heritage and an important political resource. Such activists point to situations throughout the Americas in which Afro-descendant music-dance expressions have become so popular that society has minimized their origins in Black culture, rendering these origins to a footnote within their persistent performance, for example, jazz in the United States, samba in Brazil, and candombe in Uruguay. They claim that, rather than functioning as a tool to help achieve recognition and create Afro-descendant community, the tumbe will become frivolous entertainment, insinuating that the current position of Afro-descendants within society is just fine. Lumbanga's response has been to ensure that only Afro-descendants and their families can be a part of the organization. This condition can still create difficulties, as not all Afro-descendants agree on the same political aims. And, the policy does not exclude all non-Afro-descendants from participating, since Afro-descendants may have non-Afro-descendant spouses. In general, such spouses have been incredibly supportive of Afro-descendant organizations, but some activists complain that several of the spouses have spoken out strongly in meetings without displaying an awareness of Afro-descendant-related issues. In 2016, a combination of these factors contributed to a split in Lumbanga, leading to the formation of another organization without the exclusively Afro-descendant policy in place. Lumbanga was, as of 2018, the only group with a formal policy, but other organizations, such as Oro Negro and Arica Negro, have de facto situations in which their leaders are from Afro-descendant families and manage to keep control without membership restrictions.

Few people actually advocate for the "tumbe only for Afro-descendants" perspective. Some have labeled the idea discriminatory. One individual I spoke with argued that limiting tumbe performance solely to Afro-descendants would simply be responding to discrimination with more discrimination, perpetuating differences between groups that would continue to see one another as Other. Several individuals stated that the more people that participated in the comparsas, the better, because it gives the Afro-descendant movement more strength and impact. This argument takes as default that, even if performers are participating for their own enjoyment, they are still indirectly supporting the movement. Within this discussion, the same interviewees pointed out that, even though it was ridiculous to discuss the subject in these terms, one would find few "pure" Afro-descendants among tumbe performers. What was important, several people noted, was whether the music-dance would last and whether it would serve to represent Arica or Afro-Aricans.

The ambiguity in this last point (Arica or Afro-Aricans) illustrates one of the key issues in thinking about the continuing political efficacy of tumbe performance. The political orientation of multiculturalism offers Afro-descendants certain protections and rights dependent on their ability to demonstrate their cultural difference with other parts of mainstream society. While distinct from other parts of national culture, the development of the tumbe carnaval as a stronger marker of geographic identification, that is, regional rather than ethnoracial, weakens the argument for increasing Afro-descendants' protections and rights.

Furthermore, with members of the local Afro-descendant community as the minority within the comparsas, their voices are less likely to play a role in the creative decisions of carnival performance. Their cultural memory, which functions as an important check on the adoption of diasporic resources within the tumbe, will play a less prominent role. Cosmopolitan ideas of Blackness are likely to overwhelm the unique characteristics of the Black experience in Arica, impoverishing a deeper understanding of the diversity within the African diaspora and possibly contributing to making the Chilean Afro-descendant community invisible again. When the connection of a music-dance expression to the community it is associated with is in question, then so is its heritage.

In response to the potential disassociation of the tumbe from its political aims, a few Afro-descendants and their allies in Arica have developed two approaches. The first is to follow the path of a few international Afro-descendant groups that stress a racial equality alignment over the multicultural alignment for their political purposes. As Paschel (2016) notes, the racial equality alignment is a political orientation that recognizes that a community has faced discrimination based primarily on race. Unlike the multicultural alignment, which celebrates that community for their demonstrable cultural difference, the racial equality alignment depends on a government admitting the presence of and the need to correct systemic racism—the presence of racist foundational ideas in their institutional structures and practices. The second approach is artistic, reshaping and performing the tumbe to counter the critiques of carnivalization.

Complementing Music-Dance: Efforts to Deal with Racial Inequality

Activists groups assuming the racial equality approach depend on data to call attention to the presence of systemic racism. These types of statistics are difficult to calculate without the type of information that a census can gather, which explains why the activist groups continue to emphasize the need for identification on the census (and why the government might want to deny the opportunity for such identification). I have focused on music-dance in this book because of the large part it plays in making the Afro-descendant population visible in the Chilean national imagination. Racism awareness campaigns are, to some degree, an extension of the visibility project, so that recognition of an Afro-descendant presence is a key first step to simultaneously recognizing the presence of racist attitudes. As described in chapter 3, however, Arica's Afro-descendants themselves have had a variety of experiences with discrimination, resulting in mixed attitudes toward the subject. Similar situations are also present in other countries, such as Colombia (Wade 1993, 255–56). The variety in these experiences may lead some people to doubt the presence of discrimination and the need for these visibility efforts, which in turn makes Afro-descendant activists stress the importance of a census. A census could theoretically prove, via measures such as income and employment, the presence of discrimination toward the Afro-descendant community. The pilot survey conducted by the INE in 2013 focused primarily on how many and in what ways individuals have identified as Afro-descendant. Unfortunately, while some labor information was gathered, the INE cautioned against making comparisons with national statistics, and the report presented few calculations to compare with national figures.

Afro-descendant activists, however, are not simply waiting for the government to collect such data but are working individually and in groups to address the needs of the Afro-descendant population that they understand may be a result of systemic racism. Although Cristian Báez is better known among the Afro-descendant movement as general coordinator of Lumbanga, beginning in 2014, he helped organize and participate in the Comité de Allegados Cimarrones Afroazapeños (The Committee of Afro-Azapaean Escaped Slave Kin). This committee is working with the regional offices of the Ministry of Housing and the Ministry of National Assets to solve the problem of a housing shortage in the Azapa Valley. Given that the term *cimarrones* references runaway slaves seeking shelter, the committee seeks to frame its discourse in terms of finding historically and culturally relevant solutions. In 2016, thanks to its work with the ministry offices mentioned above, the committee identified and began to develop a neighborhood in the Llosyas-Alto Ramírez sector of the Azapa Valley with housing for eighty Afro-descendant families. This development was important for families from the Pago de Gómez sector of the valley, who have been displaced by gentrification.

Similarly, to address economic issues facing members of the Afro-descendant population, Lumbanga worked with the National Company for the Promotion of Production (CORFO), a government agency aimed at supporting public and private industry to create a two-year program called the Nódo ECAFRO, or ECAFRO hub. The acronym ECAFRO abbreviated the full name of the project, which translated to "Afro-descendant Cultural Expressions: An Ethno-touristic Perspective for the Community's Productive Development." As this name implied, the project aimed to provide promotional and logistical resources to Afro-descendant entrepreneurs who run businesses related to aspects of their culture. The hope was that these businesses would entice people interested in having novel cultural experiences to participate in the local economy. In its first year, the hub produced a video featuring four entrepreneurs: Marlene Huerta, an artisan of Afro-descendant dolls; Gino Kalise, an instructor of Afro-descendant music and dance, particularly for therapeutic purposes; Las Hermanas Lara, culinary artists representing La Chimba; and Francisco Piñones, a maker of tumbe carnaval drums. Additional businesses that received support included a maker of gourd shekeres and a weaver of reed baskets. While Lumbanga helped start the project, the Lara family is connected with Arica Negro, and Piñones has worked with both Oro Negro and Arica Negro, indicating that members of other Afro-descendant organizations are participating. The hub also provided workshops in basic business skills like bookkeeping and getting loans. While some participants complained that the hub has not been as active as it could be, the main point here is that politically engaged Afro-descendant organizations recognize and try to address the existence of other types of systemic issues. While the type of data they need to make a stronger racial equality argument is lacking, Afro-descendant organizations with political orientations continue to use cultural activities to address these needs, allowing local Afro-descendants in the Arica-Parinacota region to find homes and earn income.

Figure 7.1. The entrance to the rural extension of the municipal Community Afro-descendant Office in September 2016. San Miguel de Azapa, Azapa Valley, Arica-Parinacota region, Chile. Note: while the Afro-descendant Office continues, the controversial decision to close this extension was made just a few months after this photo was taking, making it harder for Afro-descendants who live in rural areas to access the Office's services.

The Reclaiming Response: The Burgeoning of Small Performance Groups

An alternate response to the carnivalization of the tumbe has been a move to reclaim the intimacy of the smaller groups that originally performed the expression. A few of the individuals who argued that large numbers of performers in the comparsas supported the Afro-descendant movement nevertheless felt compelled to complement their participation in these groups by starting or participating in small performance troupes. Others simply quit the comparsas altogether to be in these smaller groups. In 2008, the only small group consistently performing was Sabor Moreno. By 2016, several other smaller groups had appeared on the scene, some focused more on artistry and others on politics. The artistic groups sought greater creative freedom than the current size of comparsas allowed and the sense of camaraderie that was present when the comparsas were smaller. These smaller groups also wanted to address concerns over how knowledgeable comparsa performers were and what they represented in the public eye.

One such group was Afro-Raices, founded by Angee Castillo, a former dancer for Arica Negro. Castillo identifies as an Afro-descendant from Iquique, although she grew up in Calama. She discovered the Afro-descendant movement when she came to study in Arica. Before participating in Arica Negro, she had gained dance experience as a member of the Universidad de Tarapacá's well-known Ballet Folclórico. This dance training helped her to quickly become a dance director for Arica Negro. While appreciative of everything she learned, she felt she wanted to do more, saying "In a comparsa, one always has to dance in a line, and one does not vary from that parameter and you keep doing the same thing. I have another background in dance. Because I danced in Arica Negro, I only represented one part of the tumbe. I felt limited. I said to myself—this is not just about tumbe—I know there is more, and I want to know more and through research, through participation in certain ceremonies and customary festivities, bring those to the stage" (interview with author, September 24, 2016). As an example, Castillo stated that she developed a choreography about the arrival of Afro-descendants to the former section of La Chimba. While Afro-Raices is relatively new, Castillo has gained the respect of several local Afro-descendant leaders because she has consulted with them as she constructs her choreographies and she has attended the meetings and events of the Afro-descendant organizations. Like Sabor Moreno,

Afro-Raices not only dances tumbe carnaval but also presents a range of "Afro-Latin American" dances. The recorded performances that I have seen on the internet include tumbes that chant or mention the orishas.[7] Afro-Raices, then, does follow the same styling Blackness as Afro-descendant patterns that I described earlier. However, Castillo stated, "My vision has expanded, because being a leader of a group, I am obliged to go to all the meetings. At these meetings, one goes to seminars, lectures, roundtables, sharing with people, meeting them and it is giving one the opportunity to know more about this culture than being in one troupe could" (Ibid.). Castillo pointed out that Afro-Raices differs from Sabor Moreno in that Sabor Moreno presents individual songs and dances tumbe freely, while Afro-Raices performs choreographies designed to tell specific stories—an approach informed by Castillo's background in folkloric ballet.

The focus on telling stories is also what Claudia Parra Aravena does in her role as songwriter for the group Aluna Tambo. This all-female group plays tumbe as well as what they call "Afro-Mandingue," a performance practice that they learned from a West African musician and dancer working in Antofagasta. They describe Afro-Mandingue as music performed on djembe. Because of Parra's experience playing and dancing tumbe, the group invited her to join them when they needed a lead singer for tumbe songs. Parra traces her family heritage to the South of Chile, but she grew up in Arica. Because she had danced with Oro Negro for several years, she became the spokesperson for the nongovernmental organization of the same name once she graduated with her degree in journalism. She later joined Tumba Carnaval after the split and was elected the queen of the comparsa in 2016. After years in the movement, she now identifies as Afro-descendant, in part because she discovered she had an Afro-Venezuelan ancestor several generations back and in part because of her efforts within the movement. Her songwriting efforts are relatively recent but have focused on writing tumbes based on different experiences. In "Tumbe Sanador" ("Healing Tumbe"), for example, Parra describes how a sick person discovers people dancing tumbe in the streets and heals himself through his own participation in the dance. The song uses a two-line rhyming copla format, four of which create a verse and four of which create a chorus, and a closing call-and-response section. She wrote another, much slower tumbe in response to the speeding up of the tempo over the years. The tune "Semilla" ("Seed") tells of the oral history project that discovered the tumbe. The poetic structure is slightly different, in quatrains, but the alternation of two melodic phrases is similar. Aluna Tambo illustrates the percussion skills learned via its Afro-Mandingue training in the arrangements, and the all-female makeup of the musicians is in stark contrast to the usual male-dominated drum section of other groups. This all-female focus parallels the emergence of a few all-female Afro-descendant activist groups, such as Luanda and the Afro-Chilean Rural Woman's Organization Hijas de Azapa.

Both Parra and Castillo are aware of the political efforts of Afro-descendant activists, and both think of themselves as enriching the cultural possibilities of tumbe carnaval while expressing something about local Afro-descendant culture. Although Parra has found her songwriting voice in Aluna Tambo, she continues to participate in the Comparsa Tumba Carnaval, in part because she has been involved in the movement a long time and has seen many changes. When I asked her whether she worried about the carnivalization process erasing the political reasons behind dancing tumbe, she eventually replied, "The movement is still young. That's why I am calm. Because I believe that the moment we are in now—it's an adolescent movement, at all levels. For example, at the political level, we are still trying to get the law approved—still discussing, still changing words, it is an adolescent, too" (interview with author, September 29, 2016).

Styling Blackness as Chile's Own Diasporic Resources

The emergence of these smaller groups attempts to address some of the limitations in styling Blackness as Afro-descendant within the urban carnival setting, and, once again, it illustrates how individuals style Blackness in many ways according to context. The Chilean Afro-descendant movement has largely relied on styling Blackness as Afro-descendant through the tumbe carnaval. This type of performance proved politically efficacious in the context of the initial phase of the movement, in which activists could gain visibility rapidly using selected diasporic resources—ones that resonated with the findings of the initial oral history project, that is, the elders' cultural memories. From this perspective, it was not necessary—or completely possible—to exactly replicate a (patchily remembered) tumbe carnaval. What was important was to produce a tumbe carnaval with which Afro-descendants could identify.

One of my key aims, however, has been to juxtapose this styling of Blackness with other music-dance expressions, ones that Afro-descendants historically participated in and that complemented the heritage narrative of tumbe carnaval. As Parra suggested, the movement appears to be going through growing pains, and a more complete narrative might be in order. Thanks in part to tumbe performance, local families as well as scholars have discovered more information about Afro-descendants in Arica, and this work has expanded to Chile more generally. Beyond the recent historic works cited earlier, there are several additional history-based projects, such as a FONDART musical project about the Oases of Pica, Matilla, and Tarapacá (Daponte 2010), and student theses, such as one about Coquimbo (Arre Marfull 2008). Tumbe carnaval groups have traveled to Iquique and Valparaíso to perform and teach others how to play the genre, and some physical education teachers have studied and used the genre in their classes.[8]

Afro-descendants have also started to seek out other ways to officially represent their story. In 2016–17, the members of three morenos de paso groups, the Compañías Maria Cárcamo, Manuela de Marconi, and Corazón de Maria, applied for and received the national designation of Living Human Treasures. During the Semana Afro, some Afro-descendants began more openly celebrating the feast of San Martín de Porres, a Black Peruvian saint that had already enjoyed the devotion of some local families. The celebration of San Martín de Porres now was public, complete with the performance of a morenos de paso troupe. These choices resonate with the cultural memories of other ways of styling Blackness that have a long history in the region, providing options to those Afro-descendants who may not feel comfortable identifying within the carnival troupes.

While more research needs to be done, I suspect that parallel ways of styling Blackness as moreno, criollo, and indígena are present in how Blackness has historically been styled in Chile more generally. Currently, the tumbe carnaval is the most visible way of culturally identifying as a Chilean Afro-descendant, and its strong association with Arica can contribute to the perception that the impact of Afro-descendants in Chile are limited to the Arica-Parinacota region. By opening up the vision of Afro-descendant participation in music-dance through these parallel styling strategies, Chileans are more likely to discover the historical participation of Afro-descendants is more widespread than commonly believed, thus making national recognition of Afro-descendants in Chile, both officially and culturally, a greater imperative.

Finally, Chile is currently experiencing an influx of Black immigrants from across the Americas, from Haiti, Colombia, Peru, etc. The absence of Blackness in the Chilean national imagination, aggravated by a difficult economic situation, has meant that these immigrants have become the victims of overt racism. A public awareness of Chile's own Black heritage can help change Chileans' attitudes as they begin to uncover their personal connections to Blackness. Furthermore, while these immigrants come with their own ideas of styling Blackness, local Chilean expressions of Blackness can serve as diasporic resources for these individuals. As mentioned before, some Black immigrants in Arica find comradery and support in the tumbe carnaval troupes. A knowledge of these mechanisms of styling Blackness can be useful guides in the discovery of these resources. Indeed, until the participation of Blackness in Chile's history becomes an acceptable part of the Chilean national imagination, it is unlikely that Afro-descendants will truly be accepted as full Chilean citizens.

Notes

1. Chile's FONDART program was created in 1992, which coincided with the new coalition government's policies that were being put in place in the wake of the infamous Pinochet dictatorship. Recognizing the difficulty of expressing oneself under that suppressive regime, the FONDARTs were designed to promote new creative projects. At that time, the program only gave awards in two categories, one for arts and one for literature. These arts grants have now expanded, with awards given on both the national and regional levels with specific trajectories (líneas) designated for different types of activities at each of these levels.

2. Most national grants over time have gone to the Santiago region, with other sizable percentages given to the regions of Valparaiso, Concepción, and Los Lagos, that is, those regions with large metropolitan areas and access to important institutions of higher learning. The region-specific grants are meant to combat this centralization of resources.

3. Chile's new Ministry of Cultures, Arts, and Heritage opened its doors on March 1, 2018.

4. For more on the influence of the mambo and other forms of Cuban music on the plena, see Aparicio (1998, 33).

5. For a basic description of bomba performance, see Moore (2010, 76–79).

6. The figure of the Carnavalón has parallels in other places. In Ponce, Puerto Rico, for example, carnival performers participate in a mock burial of a sardine at the end of the festivities.

7. For an example, see Larenas Urrejola, 2015.

8. Worldwide, physical education classes are the dominant educational setting in which folkloric dances are taught. See G. G. Anne, 2005. In 2008, I met a physical education student who, together with a colleague, wrote a thesis on the tumbe and won honorable mention for their work in the government's annual contest *Haz tu tesis en cultura* (Write your thesis on culture). See Ana Belén González Fuentes and Náyade Fabiola Jiménez Morales, 2008.

BIBLIOGRAPHY

Interviews

All interviews took place in Arica, Chile, with author in Spanish unless otherwise cited

Arias Cienfuentes, Manuel Omar. August 26, 2009.
Báez Lazcano, Cristian. September 12, 2009.
Báez Rios, Azeneth. September 7, 2009.
Barraza, José. September 22, 2016.
Barría Huanca, Daniel. May 13, 2010.
Butrón, Marcos. January 14, 2009.
Castillo, Angee. September 24, 2016.
Castillo, Orlando ("Nano"). March 17, 2009.
Cortés, Patricio ("Pato"). August 27, 2009.
Del Canto Larios, Gustavo. May 10, 2010.
Estévez Valencia, Francisco. Santiago de Chile: May 16, 2010.
Gallardo Díaz, Paula. September 20, 2016.
Gutiérrez, Giovanni. December 22, 2008.
Henríquez Apón, Oscar. June 16, 2009.
Llerena, Segundo Jorge ("Chilo"). July 30, 2006.
Luza, Paulina. August 27, 2009.
Mamani Huanca, Hector. September 14, 2009.
Mamani Morales, Juan Carlos. January 27, 2009.
Olis Larronda, Yoni. September 17, 2009.
Parra Araveda, Claudia. September 29, 2016.
Piñones, Francisco. September 20, 2016.
Quispe, Martin. September 18, 2009.
Ríos Sánchez, Francisca Rosa. July 26, 2006.
Rivera, Camila. May 25, 2010.
Salgado Henríquez, Marta. September 5, 2009.
Santibáñez, Rainaldo. September 14, 2009.
Vildoso Rodríguez, Sandra. September 15, 2009.
Zavala, Fernando. January 14, 2009.
Zegarra Baluarte, Miguel. July 25, 2006.

Published Sources

Abercrombie, Thomas. 1992. "La fiesta de carnaval postcolonial en Oruro: Clase, etnicidad y nacionalismo en la danza folklórica." *Revista Andina* 10, no. 2: 279–352.
A.F.C.O. and UNESCO. 2006. *Catalogación de las manifestaciones del patrimonio inmaterial carnaval de Oruro*. Oruro, Bolivia: Viceministerio de la Cultura de Bolivia.

Albizú Labbé, Francisco. 2014. "El indigenismo de la unidad popular (Chile 1970–1973). Estado y nación entre reformismo y realidad." *Amérique Latine Histoire et Mémoire. Les Cahiers ALHIM* [Online], no. 28. http://journals.openedition.org/alhim/5116.

Andrews, George Reid. 1980.*The Afro-Argentines of Buenos Aires, 1800–1900*. Madison: University of Wisconsin Press.

———. 2010. *Blackness in the White Nation: A History of Afro-Uruguay*. Chapel Hill: University of North Carolina Press.

Ang, Ien. 1998. "Can One Say No to Chineseness? Pushing the Limits of the Diasporic Paradigm," *Boundary* 2, vol. 25, no. 3, (Autumn): 223–242.

Anne, G. G. 2005. "Dance education in the 21st century." *Journal of Physical Education, Recreation & Dance* 76, no. 5: 26–35.

Aparicio, Frances R. 1998. *Listening to Salsa: Gender, Latin Popular Music, and Puerto Rican Cultures*. Music/Culture. Hanover, NH: University Press of New England.

Arre Marfull, Montserrat. 2008. *Esclavos en la provincia de Coquimbo: Espacios e identidad del afrochileno entre 1702 y 1820*. Santiago: Universidad de Chile–Facultad de Filosofía y Humanidades. http://www.repositorio.uchile.cl/handle/2250/109753.

Averill, Gage. 1994. "Anraje to Angaje: Carnival Politics and Music in Haiti." *Ethnomusicology* 38, no. 2: 217. https://doi.org/10.2307/851739.

Ayestarán, Lauro. 1967. *El folklore musical Uruguayo*. Montevideo, Uruguay: Arca.

Báez Lazcano, Cristian. 2010. *Lumbanga: Memorias orales de la cultura Afrochilena*. Arica, Chile: Herco Editores.

Bakhtin, M. M. 1984. *Rabelais and His World*. First Midland book ed. Bloomington: Indiana University Press.

Barr-Melej, Patrick. 2001. *Reforming Chile: Cultural Politics, Nationalism, and the Rise of the Middle Class*. Chapel Hill: University of North Carolina Press.

Barros Arana, Diego. (1884) 2000. *Historia general de Chile*. Vol. 3. Santiago de Chile: Editorial Universitaria.

———. 1886. *Historia general de Chile*. Vol. 7. Santiago de Chile: Rafael Jover.

Barros, Raquel. 1962. "La danza folklórica. Su investigación y enseñanza." *Revista Musical Chilena* 16, no. 79: 60–69.

Bastien, Joseph W. 2004. "Las danzas folklóricas en las 'entradas' de Bolivia: Pachamama and [sic] chora." In *Arte expresivo Quechua; La inscripción de voces Andinas* [Quechua Verbal Artistry: The Inscription of Andean Voices], edited by Guillermo Delgado Padilla and Förderverein Bonner Amerikanistische Studien. Bonner Amerikanistische Studien 38. Aachen: Shaker.

Bauman, Richard. 2004. *A World of Others' Words: Cross-Cultural Perspectives on Intertextuality*. Malden, MA: Blackwell.

Beltrán Heredia, B. A. 1956. *El carnaval de Oruro*. Colección Cultura. Editorial Universitaria.

Bendix, Regina. 1997. *In Search of Authenticity: The Formation of Folklore Studies*. Madison: University of Wisconsin Press.

Berger, Harris. 2009. *Stance: Ideas about Emotion, Style, and Meaning for the Study of Expressive Culture*. Middleton, CT: Wesleyan University Press.

Bhabha, Homi K. 1994. *The Location of Culture*. New York: Routledge.

Bosse, Joanna. 2008. "Salsa Dance and the Transformation of Style: An Ethnographic Study of Movement and Meaning in a Cross-Cultural Context." *Dance Research Journal* 40, no. 01 (June): 45–64. https://doi.org/10.1017/S0149767700001364.

Bowser, Frederick P. 1974. *The African Slave in Colonial Peru, 1524–1650.* Stanford, CA: Stanford University Press.
Brackett, David. 2005. "Questions of Genre in Black Popular Music." *Black Music Research Journal* 25, no. 1/2: 73–92.
Briones Valentín, Viviana. 2004. "Arica colonial: Libertos y esclavos negros entre el lumbanga y las maytas." *Chungará (Arica)* 36: 813–16.
Brown, Jacqueline Nassy. 2005. *Dropping Anchor, Setting Sail.* Princeton, NJ: Princeton University Press.
Brubaker, Rogers. 2004. *Ethnicity without Groups.* Cambridge, MA: Harvard University Press.
Buisson-Wolff, Inge. 1964. *Negersklaverei und negerhandel in Hochperu : 1545–1640.* Köln; Graz: Böhlau Verlag.
Burns, Kathryn. 2011. "Unfixing Race." In *Histories of Race and Racism: The Andes and Mesoamerica from Colonial Times to the Present*, edited by Laura Gotkowitz, 57–71. Durham, NC: Duke University Press.
Busdiecker, Sara B. 2006. "We Are Bolivians Too: The Experience and Meaning of Blackness in Bolivia." PhD diss., University of Michigan. ProQuest Dissertations & Theses A&I (305309236). http://libproxy.uoregon.edu/login?url=http://search.proquest.com/docview/305309236?accountid=14698.
———. 2009. "Where Blackness Resides: Afro-Bolivians and the Spatializing and Racializing of the African Diaspora." *Radical History Review*, no. 103: 105–16.
Caldwell, Kia Lilly. 2007. *Negras in Brazil: Re-Envisioning Black Women, Citizenship, and the Politics of Identity.* New Brunswick, N.J.: Rutgers University Press.
———. 2009. "Transnational Black Feminisms in the Twenty-first Century." In *New Social Movements in the African Diaspora: Challenging Global Apartheid*, 1st ed. The Critical Black Studies Series, edited by Leith Mullings, 105–120. New York: Palgrave Macmillan.
Canto Larios, Gustavo del. 2003. *Oro Negro: Una aproximación a la presencia de comunidades afrodescendientes en la ciudad de Arica y el Valle de Azapa.* Santiago de Chile: Editorial Semblanza.
Central Intelligence Agency. n.d. "Flags of the World." *The World Factbook.* Accessed January 13, 2019. https://www.cia.gov/library/publications/the-world-factbook/docs/flagsoftheworld.html.
Chasteen, John Charles. 2004. *National Rhythms, African Roots: The Deep History of Latin American Popular Dance.* Diálogos. Albuquerque: University of New Mexico Press.
Chernoff, John Miller. 1979. *African Rhythm and African Sensibility: Aesthetics and Social Action in African Musical Idioms.* Chicago: University of Chicago Press.
Collier, Simon, and William F. Sater. 2004. *A History of Chile, 1808–2002.* 2nd. ed. Cambridge Latin American Studies 82. New York: Cambridge University Press.
Cooke, B. 1972. "Nonverbal Communication among Afro-Americans: An Initial Classification." In *Rappin' and Stylin' Out: Communication in Urban Black America.* Urbana: University of Illinois Press.
Coupland, Nikolas. 2007. *Style: Language Variation and Identity.* Key Topics in Sociolinguistics. New York: Cambridge University Press.
Cussen, Celia L. 2006. "El paso de los negros por la historia de Chile." *Cuadernos de Historia* 25 (March): 45+.

———, editor. 2009. *Huellas de África en América: Perspectivas para Chile*. 1st ed. El Saber y La Cultura. Santiago de Chile: Editorial Universitaria.

Daniel, Yvonne. 1995. *Rumba: Dance and Social Change in Contemporary Cuba*. Blacks in the Diaspora. Bloomington: Indiana University Press.

Daponte, Jean Franco. 2010. *El aporte de los negros a la identidad musical de Pica, Matilla y Tarapacá*. Santiago: Gobierno De Chile, Consejo Nacional De La Cultura Y Las Artes, Fondo Para El Fomento De La Musica Nacional, Creando Chile.

Dentith, Simon. 1995. *Bakhtinian Thought: An Introductory Reader*. Critical Readers in Theory and Practice. New York: Routledge.

Díaz Araya, Alberto. 2009. "Los Andes de bronce: Conscripción militar de comuneros Andinos y el surgimiento de las bandas de bronce en el norte de Chile." *Historia (Santiago)* 42: 371–99.

Díaz Araya, Alberto, Luis Galdames Rosas, and Rodrigo Ruz Zagal, eds. 2013. *Y llegaron con cadenas. Las poblaciones afrodescendientes en la historia de Arica y Tarapacá (Siglos XVII-XIX)*. Arica, Chile: Universidad de Tarapacá.

Díaz Araya, Alberto, Wilson Muñoz, Paulo Lanas. 2013. "Censos y disensos en Arica, Azapa y Lluta. Apuntes socio-demográficos de los afrodescendientes durante el siglo XIX." In *Y llegaron con cadenoas. Las poblaciones afrodescendientes en la historia de Arica y Tarapacá (siglos XVII-XIX)*, edited by Alberto Díaz Araya, Luis Galdámes Rosas, Rodrigo Ruz Zagal, 287–337. Arica, Chile: Universidad de Tarapacá.

Durand, Luis. 1942. *Presencia de Chile, ensayos*. Santiago, Chile: Editorial Nascimiento.

Elias, Sean, and Joe R. Feagin. 2016. *Racial Theories in Social Science: A Systemic Racism Critique*. New York: Routledge.

Erlmann, Veit. 1999. *Music, Modernity, and the Global Imagination: South Africa and the West*. New York: Oxford University Press.

———. 2000. "Communities of Style: Musical Figures of Black Diasporic Identity." In *The African Diaspora: A Musical Perspective*. Garland Reference Library of the Humanities; Critical and Cultural Musicology, edited by Ingrid T. Monson, v. 1995. v. 3, 83–101. New York: Garland.

Estrella de Arica, 2003. "Carnaval de color en 'Pascua de los Negros.'" January 6, 2003. A-5.

Feld, Steven. 1988. "Aesthetics as Iconicity of Style, or 'Lift-up-over Sounding': Getting into the Kaluli Groove." *Yearbook for Traditional Music* 20: 74. https://doi.org:10.2307/768167.

Feldman, Heidi Carolyn. 2006. *Black Rhythms of Peru: Reviving African Musical Heritage in the Black Pacific*. Music/Culture. Middletown, CT: Wesleyan University Press.

Feliú Cruz, Guillermo. 1942. *La abolición de la esclavitud en Chile*. Santiago: Santiago Universidad de Chile.

Fernández Canque, Manuel. 2007. *Arica 1868. Un tsunami y un terremoto*. Santiago de Chile: Ediciones de la Dirección de Bibliotecas, Archivos, y Museos.

Floyd Jr., Samuel A. 1991. "Ring Shout! Literary Studies, Historical Studies, and Black Music Inquiry." *Black Music Research Journal* 11, no. 2: 265. https://doi.org/10.2307/779269.

———. 1995. *The Power of Black Music: Interpreting Its History from Africa to the United States*. New York: Oxford University Press.

Forbes, Jack D., 1993. *Africans and Native Americans: The Language of Race and the Evolution of Red-Black Peoples*. 2nd ed. Urbana: University of Illinois Press.

Fox, Patricia D. 2006. *Being and Blackness in Latin America: Uprootedness and Improvisation*. Gainesville: University of Florida Press.

García Canclini, Néstor. 1995. *Hybrid Cultures: Strategies for Entering and Leaving Modernity.* Translated by Christopher L. Chiappari and Silvia L. López. Minneapolis: University of Minnesota Press.
Gates, Henry Louis. 1998. *The Signifying Monkey: A Theory of African-American Literary Criticism.* 1. New York: Oxford University Press.
Gerard, Charley with Marty Sheller. 1988. *Salsa! The Rhythm of Latin Music.* Crown Point, IN: White Cliffs Media.
Gilroy, Paul. 1993. *The Black Atlantic: Modernity and Double Consciousness.* Cambridge, MA: Harvard University Press.
Godinez Quinteros, Jorge A. 1996. *Oruro: Catedral del folklore de Bolivia.* La Paz, Bolivia: Editorial Lux.
Godoy Urzúa, Hernan. 1976. *El carácter Chileno: Estudio preliminar y selección de ensayos.* Santiago de Chile: Editorial Universitaria.
Golash-Boza, Tanya Maria. 2011. *Yo soy negro: Blackness in Peru.* New World Diasporas. Gainesville: University Press of Florida.
González Fuentes, Ana Belén, and Náyade Fabiola Jiménez Morales. 2008. "Subcultura afroariqueñay tumba carnaval como un aporte al trabajo de la diversidad intercultural en la educación física." In *Haz tu tesis en cultura.* Valparaíso, Chile: Consejo Nacional de la Cultura y las Artes.
González Miranda, Sergio, Carlos Maldonado Prieto, and Sandra McGee Deutsch, 1993. "Las ligas patrióticas." *Revista de Ciencia Sociales* 2: 54–72.
González Rodríguez, Juan Pablo. 1997. "Llamando al otro: Construcción de alternidad en la música popular chilena." *Revista Resonancias* 1, no. 1: 60–68.
———. 1998. "Música popular chilena de raíz folclórica." In *Clásicos de la música popular chilena, Vol. II, 1960–1973: raíz folclórica.* Edited by Luis Advis, Juan Pablo González Rodríguez, Fernando Carrasco, and Juan Antonio Sánchez. 9–28. Santiago, Chile: Sociedad Chilena del Derecho de Autor.
———. 1999. "Historia: Clásicos de la música popular chilena 1900–1960." In *Clásicos de la música popular chilena.* 2nd ed. Edited by Luis Advis, Juan Pablo González Rodríguez, and Sociedad Chilena del Derecho de Autor. 13–49. Santiago de Chile: Universidad Católica de Chile.
———. 2011. "Posfolklore: Raíces y globalización en la música popular chilena." *Arbor* 187, no. 751: 937–46.
———. 2012. "Música chilena andina 1970–1975: Construcción de una identidad doblemente desplazada." *Cuadernos de Música Iberoamericana* 24: 175–86.
González Rodríguez, Juan Pablo, and Claudio Rolle. 2005. *Historia social de la música popular en Chile, 1890–1950.* Santiago: Ediciones Universidad Católica de Chile.
Guss, David M. 2006. "The Gran Poder and the Reconquest of La Paz." *Journal of Latin American Anthropology* 11, no. 2: 294–328.
Hall, Stuart, David Morley, and Kuan-Hsing Chen, eds. 1996. *Stuart Hall: Critical Dialogues in Cultural Studies.* Comedia. New York: Routledge.
Herzfeld, Michael. 2005. *Cultural Intimacy: Social Poetics in the Nation-State.* 2nd ed. New York: Routledge.
Hochschild, Jennifer L., and Vesla Weaver. 2007. "The Skin Color Paradox and the American Racial Order." *Social Forces* 86, no. 2: 643–70.
Jara Hinojosa, Isabel. 2016. "Nacionalismo y política artístico-cultural de la dictadura chilena: La secretaría de relaciones culturales." *Nuevo mundo mundos nuevos.* https://doi.org/10.4000/nuevomundo.68967.

Kaeppler, Adrienne L. 2000. "Dance Ethnology and the Anthropology of Dance." *Dance Research Journal* 32, no. 1: 116.
Kivisto, Peter. 2016. *Incorporating Diversity: Rethinking Assimilation in a Multicultural Age*. London: Routledge.
Larenas Urrejola, Gissella. 2015. "Afro Raices . . . Arica, Chile 1 parte." Posted November 10, 2015. YouTube video, 7:03. https://youtu.be/HEg77Of8FHc.
Lavín, Carlos. 1948. "Nuestra señora de las peñas: Fiesta ritual del norte de Chile." *Revista Musical Chilena* 4, no. 31: 27–40.
Lenz, Rodolfo. 1909. "Programa de la sociedad de folklore chileno." Santiago: Imprenta y Encuadernación Lourdes.
León, Javier F. 2005. "Ni Inga, Ni Mandinga: Reflexiones sobre el nacionalismo criollo y la música popular en Lima." In *Actas del VI Congreso Latinoamericano IASPM-AL*. Buenos Aires, Argentina. www.uc.cl/historia/iaspm/baires/articulos/javierleon.pdf.
Levine, Lawrence W. 1977. *Black Culture and Black Consciousness: Afro-American Folk Thought from Slavery to Freedom*. New York: Oxford University Press.
Lipsitz, George. (1998) 2006. *The Possessive Investment in Whiteness: How White People Profit from Identity Politics*, Philadelphia: Temple University Press.
Llanque Ferrufino, Etzhel Arturo. 2011. "Danza de los 'negritos', pasaje histórico de la vida en la colonia." *La Patria*, March 5, Carnaval de Oruro edition.
Lloréns Amico, José Antonio, and Rodrigo Chocano Paredes, eds. 2009. *Celajes, florestas y secretos: Una historia del vals popular limeño*. Lima: Instituto Nacional de Cultura: Qhapaq Ñan.
Lockhart, James. 1994. *Spanish Peru, 1532–1560: A Social History*. Madison: University of Wisconsin Press.
Loveman, Mara. 2014. *National Colors: Racial Classification and the State in Latin America*. New York: Oxford University Press.
Loyola, Margot. 1994. *El cachimbo: Danza tarapaqueña de pueblos y quebradas*. Valparaíso: Ediciones Universitarias de Valparaíso de la Universidad Católica de Valparaíso.
———. 1996. *Bailes de tierra en Chile*. 3rd ed. Valparaíso: Ediciones Universitarias de Valparaíso de la Universidad Católica de Valparaíso.
Malone, Jacqui. 1996. *Steppin' on the Blues: The Visible Rhythms of African American Dance*. Folklore and Society. Urbana: University of Illinois Press.
Manta, Coco. 1979. *¿Por que la morenada?: Una explicación sobre su origen*. Llallagua, Bolivia: Ediciones P.E.M.
Manuel, Peter, Kenneth M. Bilby, and Michael D. Largey. 1995. *Caribbean Currents: Caribbean Music from Rumba to Reggae*. Philadelphia: Temple University Press.
Maultsby, Portia. 1985. "West African Influences and Retentions in U.S. Black Music: A Sociocultural Study." In *More than Dancing: Essays on Afro-American Music and Musicians*, edited by Irene V. Jackson. Westport, CT: Greenwood Press.
McGowan, Chris, and Ricardo Pessanha. 1991. *The Brazilian Sound: Samba, Bossa Nova, and the Popular Music of Brazil*. Philadelphia: Temple University Press.
Melej, Patrick Barr. 1998. "Cowboys and Constructions: Nationalist Representations of Pastoral Life in Post-Portalian Chile." *Journal of Latin American Studies*, vol. 30 (1): 35–61.
Mellafe, Rolando. (1959) 1984. *La introducción de la esclavitud negra en Chile: Tráfico y rutas*. Santiago de Chile: Editorial Universitaria.
de Mena, José María. 1985. *Tradiciones y leyendas sevillanas*. Barcelona: Plaza & Janes.

Mendoza, Zoila S. 2000. *Shaping Society through Dance: Mestizo Ritual Performance in the Peruvian Andes.* Chicago Studies in Ethnomusicology. Chicago: University of Chicago Press.
Ministerio de Culturas. 2012. "Los creadores del caporal son reconocidos por el Ministerio de Culturas." *Erbol Digital,* July 19. http://www.erbol.com.bo/noticia/cultura/19072012/los_creadores_del_caporal_son_reconocidos_por_el_ministerio_de_culturas.
Moore, Robin D. 1997. *Nationalizing Blackness: Afrocubanismo and Artistic Revolution in Havana, 1920–1940.* Pitt Latin American Series. Pittsburgh: University of Pittsburgh Press.
———. 2010. *Music in the Hispanic Caribbean: Experiencing Music, Expressing Culture.* Global Music Series. New York: Oxford University Press.
Moreno Navarro, Isidoro. 1997. *La antigua hermandad de los negros de Sevilla: etnicidad, poder y sociedad en 600 años de historia.* Sevilla: Secretaria de Publicaciones de la Universidad de Sevilla.
———. 1999. "Festive Rituals, Religious Associations, and Ethnic Reaffirmation of Black Andalusians: Antecedents of the Black Cofraternities and Cabildos in the Americas." In *Representations of Blackness and the Performance of Identities,* edited by Jean Muteba Rahier, 4–18. Westport, CT: Bergin & Garvey.
Mörner, Magnus. 1967. *Race Mixture in the History of Latin America.* Boston: Little, Brown.
Myers, Helen, ed. 1992. *Ethnomusicology.* New York: W.W. Norton.
Nederveen Pieterse, Jan P. 1998. *White on Black: Images of Africa and Blacks in Western Popular Culture.* Reprinted. New Haven, CT: Yale University Press.
Nöth, Winifred. 1990. *Handbook of Semiotics.* Bloomington: Indiana University Press.
Nzegwu, Nkiru. 2001. "The Concept of Modernity in Contemporary African Art." In *The African Diaspora: African Origins and New World Identities,* edited by Isidore Okpewho, Carole Boyce Davies, and Ali A. Mazrui, 1st paperback ed., 391–427. Bloomington: Indiana University Press.
Oyanedel, Ivette. 2002. "El Arica que se nos fue." Archived newspaper web page. August 18, 2002. http://www.estrellaiquique.cl/site/apg/invite/pags/20020818202236.html.
Palacios, Nicolás. 1918. *Raza chilena; Libro escrito por un chileno y para los chilenos.* 2nd Ed. Santiago, Chile: Editorial Chilena.
Panfichi, Aldo. 2000. "Africania, barrios populares y cultura criolla a inicios del siglo XX." In *Lo africano eEn lLa cCultura criolla: [Ponencias],* edited by Carlos Aguirre, 137–56. Lima: Fondo Editorial del Congreso del Perú.
Paschel, Tianna S. 2016. *Becoming Black Political Subjects: Movements and Ethno-Racial Rights in Colombia and Brazil.* Princeton, NJ: Princeton University Press.
Pedemonte, Rafael. 2008. *Los acordes de la patria: música y nación en el siglo XIX chileno.* Santiago, Chile: Globo Editores.
Peirce, Charles S. 1955. *Philosophical Writings of Peirce, Selected and Edited with an Introduction by Justus Buchler.* New York: Dover.
Peri Fagerstrom, René. 1984. *Los poblados de los vientos.* Santiago: Editorial Renacimiento.
———.1999. *La rza negra en Chile: Una presencia negada.* Santiago, Chile: LOM Ediciones.
Piersen, William D. 1999. "African-American Festive Style." In *Signifyin(g), Sanctifyin', & Salm Dunking: A Reader in African American Expressive Culture,* edited by Gena Dagel Caponi, 417–433. Amherst: University of Massachusetts Press.
Plath, Oreste. 1962. *Folklore Chileno.* Santiago, Chile: Ediciones PlaTur.

Price, Sally. 2001. "The Centrality of Margins: Art, Gender, and African American Creativity." In *The African Diaspora: African Origins and New World Identities*, edited by Isidore Okpewho, Carole Boyce Davies, and Ali A. Mazrui, 1st paperback ed., 204–26. Bloomington: Indiana University Press.

Quintero Rivera, Angel G. 1986. "Ponce, la danza y lo nacional: apuntes para una sociología de la música puertorriqueña." *Música* (Habana), no. 107: 5–21.

Radano, Ronald Michael. 2003. *Lying up a Nation: Race and Black Music*. Chicago: University of Chicago Press.

Ramsey, Guthrie P. 2003. *Race Music: Black Cultures from Bebop to Hip-Hop*. Music of the African Diaspora 7. Berkeley: University of California Press.

Rengifo Lira, Eugenio, and Catalina Rengifo Grau. 2008. *Los cuatro huasos: Alma de la tradición y del tiempo*. Providencia, Santiago de Chile: Sociedad Chilena del Derecho de Autor: Editorial Catalonia.

Richards, Patricia. 2013. *Race and the Chilean Miracle: Neoliberalism, Democracy, and Indigenous Rights*. Pittsburgh: University of Pittsburgh Press.

Rivera-Rideau, Petra R. 2015. *Remixing Reggaetón: The Cultural Politics of Race in Puerto Rico*. Durham, NC: Duke University Press.

Robertson-DeCarbo, Carol E. 1976. "Book Review: Thompson, Robert Farris. African Art in Motion; Icon and Act in the Collection of Katherine Coryton White. Los Angeles: University of California Press, 1974." *Ethnomusicology*. 20, no. 3: 602–5.

Rodríguez, Romero Jorge. 2004. "Entramos negros; salimos afrodescendientes." *Revista Futuros*, vol. II (5). http://www.revistafuturos.info/futuros_5/afro_1.htm.

Rodríguez Amado, Gustavo. 1995. *Música y danzas en las fiestas del Perú*. Arequipa: Universidad Nacional de San Agustín.

Romero, Raúl R. 1994. "Black Music and Identity in Peru: Reconstruction and Revival of Afro-Peruvian Musical Traditions." In *Music and Black Ethnicity: The Caribbean and South America*, edited by Gerard H. Béhague, 307–30. Coral Gables, FL: North-South Center Press, University of Miami.

———. 2001. *Debating the Past: Music, Memory, and Identity in the Andes*. New York: Oxford University Press.

Rommen, Timothy. 2007. *"Mek Some Noise": Gospel Music and the Ethics of Style in Trinidad*. Berkleley: University of California Press.

Rondón, Víctor. 2014. "Música y negritud en Chile: De la ausencia presente a la presencia ausente." *Latin American Music Review* 35, no. 1: 50–87. https://doi.org/10.7560/LAMR35103.

Rossells, Beatriz. 2008. "Bolivia. Pepinos, ch'utas y cholas: La nueva sociedad de la paz." *Omnibus* IV, no. 21. http://www.omni-bus.com/n21/bolivia.html.

Royce, Anya Peterson. 2002. *The Anthropology of Dance*. New ed. Hampshire, UK: Dance Books.

Salgado Henríquez, Marta. 2014. *Afrochilenos: Una historia oculta*. Coquimbo, Chile: Centro Mohammed VI Para el Diálogo de Civilizaciones.

Santa Cruz Gamarra, César. 1977. *El waltz y el valse criollo*. Lima: Instituto Nacional de la Cultura.

Sater, William F. 1974. "The Black Experience in Chile." In *Slavery and Race Relations in Latin America*. Contributions in Afro-American and African Studies, edited by Robert Brent Toplin, no. 17, 13–50, Westport, CT: Greenwood Press.

Short, Thomas L. 2007. *Peirce's Theory of Signs*. Cambridge: Cambridge University Press.
Spencer Espinoza, Christian. 2009. "La invisibilidad de la negritud en la literature histórico-musical chilena y la formación del canon etnico mestizo. El caso de la (zama)cueca durante el siglo XIX." *Boletin Música* 25: 66–92.
Spivak, Gayatri Chakravorty, Donna Landry, and Gerald M. MacLean, eds. 1996. *The Spivak Reader: Selected Works of Gayatri Chakravorty Spivak*. New York: Routledge.
Stewart, Charles, ed. 2007. "Creolization: History, Ethnography, Theory." In *Creolization: History, Ethnography, Theory*, 1–25. Walnut Creek, CA: Left Coast Press.
Stone, Ruth M. 2005. *Music in West Africa: Experiencing Music, Expressing Culture*. Global Music Series. New York: Oxford University Press.
Sucesos. 1928. "El Santuario de la 'Virgen de las Peñas en Arica.'" XXVII, No. 1363, November 8, 1928.
Swann, Joan, Ana Deumert, Theresa Lillis, and Rajend Mesthrie. 2004. *A Dictionary of Sociolinguistics*. Tuscaloosa: University of Alabama Press.
Tassi, Nico. 2016. *The Native World-System: An Ethnography of Bolivian Aymara Traders in the Global Economy*. London: Oxford University Press.
Templeman, Robert Whitney.1998. "We Are People of the Yungas, We Are the Saya Race." In *Blackness in Latin America and the Caribbean: Social Dynamics and Cultural Transformations*, edited by Norman E. Whitten and Arlene Torres, 426–44. Bloomington: Indiana University Press.
Thompson, Robert Farris. 1974. *African Art in Motion: Icon and Act in the Collection of Katherine Coryton White*. Los Angeles: University of California Press.
Thornton, John K. 1991. "Legitimacy and Political Power: Queen Njinga, 1624–1663." *The Journal of African History* 32, no. 1: 25–40.
———. 1998. *Africa and Africans in the Making of the Atlantic World, 1400–1800*. 2nd ed. Cambridge: NY: Cambridge University Press.
Tijoux, María Emilia, ed. 2016. *Racismo en Chile: La piel como marca de la inmigración*. Primera ed. Estudios. Santiago de Chile: Editorial Universitaria.
Tornero, Recaredo S. 1872. *Chile ilustrado: Guía descriptivo del territorio de Chile, de las capitales de provincia, y de los puertos principales*. Valparaíso: Librerias i Agencias del Mercurio.
Turino, Thomas. 1999. "Signs of Imagination, Identity, and Experience: A Peircian Semiotic Theory for Music." *Ethnomusicology* 43, no. 2: 221. https://doi.org/10.2307/852734.
———. 2003. "Nationalism and Latin American Music: Selected Case Studies and Theoretical Considerations." *Latin American Music Review* 24, no. 2: 169–209. https://doi.org/10.1353/lat.2003.0024.
———. 2008. *Music as Social Life: The Politics of Participation*. Chicago Studies in Ethnomusicology. Chicago: University of Chicago Press.
———. 2014. "Peircean Thought as Core Theory for a Phenomenological Ethnomusicology." *Ethnomusicology* 58, no. 2: 185. https://doi.org/10.5406/ethnomusicology.58.2.0185.
Urzúa Urzúa, Luis. 1969. *Arica, Puerta Nueva*. 3rd ed. Santiago de Chile: Editorial Andres Bello.
Van Kessel, Juan. 1973. "Los bailes religiosos del norte grande: Atavismo cultural o fenómeno de desarrollo?" *Revista de La Universidad Técnica Del Estado* 13–14: 169–86.
———. 1981. *Danzas y estructuras sociales de los Andes*. Cusco, Perú: Ediciones IPA.
———. 1992. *Aica y la peña sagrada*. Iquique, Chile: El Jote Errante.

Van Vleet, Krista E. 2008. *Performing Kinship: Narrative, Gender, and the Intimacies of Power in the Andes*. Austin: University of Texas Press.

Varas, José Miguel, and Juan Pablo González Rodríguez, eds. 2005. *En bBusca de la música chilena: Crónica y antología de una historia sonora*. Santiago de Chile: Comisión Bicentenario, Presidencia de la República.

Vásquez Benitt, Erie. 1990. "Más allá del río: Santuario de la virgen del rosario de Las peñas." La Florida, Chile: Pía Sociedad de San Pablo.

Vásquez Trigo, Juan. 2002. *Arica puerto del tiempo: Memoria visual de Arica*. Arica, Chile: Universidad de Tarapacá de Arica/Gobierno Regional de Tarapacá.

Vega, Carlos, and Ercilia Moreno Chá. 1986. *Las danzas populares argentinas*. New ed. Buenos Aires: Instituto Nacional de Musicología "Carlos Vega."

Vial Correa, Gonzalo. 1957. *El africano en el reino de Chile. Ensayo histórico jurídico*. Santiago de Chile: Instituto de Investigaciones Históricas.

Vial S. J., José. 1984. "Algunas referencias cronológicas sobre la historia de la iglesia en Arica, antes de la Guerra de 1879." *Chungara: Revista de antropología chilena*, no. 13: 29–34.

Wacquant, Loïc. 1997. "For an Analytic of Racial Domination." *Political Power and Social Theory* 11, no. 1: 221–34.

Wade, Peter. 1993. *Blackness and Race Mixture: The Dynamics of Racial Identity in Colombia*. Johns Hopkins Studies in Atlantic History and Culture. Baltimore: Johns Hopkins University Press.

———. 2000. *Music, Race & Nation: Música Tropical in Colombia*. Chicago: University of Chicago Press.

———. 2010. *Race and Ethnicity in Latin America*. 2nd ed. New York: Pluto Press.

White, Shane and Graham White. 1995. "Slave Clothing and African American Culture in the Eighteenth and Nineteenth Centuries." *Past and Present* 148: 149–86.

———. 1998. *Stylin': African American Expressive Culture from Its Beginnings to the Zoot Suit*. Ithaca, NY: Cornell University Press.

Whitten, Norman E., and Rachel Corr. 1999. "Imagery of 'Blackness' in Indigenous Myth, Discourse, and Ritual." In *Representations of Blackness and the Performance of Identities*, edited by Jean Muteba Rahier, 4–18. Westport, CT: Bergin & Garvey.

Whitten, Norman E., and Arlene Torres, eds. 1998. *Blackness in Latin America and the Caribbean: Social Dynamics and Cultural Transformations*. Bloomington: Indiana University Press.

Willett, Frank. 1978. "Review: Black Gods and Kings: Yoruba Art at UCLA by Robert Farris Thompson," edited by Robert Farris Thompson. *African Arts* 12, no. 1: 11–14. https://doi.org/10.2307/3335373.

Wolf, Juan Eduardo. 2013. "Afro-Chile?!: Styles of Blackness in Music-Dance along Chile's Northern Border." PhD diss., Indiana University.

Wormald Cruz, Alfredo. 1963. *Frontera norte*. Santiago de Chile: Editorial del Pacifico.

Yelvington, Kevin A. 2001. "The Anthropology of Afro-Latin America and the Caribbean: Diasporic Dimensions." *Annu. Rev. Anthropol* 30, no. 1: 227–60. https://doi.org/10.1146/annurev.anthro.30.1.227.

———. 2011. "Constituting Paradigms in the Study of the African Diaspora, 1900–1950." *The Black Scholar* 40, no. 1: 64–76.

Zuñiga, Jean-Paul, 2001. "'*Morena me llaman . . .* '. Exclusión e integración de los afroamericanos en hispanoamérica : El ejemplo de algunas regiones del antiguo virreinato del Perú (siglos 16–18)." In *"Negros, mulatos, zambaígos." Derroteros africanos en los mundos ibéricos*. Edited by Berta Ares and Alessandro Stella, 105–122. Seville: Ediciones de la Escuela de Estudios Hispanoamericanos.

———. 2009. "Huellas de una ausencia. Auge y evolución de la población africana en Chile: apuntes para una encuesta." In *Huellas de África En América: Perspectivas Para Chile*. Edited by Celia L. Cussen, 109–135. Santiago de Chile: Editorial Universitaria.

INDEX

Achachis Morenos "Generación 90," *108*, 167, 168–69, 178, 196n12
activism. *See also* Afro-descendant organizations: Afro-Chilean recognition and, 109; elimination of Indigenous, 39; music-dance component of, 44–46, 84
Africa. *See also* Black Pacific model, of Feldman: Blackness associations with, 106; negative references to, 93
African American stepping, 150
African diaspora, 42–43. *See also* Black Pacific model, of Feldman; diasporic resources and, 79, 80, 106, 150–51, 206, 216–18; phatic music of, 53, 80n5; production of blackness and, 78–80; tumbe carnaval and, 12, 78–80, 216–18
African heritage, 9, 13, 200; music-dance and, 4, 6–7; retentions and, 42, 51; Slave Heritage Route and, *88*, 88–89; Spanish valued over Black, 22
Afro-Chilean recognition: 1990s Arica and, 11–12; activism goal of, 109; failure of Chilean state, 44; identity and, 2–3, 14n7; through music, 17; music-dance and, 211–13; Peruvian associations challenge to, 112, 113–14; proposed bill to ensure, 89, 101n4
Afro-descendant organizations (activism), 2–4, 9–10. *See also specific organizations*; Arica region, 3; Chilean government consultation with, 201–2; economic issues addressed by, 212; family connections in, 96, 99–100; first NGO, 44, 50; individual benefits of participating in, 95–96; music-dance role in, 44–46, 84 (*See also specific music-dance troupes*); racial inequality strategies of, 211–13; splits within, 98–99
Afro-descendants, 125–27, 190–93, 208–10. *See also* tumbe carnaval, styling Afro-descendant through; acculturation of, 42; carnivalization, culture and, 202–5; carnivals of, 81n19; discrimination towards, 9–10, 11; in history books, 44; multicultural turn and, 39–40; presumed decline of, 28–29; reimagined Blackness and, 40–43; terminology, 14n5
Afro-Mandingue, 215; influence on tumbe, 216
Afro-Peruvian music-dance, 50, 55, 68–69, 73. *See also* vals; revival, 62, 77, 114, 116, 130
Afro-Uruguayan carnival music, 44. *See also* candombe music
agency, styling and, 6, 12, 14n13, 106, 108
agricultural labor, 67
Alliance of Afro-descendant Organizations (Alianza Afrodescendiente), 90, 101n5
Aluna Tambo, 215–16
Anacona, Kiko 55, *63*, 98
ancestral memory, cultural *vs.*, 80n4
Andean music, 1, 36, 38; wayno (huayno) genre, 38, 48n23, 189, 190
Arak Pacha, 38
Arias, Manuel, 160, 162–63
Arias, Virginio, 24, 25
Arica. *See also specific topics*: in 1990s, 11–12; Black areas of early 1900s, *115*, 115–20; Black neighborhoods of, *115*, 115–17, 163; as part of Chile, *21*; Chilean control of, 22; criollo in 1900s, 114–20; ethnography in, 3, 9; founding of, 22; as government region, 3, *21*,141, 201, 202; as part of Peru, 50; plebiscite era, 116, 118; population of 1800s, 26–27; in tripartite region, *171*; university in, 118, 134n7
Arica Negro, 87, 200, 212, 214
assimilationist theories, 107
audience, performers as, 6
authenticity, 35, 48n16
Aymara culture, 167, 187, 189–90; language and, 168, *168*, 196n3
Azapa Valley, 29, 57, 64–65, 212; Black culture in, 117–18, *118*

231

Báez Lazcano, Cristian, 65, 66, 86–87, *90*, 98, 99, 120, 211; cueca danced by, 125–26; Gringo Chileno award from, 133

Báez Rios, Azeneth, 84, *90*, 99-100, 110, 111 133; on dance motivations, 90–91; on negative experiences of Blackness, 92–95

baile de tierra, 113, 127–33, *128*, 135n17

Bajada de Carnaval Afro (Descending of the Afro-descendant Carnival), 66, 73, 81n19, 87, 96, 192; vals performance in, 121

Baker, Josephine, 33

Bakhtin, M. M., 14n12, 169, 175–76, 182, 185, 187

Balthazar (Black Wise Man), 57

Baluarte family 126; Carmen, 111, 120, 133, *159*, 160; Cruz de Mayo 126, 191; Ester 133; in Lumbanga, 96; Religious dance troupe 138, 153, *159*, 160, 191

bandannas, 72, 73, 75

Barraza, José, 201-2

Barria Huanca, Daniel, 186, 191–92, 193

Barros Arana, Diego, 2, 23–24, 26, 29–30, 34

Black Atlantic, 66, 72–74, 78, 79. *See also* Black Pacific model, of Feldman; dances of, 68, 207; names or insults associated with, 93

Black caporales, 173–74, 176

Black Center in Periphery model, 78, 106, 208

blackface, 77, 179–80

Black Gold. *See* Oro Negro

Black immigration, assumed, 3; current, 217–18, racism and, 10, 109

Black Movement, 40, 42, 44

Black music (African American), competing scholarly models of, 51

Blackness. *See also* styling Blackness; *specific regions*; *specific topics*: absence of, 7, 10, 22, 29, 30, 37, 44, 48n13, 106–7; African diasporic production of, 78–80; ambiguity of, 78; "cerebral" qualities associated with, 26; cosmopolitan conceptions of, 2, 6, 7, 12, 14n4, 33–34, 79, 210; dance traditions and, 151; denial of, 1–2, 10, 44; erasure of, 7, 8, 12, 18, 27, 34; euphemisms for, 138; as framing concept, 41–42, 51; identity markers for Black communities, 3-4; Indigeneity and, 169, 173–75; local nature of, 79, 80; phenotypical, 42, 43, 150, 160, 180; reimagining, 40–43; Spanish heritage valued above, 22; as stigmatized, 18, 163; term usage, 13n3; tumbe carnaval and, 2–3, 12

Black Pacific model, of Feldman, 66, 186; Black Atlantic and, 42–43, 64; Black Periphery and, 7, 78, 79, 106, 208

Black Power, 76

Black religious brotherhoods, 145, 163

"Black Rhythms of Peru." *See* "Ritmos Negros del Perú"

The Blacks' Christmas. *See* Pascua de los Negros

Black Wise Man. *See* Balthazar

body: attitude, 69, 70–71, 130, 149; objectification, 93–95; as facet of style, 75–78

Bolivians, *171*; Bolivianness-Indigeneity connection and, 172, 179, 188–90, 192; major carnivals of, 178, 196n17; stereotypes of, 169, *170*, 172

bomba practice, 207

bombo (bass) drums, 54, 63, 65, 66, 80, 182

bozals, criollo *vs.*, 19

braiding (hair), 75–76

brass bands, 153, 154, 165n15; styling Indigenous in, 188

Brazilian dance, pelvic thrust in, 68–69

Brown, Jacqueline Nassy, 79, 106, 150

Brubaker, Rogers, 14n5, 91

Butrón, Marcos, *108*, 110, 145, 162

cachimbo, 129, 131, 132, 135n17

cajas (snare) drums, 65

cajón (box) drum, 50, 65, 80n1, 120; poem recited accompanied by, 101n2; vals criollo and, 114–15, 121-122, 134n10; workshop, 198

Call-Response, as master trope 52; as device, 206

candombe music, 44, 60, 61–62

Canto Nuevo (New Singing) movement, 38

cantoras (female singers), 30

caporales dances: basic drum pattern for, 185; carnivalesque facets of, 183–87, *184*; Indigeneity and, 189–90; origin and structure, 178–79; slavery and, 173–74, 185, 193, 196n8; tuntuna and, 176–77

Index | 233

caporals (captains), 147–52, 160, 161; slavery and, 173–74, 176

Carnaval Andino, 108–9, 178, 189; Aymara language and, 168, *168*; Bolivian elements of, 172; carnivalesque and, 194–95; carnivalization and, 202–3; as contested event, 175; Indigenous framing of, 167–69; 2009, 193–95. *See also* Con la Fuerza del Sol.

carnivalesque: ambiguity of, 187; Bakhtin and, 175–76; Carnaval Andino in light of, 194–95; facets of, 179–87, *184*; humor, 176, 182, 195; lens of, 195; morenada and, 179–83, *180*

carnivalization, of Afro-descendant comparsas, 202–5, 209, 214–16

carnivals. *See also* Carnaval Andino; indígena, styling Blackness as; tumbe carnaval; *specific topics*: of Afro-descendants, 81n19; in Arica, 1; Bajada de Carnaval Afro, 66, 73, 81n19, 96

castas (colonial categories), 18–19, 23, 47n2

Castillo, Orlando, 142-43, 149, 162

Catholic Church, 18, 81n9, 101n7

census, 3, 14n6, 23, 28, 37, 86, 89, 200

Chicago Boys, 38, 48n24

Chile, 11. *See also specific topics*; Arica controlled by, 22; Black immigration in contemporary, 217–18; cartography, *21*; criollo nationalism and, 132; independence, racial mixture and, 23–29; national identity of 1800s, 29–34; as part of Peru, 47n4

Chilean Independence Day Parade, 127–30, 132, 135n14

Chileanization, 134n4

Chilean National Heritage Route #79. *See* Slave Heritage Route

The Chilean Race. See Raza Chilena

Chilean state, 22; Afro-Chileans not recognized by, 44; Barros Arana vision of, 23–24, 26, 29–30; European immigrants and, 47n7; racial stereotypes reinforced by, 27–28, *28*; tumbe carnaval interest of, 199–202; Virgen sanctuaries and, 140, 164n3

Chile+Cultura (Chile plus culture), 60, 63, 86

Chile Ilustrado (Tornero), 31

La Chimba region, of Arica, 117–18, 153, 214

chingana, 124, 129

cholas (female Indigenous dancers), 181, 187

cholita, 184

choreography. *See also* facets, of style; *specific genres*: agricultural labor references in, 67; coastal labor references in, 87; common features of criollo, 130; free dance alternated with, 129; storytelling element in, 111, 112, 215; through-composed, 88, 101n3

cimarrones (runaway slaves), 211–12

clave rhythm, 61, 66, 81n11

Club de Huasos de Arica, 125, 127

colonization, Spanish, 19–23, 113

color, skin, 76–78

colorism, 76

colors, debate over costume, 73–74, 75, 78, 98

Comité de Allegados Cimarrones Afroazapeños (The Committee of Afro-Azapaean Escaped Slave Kin), 211–12

compañías. *See* religious dancers and troupes

comparsas (music-dance troupes), 45, 46, 60. *See also specific troupes*; Afro-Uruguayan, 44; all-female, 215; in Andes, 1; Arica's urban, 40, 45; Bolivian migration and, 172; carnivalization of, 202–5, 209, 214–16; identifying genre and instrumentation, 54–55; Indigeneity and, 169–73; major Bolivian celebrations, 196n17; membership policies, 209, 210; rhythm and dance formulation for tumbe, 55–56, *56*; smaller, 214–16; tourism and, 40, 89

comparsas de negros (Black dance troupes), 57

Comparsa Tumba Carnaval, 97, 98, 200, 205, 207

competition, 85, 86–87, 193–94; cueca, 125–26; political gains and risks of, 203

CONADI. *See* National Council for Indigenous Development

Con la Fuerza del Sol, 40, 45, 196n11; Bajada de Carnaval Afro and, 81n19; La Ginga and, 85, 100n1; Lumbanga decision not to perform in, 86–87; opening day, 167; Oro Negro and, 67, 86; translation, 195n1. *See also* Carnaval Andino.

Conservation and Advancement of Intangible Cultural Heritage, 200
conventillos, 114, 116, 134n2
Convention 169 on Indigenous and Tribal Peoples, 201
coolness, 150–51, 161
Copiapó, 21, 22, 93
CORFO. See National Company for the Promotion of Production
Cornejo Albarracín, Pedro, 65-66
Corvacho family 93; 96; Club Julia 201, 207; Cruz de Mayo, 97;in Lumbanga, 96; Rosa 157
cosmopolitan conceptions, of Blackness, 2, 6, 7, 12, 14n4, 33–34, 79, 210
costumbristas, 31
costumes, 71–72; baile religiosos uniforms and, 139, 144–46, 165n6; caporales, 183–84, 185; cross-dressing and, 197n19; morenada, 181–82; slavery references of, 73, 82n21, 82n23; tumbe carnaval debate over, 73–74, 75, 78, 98
Council of Culture and the Arts, 200, 201–2
Coupland, Nikolas, 6, 14n14
couple dances, 129–30
courtship, dances based on, 130
cowbell pattern, 56, 58
creolization theories, 107
criollistas (criollo writers), 31
criollo, 29, 34, 114, 130, 133; Black influences on, 123–24, 134n11; Gómez on, 19; in Peruvian and Black contexts, 114–20, 132
criollo, styling Blackness as, 8, 95, 105; Afro-descendant participation in, 125–27; baile de tierra and, 127–30, 128, 135n17; Chilean vision and attributes of, 123–24; Independence Day and, 127–30, 132; vals and, 113–15, 119–24, 133–34
cross-dressing, in costuming, 197n19
Cruz de Mayo (May Cross), 97, 101n6, 126–27, 166n16; Indigeneity, Afro-descendants and, 191
Cuban dance, rumba hip movements and, 69
cueca, 1–2; competition, 125–26; in Cruz de Mayo, 127, folklore significance of, 30; pies in, 128, 131, 135n15; public version of, 134n13; structure of, 135n15

cultural intimacy, 105, 112–15, 133–34; military dictatorship, music and, 124; of Peruvian criollo, 132
cultural memory, 53, 64–67, 80; ancestral vs., 80n4; baile de tierra in local, 130–33; carnivalization and, 202; of elders, 106, 121, 130–31, 134n5; hip movements and, 69; personal, 10–11; signifyin(g) and, 52; tumbe performance invoking, 7, 9, 14n15, 62
cumbias, 127, 134n12

dance. See also choreography; music-dance: of Black Atlantic culture, 68, 207; facets of, 67–75; intergenerational participation in, 111–12; Latin American popular, 70–71; leaders (guías), 67, 161, 192; religious, 73, 108 (See also moreno styling, baile religiosos and); saya, 78, 186, 191, 194; sexual connotations of, 93–94
dancers. See also female dancers; male dancers: in FONDART project, 56; retired, 148–49; second-in command, 67, 161, 192
dance troupes. See also comparsas: religious, 53, 84, 138, 207 (See also moreno styling, baile religiosos and)
Day of the Dead, 97, 101n7
decency, 105, 138, 141–44, 146, 151, 152
del Canto, Gustavo, 45, 46, 50, 60, 81n9. See also; Fondo Nacional para el Desarrollo Cultural y las Artes; on barrel significance, 64; compositions of, 128, 129
despedida (farewell), 139–40
Diablada de Arica, 157
diasporic resources, 79, 80, 106, 150-151. 206, 216–18
dicent indexes, 7
discourse, styling as, 5
discrimination, 9–10, 11; of Blacks against Blacks, 77; Durban international conference on, 40; name calling and, 92–93, 101n5; pilot study on, 101n5
donkey jaw bone. See quijada
drummers, 56, 81n10; dancer interaction with, 207; limited number of, 99
drums, tumbe carnaval. See also cajón drum: barrels used in making, 64–67;

bombo drums, 54, 63, 65, 66, 80; deciding on types of, 54–58; fabrication of, 64, 65, 81n17; Indigenous performance, 65, 66; repique pattern, 59; sizes of, 58; skin of, 58–59, 64; visual characteristics of, 63–64; voicing and pitch of, 61, 81n10
Durban International Conference on Racism, Xenophobia and Discrimination, 40

economic problems, 211–12, 213, 217–18
economics, Chicago Boys, 38, 48n24
elders, 96, 204, 207. See also Achachis Morenos Generación 90; cultural memory of, 106, 120, 130–31, 134n5; irony of criollo styling based on, 120; as libraries, 120; tumbe described by, 54, 55, 62, 100; vals and, 111–14, 120, 121
encomienda, 37, 48n19
entradas, 147–48, 188
entrada-saludo-retirada, 147–48
entrepreneurs, 212
español, as casta category, 18
ethno-racial Other, music-dance introduction of, 34–36
European immigrants, Chilean state and, 47n7

facets, of style, 53, 105–6; body as, 75–78; carnivalesque, 179–87, 184; facets concept and, 80n7; instrumental, 62–64; kinesthetic, 67–75, 146–52; sonic, 58, 58–62, 59, 152–57, 182–83, 187; tumbe costuming and, 71–75
families, Afro-descendant organizations and, 96, 99–100
Feast of San Miguel, 146
Feast of St. John the Baptist, 119, 134n8
Feast of the Virgin of La Tirana. See Virgen de la Tirana
Feldman, Heidi, 7, 106, 116; Black Pacific model of, 42–43, 64, 66, 78, 79, 186, 208
Feliú Cruz, Guillermo, 37
female dancers: in baile religiosos, 144; of caporales, 178, 184, 184; cholas, 181, 187; costuming of, 71–72; headwraps of, 72–74, 75; in male costumes, 197n19; in morenada, 187; pelvic contact between male and, 68–69; troupe of only, 215

festejo, 89
festivals and festivities, 114, 124, 172, 184
Festividad de la Virgen de la Candelaria, 172
Flores Corvacho, Guillermina, 131, 132
folklore (folclórico), 136–37, 203; authenticity and, 35, 48n16; cueca in folkloric ballet, 125; huasos in, 32–34, 33; institutionalization of, 34–35; moreno styling influenced by, 157–58; physical education and, 217, 218n8; troupes, 145
folklorists, academic, 30, 34, 129
Fondo Nacional para el Desarrollo Cultural y las Artes (National Fund for the Development of Culture and the arts) (FONDART), 50, 54, 55–57, 121; creation of, 217n1; grants awarded by, 218nn1–2; tumbe carnaval and, 200, 201
free Blacks, 19
funerals, tumbe performances at, 97, 101n7

La Ginga, 85, 100n1, 157, 172, 203
Gitanos (Gypsies) troupes, 57, 137, 164n4
Gómez de Vidaurre, Felipe, 19, 47n2
González, Juan Pablo, 35, 123
Great Feast (Virgen de las Peñas), 141, 165n9
Guerrero Honores, Hugo, 158, 159, 159
guías (second-in-command dancer), 67, 161, 192
Güisa Lanchipa, Rosa 38, 117, 134n5

habanera, 117, 134n6
hair styles, Blackness and, 75–76, 93
Hall, Stuart, 41
headwraps, 72–75
"Hero of the Pacific." See "Roto Chileno"
Herzfeld, Michael, 112–13
Henríquez Apón, Oscar 144, 149, 150, 153-54, 160-62
Hijos de Azapa, 99, 148, 148, 158–59, 159; skin color and, 160–61; sponsor and predecessor, 140–41
hip movements, 70–71, 186; hip bump and, 55–56, 68–69, 81n20
Historia general de chile (Barros Arana), 26
historiography, Chilean, 123–24
Holy Cross celebration. See Cruz de Mayo
housing projects, 211–12, 213

Huanca Baluarte, Gabriel, 190–91
huasos, 33–34, 125, 127–28; early conception of, 31; racial ambiguity of, 31–32
Huasos Quincheros, 32
hybridity theories, 107

identity. *See also* Afro-Chilean recognition: Afro-Chilean, 2–3, 14n7; Brubaker on, 14n5; census self-identification and, 3, 14n6, 23, 28; national, 29–34; self-understanding reframing of, 90–92; styling concept for understanding, 106–8
immigrants: European, 47n7; racism toward current Black, 217–18
improvisation, 188, 198
indexical cluster, 48n11, 75
Indígena (Indigeneity), 13n3; Bolivianness association with, 172, 188–90; current attitudes toward, 169–73; encomienda and, 37, 48n19; religious dances and, 138, 177
Indígena, styling Blackness as, 8, 9, 105. *See also* Carnaval Andino; Afro-descendant similarities with, 65; Afro-descendants in carnival genres and, 190–93; Bolivia and, 179, 196n15; caporales genre and, 178–79, 189–90; carnivalesque and, 105, 175–77, 179–87, 194–95; drums used in, 66; invisible Blackness and, 169; morenada and, 177–78, 188–89, 196n11; racial order and, 194–95; stereotypes and, 169, *170*, 172, 196n4; style shift in 2009 carnival, 193–94; tensions and connections in, 169, 173–75, 195
Indigenista, 134n2
Indigenous Law (*Ley indígena*), 3, 39, 172, 179
Indigenous Rights movements, 134n8
indio, as casta category, 18, 19
INE. *See* National Institute of Statistics
Institute of Folkloric Music Research, 34
instruments. *See also specific instruments*: Afro-Peruvian music and, 50–51, 55, 62; moreno dance and, 147; in moreno styling, 152–57; sounds and signs of, 62–63; style facets of, 62–64; tumbe genre and, 54–55; Uruguayan, 61
intergenerational dancing, 111–12
International Labor Organization, 201

interracial intercourse, 71
intertextuality, styling and, 5, 14nn12–13
Intin Ch'amampi 195n1; *see also* Carnaval Andino
Iquique, *21*, 120, 131, *171*, 214

jaranas (all-night festivities), 114, 124

kineme (movements with social meaning), 151
kinesthetic facets, of styling, 67–75, 146–52

Latin America: colonial, 19–23, 113; popular dance of, 70–71; religious dances in, 73
laundresses, 120, 121
"Las Lavanderas" (laundresses), 121
Leal, Antonio, 89, *90*
legislation, proposed, 89, 101n4
Letelier Salgado, Carolina, 50, 56
Lima, 115, 133
Little Feast (*Virgen de las Peñas*), 141, 148, 157
Living Human Treasures (*Tesoros Humanos Vivos*), 201, 217
Llerena Corvacho, Segundo "El Chilo" 119, 146
Lluta Valley 29, 115, *115*, 117; San Geronimo de 157
Loyola, Margot, 129, 131, 132
Lucas Gómez (Quevedo), 31
Lumbanga comparsa, 66, 69–70, 191, 212; Blacks in Oro Negro compared with, 77; Carnaval Fuerza del Sol and, 86–87; criollo styling of, 120–22; elders as resource for, 131; family line formations of, 96; Oro Negro and, 86, *90*, 132; participant motivations, 83–84; politics, membership and, 209; private celebration of, 110–14; vals use by, 111–14
Lumbanga neighborhood, *115*, 115–17

machas (females in male costume), 197n19
Magi, Black African, 81n9
malaria, 47n5
male dancers, 73, 77–78, 94, 126; in baile religiosos, 144; in cachimbo, 132; caporales, 186–87; pelvic contact between female and, 68–69

Mamani Huanca, Hector, 203
Mamani Morales, Juan Carlos, 189–90, 204
marches: military, 129, 138; music-dance with activist, 44; in religious dances, 147–48, 151, 178; slavery references of, 182, 183
marching bands, 65, 66, 127, 182
marineras, 114, 130
La Marseillaise, 29
masks, moreno, 180, *180*
matracas (ratchets), 147, 152–53, 161, 183
May Cross. *See* Cruz de Mayo
Mendoza, Zoila, 141-142, 164n2, 176-77
mestizaje. *See* racial mixture
mestizo casta, 18
military bands, 154
military marches, 29, 138, 152
military music, 29, 124, 154, 165n15
miscegenation, 70–71
morenada dance: carnivalesque facets in, 179–83, *180*; improvisation in, 188; Indigeneity and, 188–89; origin of, 177–78, 196n11; skin color and, 76
Morenos de Marconi, 144, 149, 153, 155, *156*, 158, 217
Morenos de Tacna, Compañía No. 1, 154, 164n9
morenos pitucos (snobbish morenos), 144
moreno styling, baile religiosos and, 8, 73, 105, 108, 191; Bolivian carnival and, 179, 196n15; Chilean *vs.* Peruvian, 149; commitment of, 162, 165n6; compañías, 140–41; decency, 138, 141–44, 146, 151, 152; devotion and, 143, 163; folclórico influences on, 157–58; genre sets, 136–37; Indigenous framing of, 177; kinesthetics of, 146–52; morenos de paso performance and, 137–38, 141, 144–46, 155; moreno term and, 138; relationships and, 162–64; religious feasts and, 139–41, 148, 157 (*See also* La Virgen de las Peñas); retired dancers of, 148–49; rhythm and, 160, 166n18; seniority, 141; societies (sociedades), 141, 149; sonic facets of, 152–57; sponsorship, 140–41; stereotypes associated with, 164n4; time limits on performing for Virgin, 147, 160, 165n11; uniforms, 139, 144–46, 165n6; younger dancers and, 157–58

mulato/mulata: casta, 18; interracial intercourse and, 71
multicultural alignment, 3, 18, 46–47, 199; racial equality distinguished from, 10, 210
multicultural turn, 39–40
Mundo Afro, 40, 44, 60, 89
music: Afro-Peruvian, 50; Andean, 1, 36, 38, 48n23, 189, 190; military, 154, 165n15; military dictatorship and, 124; *música criolla*, 114; participation and, 44–45, 49n29; phatic, 53, 80n5; plebiscite-era Azapa Valley, 119–20; recognition through, 17
Música Tipica Chilena (Typical Chilean Music), 32
music-dance. *See also* Afro-Peruvian music-dance; dance; political use, of music-dance; styling; *specific genres*: African heritage and, 4, 6–7; Afro-Chilean recognition and, 211–13; Afro-descendant activism importance of, 44–46, 84; authenticity and, 35, 48n16; Barros Arana vision reinforced through, 29–30; ethnoracial other in, 34–36; huaso significance in, 32–34; participant motivations and, 83–84; racial mixture in early state, 29–34; redundancy and, 29; troupes, 45, 46 (*See also* comparsas, religious dancers and troupes); tumbe carnaval as, 1

name calling (insults), 92, 93, 101n5
National Company for the Promotion of Production (CORFO), 212
National Council for Indigenous Development (CONADI), 39, 173
National Cueca Competition, 125–26
National Heritage Day, *88*, 88–89
national identity, in 1800s, 29–34
National Institute of Statistics (INE), 208
negra (Black), as insult, 92
"Negra" (poem by V. Santa Cruz), 86, 101n2
negritos, 179, 194, 196n15
negro: azapeño, 92, 93; bozal, 19; as casta category, 18
neofolklore, 35
neoliberalism, 38–40
neoliberal multiculturalism, 39, 40, 49n25, 86

New Song movement. *See* Nueva Canción
NGOs. *See* nongovernmental organizations
Ño Carnavalon, 208, 218n6
Nódo ECAFRO, 212
nongovernmental organizations (NGOs). *See also* Afro-descendant organizations; *specific organizations*: first Afro-descendant, 44, 50
Nueva Canción (New Song) movement, 36, 37

objectification, body, 93–94
Office for Afro-descendant Development, 3
Oficina Comunal Afrodescendiente (Community Afro-descendant Office), 208, *213*
O'Higgins, Bernardo, 23, 57–58
Olis, Yoni, 50, 60, *63*
olive barrels, 64–67
olive production, 79, 118; cultural memory and, 64–67, 80
orishas, 207, 215. *See also* Yemayá.
Oro Negro (Black Gold), 13n1, 17, 42, 85, 215; candombe and, 60; creation of, 44; FONDART project of, 50–51; music-dance component of, 45, 46; new organizations arising from, 86
Oro Negro comparsa, 45, 46, 54–56, *56*, 200; Arica Negro tensions with, 87; baile de tierra and, 127–31, *128*, 132; Black-skinned dancers in, 77; bloc formations and choreography, 67–68; costuming and, 73–74, 98; dance styling of, 67–75; hip bump in, 68–69, 81n20; Lumbanga and, 86, *90*, 132; older songs of, 206; relations with other groups, 74; split into separate troupes (comparsas), 86, 87, 98; 2009 performance of, *63*, 73
Oruro, 177, 191, 196n17

Palacios, Nicolas, 23, 25, 26, 47nn7–8
panpipes *(zampoñas)*, 66, 153, 154, 191
pasacalle (street parade), 65, 81n18, 112
Paschel, Tianna, 3, 10, 210
Pascua de los Negros (The Blacks' Christmas), 56–59, 71, 73, 205; "pascua" meaning in Chile, 81n9; 2009, *63*, 73
"El Payande," 117, *118*, 134n6
pelvic thrust, 68–69

performers, as audience, 6
Peri Fagerstrom, René, 117, 146
Peru. *See also* Afro-Peruvian music-dance: Afro-Chilean recognition and links with, 112, 113–14; Arica and, 50; Blackness in mid-1800s, 26–27; Black representations of, 172; Chile as part of, 47n4; coastal culture of, 114; moreno dance and, 149, 157; 1900s Arica, criollo and, 114–20; vals, nationalism and, 111, 112–13 (*See also* vals (Peruvian waltzes))
phenotype, Blackness, 42, 43, 150, 160; slavery and grotesqueness, 180
physical education, folkloric dance and, 217, 218n8
pies (poetic structure), 128, 131, 135n15
pilgrimage, to La Virgen de las Peñas, 136, 164n1
Pinochet, Augusto, 37
Pinochet regime, 18, 37–39, 124, 142, 218n1
Piñones, Francisco ("Pancho"), 205, *205*, 206, 208
pipe-smoking, 180, 196n16
poems, 86, 101n2, 110; *pies* structure of, 128, 131, 135n15
political cartoons, 28, *170*, 172
political use, of music-dance, 90–91; competition and, 203; of styling Blackness through music-dance, 9–11; tumbe and, 208–10, 216–18
Popular Unity, 37
pregones (street cries), *118*, 118–19
protests, 89–90
proyección folclórica (staged folklore), 34–35, 50; comparsa building and, 54–55
Puerto Ricans, 206–7

quijada, 55, 57, 58, 62
Quintana family; in Lumbanga, 96; Segundo, 111, 121

race: carnivalesque and, 194–95; racial ambiguity and, 31–32; as social construction, 2
Race Music (Ramsey), 52
racial equality alignment, 10, 210
racial inequality, Afro-descendant activism and, 211–13

racial mixture (mestizaje), 8, 22, 185; Chilean independence and, 23–29; early music-dance representations and, 29–34
racial self-identification, 106, 200–201; census and, 3, 14n6, 23, 28
racism: colonial, 19, 22, 23; toward immigrants, 217–18; racial mixture as downplaying, 22
raíma (olive harvesting). *See* olive production
Rapa Nui, 35, 48n17
Rastafarianism, 74, 75, 82n22
ratchets. *See* matracas
Raza Chilena (The Chilean Race) (Palacios), 24
Reales Brillantes, Caporales 193
redundancy, Turino concept of, 29, 48n11
reggae, 74, 82n22
Regional Cultural Advancement, 200
relatedness, sense of, 100
religious brotherhoods, 120–21
religious dancers and troupes, 53, 84, 207. *See also* moreno styling, baile religiosos and; Indigeneity and, 138
religious feasts, 119, 134n8, 146; moreno styling and, 139–41, 148, 157
repique (lead) drum, 58, 59, 61
retentions, African cultural, 42, 51
retired dancers, 148–49
rhythm: moreno styling and, 160, 166n18; saya, 191
rhythm, tumbe carnaval, 55–56, 56, 58, 68. *See also* drums, tumbe carnaval; Arica Negro variations on, 87; clave pattern and, 61, 66, 81n11; *cuá* in new tumbe, 207; repique pattern, 59
Ríos, Francisca "Rosa," 111, 118, 119, 132
"Ritmos Negros del Perú" (Black Rhythms of Peru) (Santa Cruz, N.), 110
Rivera, Camila, 92–94, 96, 110, 125, 192–93
Rodriguez, Romero Jorge, 40–41, 42, 89, 90, 101n4
Rondón Víctor 123–24
"Roto Chileno" ("Hero of the Pacific"), 25. 196n4
rumba, 69

Sabor Moreno (Moreno Flavor) troupe, 60, 63, 86, 198, 207
Salgado, Marta, 17, 41, 44, 46, 73, 74, 92, 99; in independence day parade, 128; on Lumbanga neighborhood, 115–16
Salgado, Sonia, 43, 44, 45
salsa, 60, 61
samba music, 100n1
San Pedro de Totora, 190, 193, 194
Santa Cruz, Nicomedes, 110, 111
Santa Cruz, Victoria, 86, 101n2, 111
Santiago (Chile's capital), 20, 21, 22, 44, 135n14, 163, 208, 218n2
Sater, William F., 20–21, 27
saya dance, 78, 186, 191-194
self-understanding: identity reframed as, 90–92; negative experiences leading to, 92–95; tumbe, tradition and, 96–98
Semana Afro (Afro Week), 202
semiotics, 48n11, 53
senior citizens, 204, 207
Señor del Gran Poder, 172, 178, 196n17
sex: dance connotations of, 93–94; interracial, 71
signifyin(g), Gates theory of, 52
signs: of costume colors, 73–74, 75; iconicity of, 60–61, 82n23; indexical cluster of, 48n11, 75; instrumental sounds as, 62–63; performance facets and, 53; signifiyin(g) and, 52, 64, 66–67; sign-vehicles and, 53, 84, 207; sonic, 58–62
silver mines, 22, 178
singers, female. *See* cantoras
singing, for Virgen de las Peñas, 155–57, 160, 166n16
skin, drum, 58–59, 64
skin color, 76–78, 92, 160–61
Slave Heritage Route, 88, 88–89, 99, 116
slavery, 19, 20–22, 211–12; abolition of, 40–41; advance in scholarship on, 37; caporales carnival dance and, 173–74, 185, 193, 196n8; costume references to, 73, 82n21, 82n23; Indigenous, 37, 48n19; morenada genre linked with, 178, 180–81; Peruvian abolishment of, 26–27; racial mixture and, 23, 25
snobbish morenos. *See* morenos pitucos
social policy, 208

soldiers, 28, 36, 164, 166n19
sonic facets: Indigeneity and, 187; of morenada, 182–83; of moreno styling, 152–57; tumbe carnaval, 58, 58–62, 59
Spencer Espinoza, Christian, 124
Spivak, Gayatri Chakravorty, 14n16
spouses, in music-dance troupes, 209
staged folklore. See proyección folclórica
stepping, African American, 150
stereotypes, racialized, 93–95, 96, 164n4, 177, 196n4; of Bolivians, 169, 170, 172; Chilean state and, 27–28, 28; performance groups affording freedom from, 96; racial mixture and, 185
storytelling, in choreographies, 111, 112, 215
strategic essentialism, 9, 14n16
street cries. See pregones
street parade. See pasacalle
styling. See also facets, of style: definitions of, 4–6, 14n8, 14n10; identity and, 106–8; intertextuality and, 5, 14nn12–13; multiple modes of, 107–8, 108; performance and, 5, 14n14
styling Blackness. See also criollo, styling Blackness as; indígena, styling Blackness as; moreno styling, baile religiosos and; tumbe carnaval, styling Afro-descendant through: carnivalesque racial order and, 194–95; cultural intimacy and, 133–34; politics of music-dance and, 9–11; tumbe carnival allowing, 6–7, 12
Sucesos, 28, 154, 170

Tajadillo, Richard "Alex," 110-11, 122
tambora drums, 54–58, 65
tamboril, Uruguayan, 63–64
Tarapacá, town, 131, region 135n17, Feast of San Lorenzo in 131
Temuco, regional map of Chile and, 21
tenant farmers. See huaso
Thompson, Robert Farris, 151–52
"Tiempos de Guarapo," 205, 205, 206
Tornero, Recaredo, 31
tourism, 40, 49n25, 89
training, carnival dance, 205
Treaty of Ancón, 27
tumbe carnaval (tumba): Afro-descendant participation in, 208–10; funeral performances of, 97, 101n7; government interest in, 199–202; healing through, 215; as music-dance, 1; political efficacy of, 208–10, 216–18; training, 205
tumbe carnaval, styling Afro-descendant through. See also drums, tumbe carnaval; rhythm, tumbe carnaval: African diaspora and, 12, 78–80, 216–18; Blackness and, 2–3, 12; changes in style of, 198–99; comparsa (troupe) building for, 54–56; critics of, 9; cultural memory and, 7, 9, 14n15, 62; elders consulted in construction of, 100; facets of style in, 53, 58–78, 80n7 (See also facets, of style); first public, 56–57; genre and instrumentation for, 54–55; hip movements in, 55–56, 68–70; Indigenous overlap and, 65; instrumental facets of style in, 62–64; jam session, 198; move associated with name of, 68; origins of, 51; performance contexts and motivations for, 84–90; personal meanings and uses of, 97–98; protests and, 89–90; public awareness of, 17; recent ways of, 205, 205–8; signs and signifyin', 52–53; skin color and, 77–78; styling Blackness through, 6–7, 12; terminology, 13n1; tourism promoted through, 89; traditions incorporation of, 96–98; turban in, 72–73; vals mixed with, 121
Tumbe Sanador (Healing Tumbe), 215
Tuntuna 176-177, as rhythm 185
turbans (turbantes), 72–73, 137
Turino, Thomas, 29, 48n11, 53
Typical Chilean Music. See Música Típica Chilena

UN. See United Nations
UNESCO, 88, 88–89
United Nations (UN), 44
United States (US), slave dress and, 73, 82n21
Uruguayan instrumentation, 61, 63–64
US. See United States

vacunao (male pelvic thrust), 68–69
vals (Peruvian waltzes): cajón drum and, 114–15, 122, 134n10; in criollo styling,

113–15, 119–24, 133–34; elders' participation in, 111–12; tumbe styling mixed with, 121
Van Kessel, Jan, 140, 153,163
"La Vendedora de Azapa," 111, 120
Vendimia Festival, *184*
Vial Correa, Gonzalo, 37
La Virgen de las Peñas, 136, 164n1, 164n3; celebrations, 139–40; compañías and, 140–41; dancing for Virgin, 142–43; early bands playing for, 165n15; entrada-saludo-retirada, 147–48; new entrance song for, 158, 159, *159*; origin stories, 140, 165n7; sanctuary, *137,* 140–41, 164n5; singing for, 155–57, 160, 166n16
Virgen de la Tirana, 137, 141, 154, 157, 164n3
Virgen del Rosario de las Peñas. *See* La Virgen de las Peñas
voicing, in drums, 61, 81n10

waltzes. *See* vals
wankaras (hide-head drums), 65

War of the Pacific, 22, 23, 137, 154
wayno (huayno), 38, 48n23, 127, 135n19, 172, 189, 190
Whiteness: absence of Blackness as, 48n13; criollo as, 114, 133; fashion and, 146; racial ambiguity and, 31–32; valuing of, 77
Whitening, 8
wiphala (flag), 167, 172, 196n2
Wormald Cruz, Alfredo 116–17, 152–53

Yemayá, 207
Yungas region, 184, 194

zamacueca, 129, 130, 132
zambos, casta category of, 19
zampoñas. See panpipes
zapateado, 129, 130, 132
Zavala, Fernando, 126
Zegarra family, 138, *159,* 160; Miguel 145, 153
Zuñiga, Jean-Paul, 20

JUAN EDUARDO WOLF is Assistant Professor of Ethnomusicology at the School of Music and Dance at the University of Oregon. He also serves as a core faculty member in the university's Folklore and Public Culture Program.

www.ingramcontent.com/pod-product-compliance
Lightning Source LLC
Chambersburg PA
CBHW061937220426
43662CB00012B/1935